EDP PROJECT MANAGEMENT CONTROLS

M. D. Wadsworth

Prentice-Hall, Inc.

Englewood Cliffs, N. J.

Prentice-Hall International, Inc., *London*
Prentice-Hall of Australia, Pty. Ltd., *Sydney*
Prentice-Hall of Canada, Ltd., *Toronto*
Prentice-Hall of India Private Ltd., *New Delhi*
Prentice-Hall of Japan, Inc., *Tokyo*

Library of Congress
Catalog Card Number: 78-179446

Printed in the United States of America

ISBN-0-13-237008-5
B&P

About the Author

M. D. Wadsworth is currently a principal in the management consulting firm of Knight, Gladieux & Smith, Inc. In this post he is primarily responsible for solving problems and providing counsel in all aspects of computerized management information systems. Previously, Mr. Wadsworth has been an independent EDP Consultant after serving for several years in managerial capacities for a wide variety of firms. His experience features the management of analysts, programmers, operations personnel, systems maintenance personnel, and various clerical groups in some of the nation's largest companies. At *Reader's Digest,* for example, Mr. Wadsworth, as Internal Manager, directed all EDP in subscription fulfillment activities and a budget in excess of eight million dollars annually.

Mr. Wadsworth's education includes a Bachelor of Arts in Mathematics Education from the University of Michigan and a number of graduate courses in Operations Research and Business Administration. The author has lectured before EDP groups on the evaluation of a management system and has developed several cycles of a ten-day course on EDP Project Management.

What This Book Can Do for You

This book presents a master plan for controlling EDP projects. It is intended for any person responsible for or concerned with the implementation of EDP projects. By implementing this plan, the reader can ensure that data processing projects are implemented on time, within costs, and in a profitable manner. Regardless of your position, the size of your company, or the size of your projects, the proven, practical controls which comprise this plan can be used to increase the profitability of data processing and the company.

As an example of what this book can do for you, the following listing shows how you can use a few of the controls presented here to solve your problems and become more profitable. Within this book you can find out how to:

1. Organize the people in EDP so that project functions can be performed and so that you can perform your managerial functions effectively and efficiently. See Chapter One.
2. Assign general project responsibilities among the various groups involved in project implementation so that controls can be maintained and so that the benefits expected from the project are achieved. See Chapter Two.
3. Elicit, evaluate, and maintain control over new ideas for potentially profitable projects. It also describes how to begin a feasibility study and develop a conceptual design when the profitability of the project appears to justify the study. See Chapter Three.
4. Analyze a project, evaluate its potential and request project authorization. See Chapter Four.
5. Develop and validate a detailed project schedule which illustrates in a clear and understandable manner when, and by whom, each project activity will be accomplished. It also describes how you can obtain periodic, benchmark, and exception reports from your people and how these can be used to ensure that the project is completed on time. See Chapter Five.

6. Ensure project quality during all stages of the project by the involvement of the user group, systems maintenance, and computer operations personnel. In addition, this book describes how to plan and control the various types of testing so that they are accomplished efficiently and economically, thereby providing maximum training for all operational personnel. See Chapter Six.
7. Manage conversion efforts so that schedules are met, accuracy is maintained and resources are used efficiently. See Chapter Seven.
8. Estimate project costs, system operation cost, project cash flow, payback period, and project payoff. It also describes how various financial reports produced during and after system implementation can be compared to these estimations to effect control over the project's profitability. See Chapter Eight.
9. Increase your control over all schedule, quality and cost elements by efficiency in your daily activities and by conducting effective meetings. In addition, this book describes how to gain top management's support by providing it with understandable reports on single and multiple projects. See Chapter Nine.
10. Evaluate and control computer operations and systems maintenance areas so that the benefits expected from a project are achieved. This book also describes methods and techniques of evaluating and controlling the various types of modifications to production systems so that these modifications can be implemented efficiently and profitably. See Chapter Ten.
11. Combine the various control elements into an overall master plan and use it in a typical project. See Chapter Eleven.
12. Install the master control plan in an efficient manner and maintain control while the plan is being installed. See Chapter Twelve.
13. Overcome other groups' resistance to the master control plan and the changes in organization, responsibility, and methodology which it represents. See Chapter Thirteen.

In addition to the major benefits described above, this book contains many additional controls, the reasons why individual controls are required, and illustrations of the various control formats which will assist you in developing a master control plan that increases the profitability of your projects and company.

HOW THIS BOOK IS ORGANIZED

EDP Project Management Controls is organized so that it can be understood by any person concerned with data processing project implementation regardless of his understanding or knowledge of EDP itself.

The book consists of thirteen chapters organized into five basic segments. The first segment includes Chapters One and Two and provides an overview of data processing, a definition of the terms used, the groups that will be encountered, and a description of how the various responsibilities involved in implementing an EDP project should be assigned. The second section, comprised of Chapters Three and Four, outlines the controls that must be established during the feasibility or planning portion of the project and that are necessary for top management to logically and effectively evaluate the project's worth and assign it a priority for implementation. The third segment, comprised of Chapters Five through Ten, describes in detail how the various controls are developed during the planning portion of the project and utilized during the remainder of the project to ensure that schedule, cost, quality, and payoff expectations are actually achieved. The fourth segment of the book, consisting of Chapter Eleven, describes and illustrates exactly how the master control plan could be applied to an actual project. The fifth, and final, segment of the book, which consists of Chapters Twelve and Thirteen, describes step-by-step methods for implementing the master control plan and for avoiding problems that will occur during the implementation of the control plan.

To provide continuity, and to make the book more understandable, fifty illustrations have been included. These illustrations begin with the request for a study of an inventory system (sample) and illustrate the controls that would be prepared at each step of the project study, evaluation, implementation, and operation. Because the sequence of the book and the illustrations parallel the actual sequence of events in a project, the reader is led step by step through the development of all controls. This development is summarized and illustrated by Chapter Eleven which describes the chronological sequence of events as they might have occurred in the sample project. Both EDP experts and novices can develop, therefore, an understanding of how, why, and when each control should be used. The plan and the methods presented do not require special knowledge or training to be useful. Their usefulness is limited only by the resourcefulness of the person who wishes to implement them and his dedication to achieving the benefits that they can provide.

Because it is written with a minimum of technical language, this book provides a basis for eliminating the communications gap that exists between EDP managers, top management, and user personnel. By using the controls that are presented in this book, each project's potential is described in terms that are understandable and meaningful to top management. This allows top management to assign project priorities in a logical, consistent fashion. Likewise, the controls and reports utilized during and after implementation of the project enable top management, user management, and others in the company to assess EDP's activities, achievements, and potential for the future.

As top management and others in the company gain a better understanding of EDP's work, problems, achievements, and potential, they learn how to communicate the company's goals and EDP's potential for assisting in achieving these goals. Therefore, this book can provide a common meeting ground where the interests of top management, EDP management, user personnel and EDP technicians can be logically joined for the advancement of the company.

M. D. Wadsworth

Table of Contents

List of Illustrations

1

Projects and Controls in Perspective to the Overall EDP Effort

It is no secret that electronic data processing has not realized its full potential. While some EDP managers accept the rationalization that EDP's shortcomings are the fault of top management because top management has not learned what EDP can do, most EDP managers agree that the basic problem is that, in general, EDP areas are poorly managed. This poor management is reflected by late projects, high costs, a growing distrust of EDP on the part of top management and, most importantly, top management's lack of knowledge of EDP.

Few businessmen are uninformed about accounting, sales, production or even building maintenance, and yet many EDP managers are asked the following questions, sometimes by top management personnel:

> What is really going on in EDP? Your personnel have doubled in the last year. What are you doing with all those people? The only things I ever hear about your operation are complaints about the things that you either have or haven't done. What's the problem?

These questions usually produce humorous, indignant, or very technical answers. However, intelligent EDP managers usually translate these questions into the following questions:

1. What are the functions of EDP?
2. What do your people do and how are they organized?
3. What management techniques are being used to eliminate problems?

The remainder of this chapter describes the functions, organization and management of a typical EDP area. It provides a logical and understandable overview of EDP that is used as the basis for the project control plan presented in the remaining chapters of this book. Experienced EDP personnel will skim the remainder of this chapter to note how the description differs from their company. Readers not familiar with EDP will, it is hoped, gain a general insight into its functions, organization, and management.

EDP FUNCTIONS

The main purpose of all EDP areas is to harness the fantastically high-speed calculating capability of the computer to replace, or to institute, new business activities. To accomplish this purpose, the EDP area must develop methods (called computer systems) for communicating with the computer and accomplishing the business activities on the computer. In addition, the EDP area must also operate these computer systems on a periodic or routine basis.

Development Efforts

The successful development effort is composed of seven major functions. These are:

1. Study
2. Analysis
3. Detail design
4. Programming
5. Testing
6. Conversion
7. Manual system implementation

Each of these functions is briefly described in this chapter and is also described in more detail in later chapters.

1. **Study.** The purpose of the study function is to gather basic information about operational or proposed business activity. This basic information is used during later development effort functions to determine whether, why, and how the particular business activity should be accomplished by means of a computer system.

The study function, properly managed, is composed of an initial study and, when warranted, a feasibility study. These two studies provide basic information about how the business activity would be computerized and detail the benefits to be derived from such computerization. Further details on the study function are in Chapters Two and Three.

2. **Analysis.** The purpose of the analysis function is to analyze the information gathered during the study function. The analyses provide top management with the knowledge they require to authorize project inception and to concur on project priority. This information includes project schedule, costs, payoff, other benefits, risk, manpower, and other restrictions.

Properly managed, the analysis function provides quickly the information necessary for project authorization and rating in a format that is consistent (standardized) and completely understandable by top management. Further details about the analysis functions are in Chapters Two and Four.

3. **Detail design.** The detail design function provides a step-by-step description of how the computer system will actually operate (or harness the capacity of the computer). It describes how every job, task, calculation, data storage, data transformation, or other element of the business activity will be handled in the computer system.

In addition to providing layouts of all inputs to and outputs from the system, and data files used by the system, the detail design function subdivides it into a specified number of programs, states the purposes of each, and describes (by means of flow charts or decision tables) the internal logic of each. Additional information about this function is in Chapters Two and Six.

4. **Programming.** The programming function translates the detail design into a code or language that causes the computer to perform the elements required for the business activity. For the first time, during this project function, each program in the computer system is operated and tested by its programmer to ensure correct operation.

Although simple in concept, programming is a time-consuming and error-prone activity because of its extreme complexity. Chapter Five illustrates the relationship of programming time to total project time. Chapters Two and Six describe some methods of reducing errors during programming.

5. **Testing.** The testing function provides the ultimate quality control for the project. Utilizing test data that is prepared by someone other than the programmer, each program, sets of programs called links, and the system are tested to ensure proper operation. In addition, systems are usually tested by using actual production data as test data. This is done either in a pilot test operation where full production of the old system is simulated or in a parallel operation where full production of the old system is duplicated for a period of time.

During testing, all errors in logic, commission and omission should be uncovered, remedied and retested. Because of the complexity of the programming, changes must be made with extreme caution or the remedy of one problem may cause another, usually more serious, error. Chapters Two and Six describe some methods for conducting efficient testing.

6. **Conversion.** The conversion function consists of changing all of the basic data files utilized in the system from the form and format in which they normally exist into those required by the system. Because these conversions deal with basic data, they must be extremely accurate.

The conversion function usually includes all of the development functions and is, in effect, a small project within a project. Because the data files to be converted are generally used constantly, the time period when the files' forms and formats finally undergo change is usually quite short. The combination of extreme accuracy and a very short conversion period adds additional problems to the conversion function. Chapters Two and Seven provide more information about conversions and how to control them.

7. **Manual system implementation.** The manual system implementation function parallels all of the previously described development functions. It is composed of the study, design, writing, testing and installation of the manual procedures that will interface with and support the computer system.

Because the procedures developed during the manual system implementation function greatly determine the number and types of personnel required to effectively operate the overall system, they have an important effect on the total salaries required for system operation. Details on how to determine these costs and how to use them are in Chapter Eight.

Operations Effort

The operations effort includes eight functions that ensure that computer systems, when developed, are operated on a schedule and in such a manner that all of the benefits expected from the systems are realized. The eight functions in the operations effort are:

1. Computer operations
2. Data preparation
3. Information dissemination
4. Scheduling
5. File library
6. Quality control
7. Application systems modification
8. Manufacturers' systems modifications

Each of these functions will be briefly described in this chapter and more fully described in Chapters Two and Ten.

1. **Computer operations.** The first of these functions includes the activities necessary to physically operate (or run) the programs and systems on the computer equipment. These activities include, but are not limited to, card or queue loading, tape and disk (file) mounting, console monitoring, output set-up and alignment, and administrative control.

The high cost of computer equipment mandates its efficient operation. Proper management of the computer operations function provides the necessary basis.

2. **Data preparations.** The second function includes the activities necessary to translate the required business data into a form acceptable to computer equipment. Historically, and even today, keypunching of cards provides the basic or most used means. However, within the last few years, viable new data preparation media such as key-to-tape, on-line input, and optical and magnetic ink scanners have proliferated. The future will probably provide even more alternatives.

The data preparation function includes all activities connected with entering the required business data into the computer. For this reason, activities such as mail opening, input editing or copying, order processing, complaint classification, etc., may well be included in this function. Even though the departments in which activities take place are not included in the EDP area, it must maintain some controls over these activities. Schedule controls are discussed in detail in Chapter Eight.

3. **Information dissemination.** This function provides the means for distributing the outputs (products) of the computer system to the places where they can be used. As with inputs, there has been a recent proliferation of output media. From basic printers, output media have expanded to include such items as x-y plotters, microfilm, cathode ray tube (video) display, on-line teletype and video, and audio response.

For internal information such as reports, the activities in this function include the decollation, bursting, addressing, and delivery of the reports. For outputs such as bills, the activities include insertion of the form and other material, application of postage, and mailing. Again, EDP must maintain some control over these activities, and Chapter Eight describes scheduling controls.

4. **Scheduling.** The scheduling function controls the flow of work to, through, and from the computer. It includes the scheduling of all data preparation activities, inter-computer and intra-computer operations, and information-dissemination activities.

The scheduling function is one of the main methods used to improve the efficiency of the computer operation function. In addition, scheduling ensures that the totality of computer work is performed with the shortest possible throughput time and in the most efficient manner possible. Additional details on scheduling are contained in Chapter Eight.

5. **File library.** This next function consists of the activities necessary to ensure that all program, system, language and required data (master, input and output) files are correct, usable, and available when required. The format for these files may be cards, tape, disk or drum.

The activities associated with this function include identification, cataloguing, storage, assembly, reproduction and elimination of files. These activities can be done manually or, in some cases, by means of computer systems. Because of the vital nature of these files, the file library function must always be performed in an extremely accurate and thorough manner.

6. **Quality control.** This is the function that ensures that all outputs are correct and accurate. The activities comprising this function include: output sampling, comparison with specifications, checking for reasonableness, input and process review, and legibility checking.

This function ensures that errors in inputs, processing, or outputs are corrected before the outputs are transmitted to the user complaints.

7. **Application system modification.** More commonly called program maintenance, the application system modification function provides a means of changing any (or all) programs in a fully developed and operational system. Changes are required in operational systems because of changes in user requirements, changes in manufacturers' programs and equipment, previously undiscovered errors, and a desire for improved system efficiency.

This function is of prime importance because it enables continual updating and improving of systems while in operation. All the functions in the development effort are also found in the application system modification function. For this reason, the author has chosen to discard the more common and somehow demeaning title of program maintenance.

8. **Manufacturers' system modification.** With their equipment, manufacturers provide a wide variety of systems and programs (software) to assist in the equipment's utilization. The manufacturers' system modification function provides the ability to select, install, modify and update the manufacturer's software.

Because manufacturer software is extremely complex, not of consistent quality, or not thoroughly (or correctly) documented, this function requires constant attention. Because the manufacturers' software determines, to a large extent, the success and efficiency of operation of all application programs, the critical nature of this function can not be overemphasized.

SUMMARY

Figure 1-1 presents an overall listing of the functions and activities of both the development effort and the operations effort. Experienced EDP managers will modify (add, delete, or change) this listing to approximate more closely the important functions and activities in their company.

EDP ORGANIZATION

Although there are vast differences in the manner in which EDP areas are organized, dependent primarily on the size of the area, the typical EDP area is organized approximately as shown in Figure 1-2. This organization is very easy to understand and the job descriptions are quite straightforward. In addition, unless the number of personnel in any section varies significantly, it tends to be relatively static.

The main problem with the typical EDP organization is that it does not reflect the way the personnel really interact. Figure 1-3 presents a functional EDP organization that takes into account the differences between development efforts and operations efforts. The functional EDP organization also demonstrates more clearly the organization of development efforts.

There are, however, two main problems with the functional EDP organization. The organization of the development area will tend to be very dynamic depending on the type and number of projects being implemented, and job descriptions will have to be modified for each new project.

Despite significant problems, the advantages of this type of organization predominate. In the next few years more and more EDP areas should be organizing and reorganizing along functional lines. For this reason, the functional (rather than the typical organization) will be referred to throughout the remainder of this book.

DEVELOPMENT EFFORT

Function	Activity
Study	Review Request
	Interview
	Prepare prima facie case
	Begin feasibility study
	Determine inputs
	Determine outputs
	Develop data base
	Prepare conceptual design
Analyze	Operations scheduling
	Development scheduling
	Estimate operational costs
	Estimate development costs
	Determine priority
	Obtain authorization
Detail Design	Input layout
	Output layout
	Master file layout
	Program flow or Decision tables
	Document
Programming	Study
	Flow chart
	Code
	Test
	Document
Testing	Programs
	Linkage
	System
	Pilot
	Parallel
Conversion	Study
	Analyze
	Design
	Program
	Test
	Convert
Manual Systems	Study
	Write
	Train
	Condition

OPERATIONS EFFORT

Function	Activity
Computer Operations	Card or queue loading
	Tape or disk mounting
	Console monitoring
	Output setup, alignment
	Administrative control
Data Preparations	Keypunching
	Mail opening
	Input editing
	Order processing
	Complaint classification
Information Dissemination	Printing
	Decollation
	Bursting
	Addressing
	Insertion
	Postage application
	Mailing
Scheduling	Input scheduling
	Computer scheduling
File Library	Identification
	Cataloging
	Storing
	Assembling
	Reproducing
	Eliminating
Quality Control	Output sampling
	Comparison with specifications
	Check for reasonableness
	Input and process review
	Legibility check
Application Systems Modification	Study
	Analyze
	Detail design
	Programming
	Testing
	Conversion
	Manual Systems
Manufacturers'Systems Modification	Study
	Analyze
	Detail design
	Programming
	Testing
	Conversion
	Manual systems

Figure 1-1. Functions and Activities List

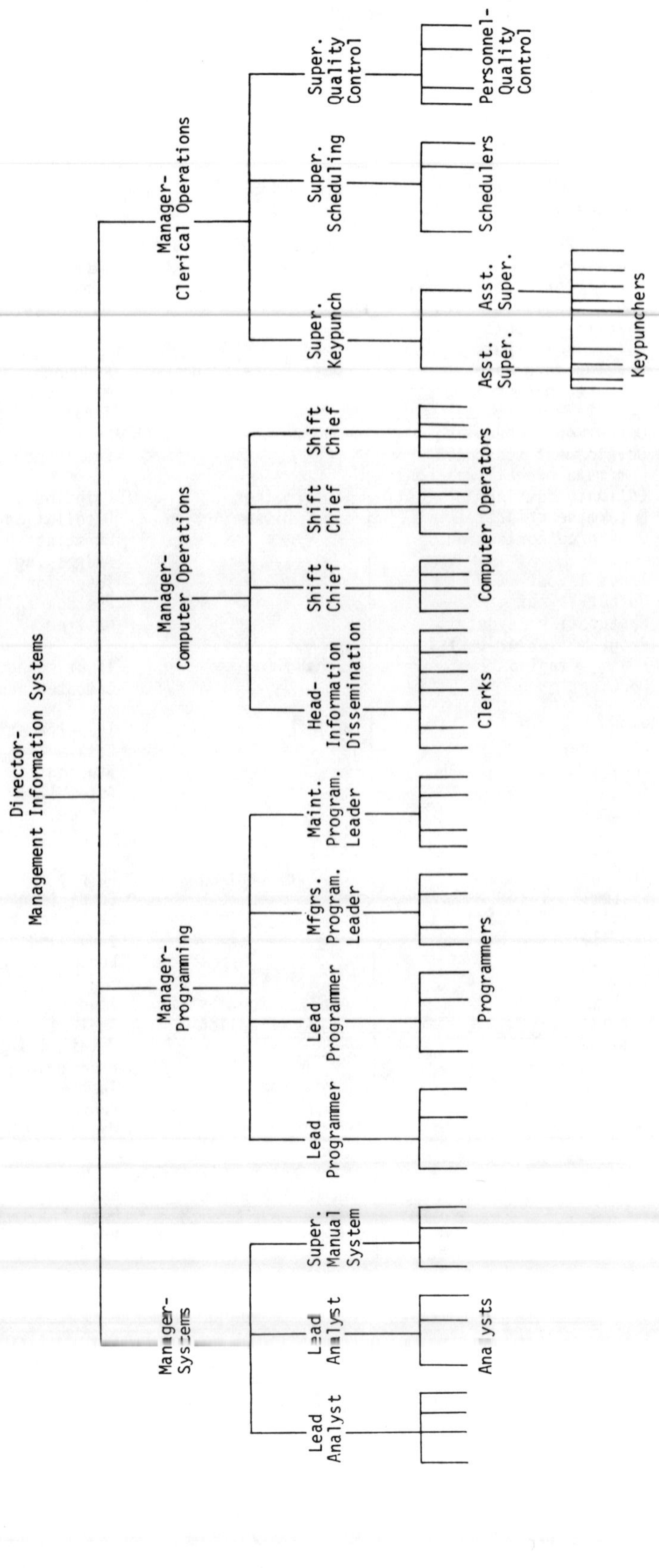

Figure 1-2. Typical EDP Organization

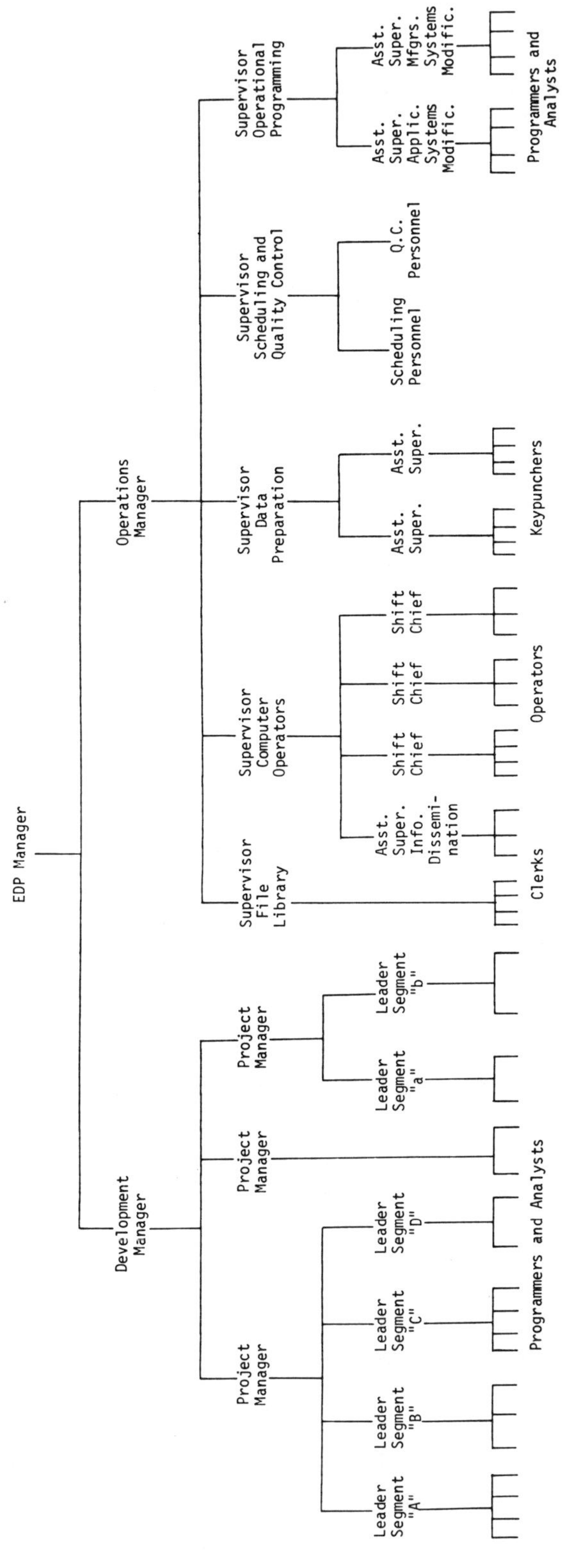

Figure 1-3. Functional EDP Organization

MANAGING EDP

The basic functions of an EDP manager are exactly the same as those of any other manager. He must plan, organize, motivate or direct, and control the efforts, functions and activities of the people in his area. However, management of operations efforts and development efforts differs widely.

Operations Efforts

For operational efforts, the EDP manager's activities, methods and tools are almost exactly the same as those of any production manager. He has specific (budgeted) amounts of resources (personnel, equipment and materials), specific tasks to accomplish (stated computer and attendent jobs to conduct), and finite time periods within which the tasks must be accomplished (production deadlines or timetables). Within this framework, it is the EDP manager's task to produce top quality products (outputs), as timely as possible (at the optimum schedule), and at the lowest possible cost (budget). All of this, naturally, must be accomplished regardless of problems with personnel (turnover), equipment (downtime), fluctuation in volume (excessive input) and new requirements (unexpected test time). Realistically, the EDP operations manager's task is very much the same as any other critical line management position in your business.

Development Efforts

A review of the development portion of the functions and activities list (Figure 1-1) will indicate that, for each project, all development functions and activities must first be planned. The number and types of personnel must be determined, the people must be organized, their roles must be defined, and the project must be staffed. The staff must be motivated to accomplish the project in the manner prescribed within the given schedule. Finally, controls must be established which ensure that the project is proceeding according to plan.

The EDP development manager's activities, methods and tools can only be approximated by other one-time-only management endeavors. For example, initiation of new product lines, implementation of fashion items and construction of single items such as large buildings and bridges provide the EDP development (and project) manager with compatible methods of management.

In comparison with the wealth of material written to assist (line) production managers, there is relatively little written on the management of one-shot projects. The main assistance comes from the body of literature on PERT (Project Evaluation Review Techniques), PERT/COST, and CPM (Critical Path Method). Unfortunately, EDP managers' attempts to apply these techniques have usually *not* provided the necessary assistance and have been abandoned.

The outline of the development effort functions and activities presented earlier is based upon a review of one-time-only management techniques, in-depth experience in EDP development efforts, and general management techniques. The control techniques presented in the remainder of this book have the same bases but, most importantly, have been developed specifically for the management of EDP projects.

EMPHASIS ON CONTROL

There are three cardinal sins of management:

1. To be in serious trouble.
2. To be in serious trouble and not know it.
3. To be in serious trouble, know it, and not report it.

In managing EDP projects the first sin is, unfortunately, a common occurrence; the second sin should be cause for demotion from management to worker; the third sin should be cause for dismissal.

An overall system of controls that is logical, that applies to your projects and that can be implemented and administered, lets you know when you start to get into trouble and provides a reporting mechanism. It provides sufficient warning so that you can, generally, avoid serious trouble entirely. The remaining chapters present an overall system of controls that:

1. Is logical.
2. Can be applied to your project.
3. Can be implemented by following this general implementation plan and heeding the warnings about the problems that will be encountered.

One warning must be given. The remaining chapters describe the basis, purpose, usage and format for the controls to be used. *Do not simply use the forms!* In almost every case the formats are only used for illustration and should be modified to fit the specific needs of your company and project. Blind utilization of control formats is worse than an absence of controls because you will believe that the project is under control without really understanding the information provided or its use.

2

Determining and Assigning Project Responsibility

The most effective control mechanism is to make reliable people responsible for achieving specific segments of the desired end result. Before they will authorize the implementation of a new EDP project, the top management personnel in many companies require an estimation of the project's potential payoff. Unfortunately, after the project has been approved, very few companies determine or assign the various responsibilities for achieving the expected results. Consequently, when the system has been installed, no one bears the responsibility for achieving the results expected from the project.

Unless specific people assume or are assigned the responsibilities for achieving the results expected, discussions similar to the one that follows are guaranteed:

Treasurer: It has been several months since the ledger system was installed. The system was supposed to save $100,000 a year. So far, the figures indicate a total saving of less than $50,000. What's the trouble? Will we save the money eventually?

Project Manager: I have no knowledge of what's happened. We installed the ledger system on time and it should have saved the amounts indicated. However, since installation, I've been tied up trying to implement the inventory system.

User Manager: I'd guess that the estimate was overly ambitious. I don't know how you could save $100,000 a year and still perform the required functions. My people are killing themselves to give you the savings that have been achieved.

Treasurer: Then, if I understand you correctly, I should estimate $40,000 savings per year rather than $100,000 per year.

Project Manager: That sounds awfully low.

User Manager: That's about right based on our experience.

Treasurer: O.K. We'll use the $40,000 per year figure.

In many companies this discussion would not really take place. Accounting would simply note that the estimated savings were not forthcoming and would adjust their forecasts accordingly.

In the rare instances where follow-up studies have been conducted to determine why projects did not pay off as estimated, the investigators usually encountered great difficulty in determining the actual project costs and savings because the company's normal accounting practices tended to group costs and income by responsibility areas. When valid results were obtained, they indicated that "if no one is responsible for each step leading to the company's actually realizing a projected benefit, the benefit will usually not be realized."

Because of these experiences, the controls described and recommended in this book assume specific responsibility relationships. This chapter describes:

1. The responsibility relationships recommended for each stage of the system's development and operation.
2. The benefits to be derived from using these relationships.
3. The methods and procedures for fulfilling these responsibilities.

These descriptions provide sufficient information so that valid responsibility relationships can be defined and assigned if those recommended cannot be directly implemented. Until these responsibility relationships are defined, no valid controls can be established.

To control an entire project, the controls must begin with the submission of new ideas and do not end until top management is assured that the project's benefits will be realized. Therefore, the description of the responsibility relationships for an entire project is segmented as follows:

1. Study
2. Development
3. Operations

The Study segment describes responsibility relationships beginning with the preliminary request evaluation and ending with the request for authorization. The Development segment describes the responsibility relationships from detail design through conversion. The Operations segment describes the responsibility relationships for user operations, computer operations, and for achieving the expected benefits. In all cases, the responsibilities for accomplishing and reviewing the overall function, activity, or achievement are described and the benefits of and procedures for these relationships are indicated.

STUDY

During the Study segment, good ideas for improving the company's activities are analyzed, assessed and expanded into requests for project authorization. Included in the Study segment are:

1. Preliminary request evaluation and request follow-up
2. Initial study

3. Conceptual design
4. Analysis
5. Project justification
6. Request for authorization

Each of these six functions, activities and achievements requires a different responsibility relationship if it is going to be accomplished, reviewed, and controlled in the most efficient manner. More detailed descriptions can be found in Chapters Three and Four.

Preliminary Request Evaluation and Follow-Up

The preliminary request evaluation and follow-up is conducted to ensure that the request contains sufficient information, to evaluate the general worth of the project requested, to inform the requester of the evaluation, and to motivate the requester and others to submit worthwhile ideas. Chapter Three details the methods, procedures and controls for accomplishing these purposes.

The responsibility for the preliminary request evaluation and follow-up is very straightforward. The EDP manager conducts the evaluation, and the person who has requested the study conducts the only review of the EDP manager's evaluation. This very basic responsibility relationship provides the following benefits:

1. The request is reviewed by the person who has overall responsibility. Therefore:
   a. Information is communicated directly.
   b. The information can be viewed in perspective to overall requirements.
   c. The evaluation can be accomplished quickly.
   d. Decisions are made by one person.
   e. Motivation is engendered by the high level review.
2. The requester is directly informed of, and reviews, the EDP manager's decision. Therefore, he is given the opportunity of:
   a. Understanding and agreeing with the basis for the decision.
   b. Protesting the decision to the EDP manager.
   c. Adding any new or omitted information.
   d. Submitting his request to his direct superior or another manager.

These benefits, with the controls and procedures recommended in Chapter Two, increase the probability that more requests will be submitted in the future and ensure prompt and efficient evaluation and follow-up.

Initial Study

The initial study, as described in Chapter Three, is conducted to roughly determine the scope of the project and to substantiate the requester's concept of the benefits to be derived. It usually consists of a few hours of interviewing and data analysis.

During the initial study, the interviewing, data analysis, and reporting are performed by an analyst selected by the development manager. This analyst is responsible for accomplishing the work and reports directly to the EDP manager.

The EDP manager has the primary responsibility for the accomplishment of the initial study. He, therefore, plans the project, thoroughly checks all results provided by the analyst, and decides whether to continue studying the feasibility of the project. In addition, the EDP manager maintains overall responsibility for the review of the results by the development manager and by the requester.

The development manager reviews the analyst's work to ensure the consistency of the project scope and benefits with the results of the interviews and data analysis. Based on this review, the development manager must be prepared to support or contest the preliminary decision of the EDP manager with regard to continuing study of the project's feasibility.

The requester reviews the analyst's work to increase his own knowledge and understanding of the project's scope and benefits. Based on this review, the requester must also support or contest any decision made by the EDP manager. Unless he is satisfied with the results of the initial survey, the requester must initiate further studies, either through his immediate superior or by working with the EDP manager.

By assigning the responsibilities in this manner, the following major benefits are realized:

1. The primary responsibility for accomplishment remains with the EDP manager. Therefore:
   a. The results can be viewed in perspective to the broadest overall knowledge of the company's EDP needs.
   b. The EDP manager develops individual knowledge of the EDP analyst's abilities and can personally direct the project.
   c. Because of his position, the survey is given prestige and can be used as a motivating factor.
2. The primary responsibility for reviewing the results is assigned to the development manager. This ensures that the development manager:
   a. Can assess his analysts.
   b. Contributes to the final decision.
   c. Is informed of potential projects.
   d. Meets and assists in motivating requesters.
3. All time and costs for activities can be charged to the EDP manager's account code (EDP overhead). This:
   a. Isolates the cost of initial surveys from Development costs without charging the user.
   b. Provides a direct measure of the cost of evaluating potential projects.
   c. Ensures that costs and responsibility coincide.
4. The requester's importance and status are recognized by assigning the responsibility for reviewing the results of the survey. This is motivational for as it increases the requester's knowledge, so it increases the probability of significant contribution in the future.

If the initial survey is conducted as described in Chapter Two, few additional procedures are required to ensure that all responsibilities are understood and accepted. Usually all that is required is an explanation by the EDP manager of each individual's responsibilities. An additional procedure which can be implemented at the conclusion of the follow-up meeting is the completion and submission of written approval statements by the requester and the development manager.

Conceptual Design

The completion of a conceptual design of the proposed system concludes the first portion of the feasibility study. The contents, conduct, and control of this portion of the study are described in greater detail in Chapter Three.

The primary responsibility for developing an effective and efficient conceptual design is assigned to the study manager (or lead analyst). The study manager is responsible for planning, organizing, motivating, and controlling the data gathering, interviewing, analysis, and design activities so that the resulting conceptual design meets all project objectives, performs all project functions, and is technically sound.

The study team is responsible for conducting the actual study under the direction of the study manager. Each individual is assigned a specific area (or areas) of responsibility and is expected to complete his assignment under the direction and control of the study manager.

The activities of the study manager and study team are monitored by the development manager who reviews the design and is responsible to the EDP manager for its successful accomplishment.

The EDP manager retains overall responsibility for accomplishment and review of the conceptual design. To achieve this, the EDP manager must, himself, review each element of the design as it is completed.

The primary responsibility for reviewing the conceptual design to ensure its functional accuracy is assigned to the user group, consisting of individuals selected from the user departments to perform this specific review function. The user group reviews the conceptual design documentation and participates in the in-depth review of the conceptual design.

The EDP technical review team consists of personnel selected from the Development and various Operations areas by the managers of Development and Operations. This team is responsible for reviewing the technical aspects of the conceptual design and determining whether the design is technically sound.

By assigning the responsibilities for accomplishing and reviewing the conceptual design in this manner, the following benefits are obtained:

1. The EDP manager retains overall control of the study segment. Therefore:
   a. The control of the EDP areas and groups is facilitated.
   b. The prestige of his position improves the initial contacts and communication with the user departments.
   c. Conceptual design efforts can be charged directly to the EDP manager's account code.

2. Primary responsibility for accomplishing the design is assigned to the lowest possible management level (the study manager) without abridging the development manager's responsibility.
3. The development manager is involved and can contribute prior to the completion of the design, but his time is not absorbed by direct management activities.
4. The user group is formed early in the project and its personnel are forced into involvement in the project because they must assess the functional soundness of the design.
5. The technical review team is also involved at an early date and must assess the design's technical soundness.
6. When the in-depth review of the conceptual design has been completed, independent approvals of the design's functional and technical soundness are documented by representatives from the groups that will eventually be responsible for the system's operation.

The procedures required to ensure acceptance of assigned responsibilities are generally outlined in Chapter Three. However, it is advisable for the EDP manager to conduct a short study initiation meeting with the study manager, the development manager, and the study team during which their various responsibilities are discussed, outlined, and agreed upon. Similarly, as the user group and technical review team are formed, the EDP manager should coordinate with the user manager and the operations manager (respectively) to conduct the same type of meeting.

Analysis

Analysis consists of the activities necessary to translate the conceptual design into project costs, schedule, resource requirements, benefits, and risk. The final analysis as described in Chapter Three, is a weighted point evaluation that permits ranking of potential projects in relation to their overall importance to the company.

During analysis, the primary responsibility for accomplishing the activities is assigned to the development manager. The development manager must:

1. Determine the analysis that will be performed.
2. Define the detail that will be included in each analysis.
3. Evaluate the manpower required.
4. Staff and schedule the analyses.
5. Review the results.

The study manager assists the development manager during analysis by providing working leadership and by directing and controlling the analysts, each of whom is responsible for performing specific analyses. Because of his primary responsibility to the conceptual design effort, all planning and organizational activities for analysis are the responsibility of the development manager.

The EDP technical review team is assigned the primary responsibility for reviewing the analyses to ensure that they realistically portray the efforts required and the benefits to be received from development and operation of the system. Naturally, the Development personnel on the team concentrate on the Development estimates and the Operations personnel concentrate on EDP Operations estimates.

The user group also reviews the analyses pertaining to non-EDP Operations and expected benefits. They ensure that the operations can be conducted as described in the analyses and that the benefits can be obtained.

The EDP manager provides a final review of all analyses and is responsible for top level coordination of EDP and user personnel during the analysis effort. Additionally, the EDP manager provides any subjective managerial judgment that is required to establish the project's priorities.

By assigning analysis responsibilities in this manner, the following benefits are realized:

1. The development manager's knowledge and experience in providing analyses are fully utilized in planning, organizing, and reviewing the analysis effort. Therefore:
   a. The analyses are completed in the most efficient manner.
   b. Gross errors are eliminated before the analyses are presented to the reviewing groups.
   c. The importance of the analyses is emphasized.
   d. Approved analytical techniques are described directly to each analyst.
2. The study manager's involvement in the working leadership of the analysis provides:
   a. Opportunity for the study manager to learn more analytical techniques.
   b. Relief of the development manager so that he can concentrate on other responsibilities.
   c. A method whereby the study manager can manage the entire feasibility study without overburdening himself or requiring a study manager who is completely knowledgeable about all analytical techniques.
3. Assignment of primary review responsibility to the EDP technical review team. This involves Development and Operations in the approval of all initial estimates. Then upon project authorization, the areas that are responsible for project implementation will have faith in the accuracy of the estimation, and will accept the responsibility for meeting the overall commitments made during analysis.
4. Assignment of responsibility for approving non-EDP operations to the user group. As with the EDP areas, this precludes later rejection of the estimations by the user areas.
5. Assignment of an overall responsibility to the EDP manager:
   a. Permits direct costing to the EDP manager's account code.
   b. Provides continuity of overall management of the Study effort.
   c. Permits utilization of his contacts, status, and prestige to ensure cooperation and coordination of the various groups.

To achieve these benefits, the general procedures for analysis that are outlined in Chapter Four should be supplemented by:

1. Analysis initiation meetings similar to the initiation meetings described in the section on conceptual design.

2. Each analyst forwarding a copy of each analysis to the development manager upon completion of the analysis.
3. Review, copying, and distribution of the analyses to the review groups by the development manager.
4. Immediate review of each analysis as it is received by the review groups. All questions and errors should be directed to the development manager.
5. Issuance of complete sets of analyses to the review groups when all individual analyses have been completed and corrected.
6. Total review by the review groups (technical and user) culminating in in-depth reviews of analysis and written approvals.

These general procedures can be supplemented by statistical chronological controls similar to the controls on the request process (Chapter Three). These controls would be instituted by either the development manager or the EDP manager to document and improve the efficiency of the analysis process.

Project Justification

Project justification is the final report summarizing the conclusions, recommendations and details of the feasibility study. Its preparation is relatively simple if each step of the feasibility study was correctly documented.

The study manager is responsible for actually preparing and directing the preparation of the project justification. All errors, ommissions, unclear phraseology, and poor organization of the feasibility studies' documentation must be corrected.

The primary responsibility for completing the project justification rests with the EDP manager. As he reviews each segment of the documentation to meet his overall study responsibilities, the EDP manager should note any problems and return them to the study manager for correction. Finally, the EDP manager must grant final approval to the project justification.

Top management, the user groups, and the EDP technical review team all review the completed project justification.

Top management's responsibility is to understand the information provided, to measure the realism of the information with respect to their knowledge, and to assess the worth of the project.

The user group and the EDP technical review team review the project justification to ensure that it conforms to the documentation that they previously approved.

The major benefits provided by assigning project justification responsibilities in this manner include:

1. Assignment of the primary responsibility for completing the project justification to the EDP manager who:
   a. Best knows how to present the information to top management.
   b. Must accept the overall responsibility for improper study documentation and, therefore, for inefficient completion of the project justification.
2. Assignment of the responsibility for all additional work in preparing the project justification to the study manager who was primarily responsible for its correct completion during the feasibility study.

3. Recognition of organizational structure realities and the development manager's primary responsibility for the analysis effort by assigning him secondary responsibility for the project justification.
4. Assignment of primary review responsibilities to top management as they must approve the project.
5. Allowance for final review by the user group and EDP technical review team.

Additional procedures necessary to ensure acceptance of the recommended responsibilities are described in Chapter Three.

Request for Authorization

The request for authorization is prepared by the EDP manager and is submitted to top management with the project justification. A second copy of the request for authorization and the project justification are sent to the user manager. When signed by top management, the request for project authorization gives the EDP manager the authority to begin the indicated project implementation.

To centralize the function, the EDP manager should be the only person involved in requesting project authorization and, therefore, has the primary responsibility for this function. Only top management can authorize projects and, therefore, must conduct the primary review.

The user manager is sent a copy of the request for authorization and the project justification so that he is fully informed of the scope, schedule, costs and benefits of the project.

The assignment of responsibilities for the request for authorization places the primary responsibilities for review and accomplishment on the people who will actually be doing the work. This reduces the time required and facilitates communication.

By informing the user manager of the impending authorization, his involvement and cooperation are maintained. Additionally, the user is requested by top management either to refute any points in the project justification with which he does not agree or submit a written concurrence memorandum.

In the area of procedures, logging and statistical summaries similar to those used for requests (Chapter Three) can be employed, but usually all parties know and understand their responsibilities.

DEVELOPMENT

After project authorization has been granted, the Development segment begins. During Development, the conceptual design is transformed into an operational system. The following functions and tasks are included in this segment:

1. Detail design and programming.
2. Testing and conversion.
3. Manual systems—study and writing.
4. Manual systems—training and conditioning.

By realigning the responsibility relationships of each of these four groupings of functions and tasks, the most efficient control of the project can be achieved. Chapters Four through Nine describe specific methods of controlling these groupings. Chapter One describes the functional activities in greater detail.

Detail Design and Programming

During the detail design and programming functions, the conceptual design of the system is translated into specific instructions that can be understood and performed by the computer. These activities generally account for more than 80 percent of the entire Development effort.

The project manager is assigned the primary responsibility for successfully accomplishing the functions. This responsibility encompasses planning, organizing, directing, and controlling the efforts of the project staff so that their individual responsibilities are completed in a satisfactory manner relative to all cost, schedule and quality parameters.

The overall responsibility for accomplishment and review is assigned to the development manager. In fulfilling this responsibility, he must coordinate the efforts of the project staff, the operations group and the user group. Additionally, the development manager must monitor the progress of the project and must integrate these efforts to maintain multiproject controls.

Each person on the project staff is assigned a specific set of activities and is responsible for the successful completion of these activities.

The operations group is selected from the EDP Operations personnel by the operations manager. This group should include personnel from operational programming, computer operations, scheduling and quality control, data preparation, and file library. This group is assigned the primary responsibility for monitoring and reviewing the design, program listings, program (programmer) tests, and documentation to ensure that each system element can be efficiently operated and modified after implementation.

A user group, similar in composition to the user group formed during the feasibility study, is formed to review the detail design and programming documentation to ensure that the system will function in the manner described by the conceptual design. In line with this review, the user group also plans and begins preparation of test data during the early stages of the detail design and completes all test data preparation by the end of programming. Chapter Six contains additional details about these efforts.

By establishing responsibility relationships for detail design and programming in this manner, the following benefits can be realized:

1. The assignment of the primary responsibility for accomplishment to the project manager:
    a. Centralizes the management of the project functions in one individual who can concentrate on this responsibility.
    b. Relieves the development manager of most project management tasks.
    c. Promotes "esprit de corps" among the project staff.

2. The development manager's overall accomplishment responsibilities:
   a. Permit monitoring without interference so that multi-project controls can be effected.
   b. Provide a coordinating influence with more prestige than that of the project manager.
   c. Correlate the overall responsibility with the area that is charged (Development) with the activities.
3. The assignment of primary and secondary review to the operations group and user group respectively:
   a. Coincides with the strong need for technical (EDP-oriented) review during these functions.
   b. Provides a basis for functional review.
   c. Ensures the preparation of test data—by the groups which will have to assess the results of the tests and who will be most affected by errors in the operational system.

The procedures required to ensure that all personnel understand and can accomplish their responsibilities are generally described in Chapters Five through Nine.

Additionally, initiation meetings are recommended for review personnel and a method should be established for obtaining cost distribution figures (from Accounting) within two working days of the close of a payroll period. If the cost distribution figures cannot be obtained within this period of time the project manager should consider establishing an easy method of manually estimating project costs or should suggest that the cost distribution system be improved immediately.

Testing and Conversion

Testing and conversion ensure that the system is functionally and technically sound and that the data base and programs are ready for operation. These functions are described in greater detail in Chapters Six and Seven.

The responsibilities for accomplishing the testing and conversion functions are assigned to the project manager, development manager, and project staff in exactly the same manner as during the detailed design and programming functions.

The primary review responsibility, however, is assigned to the user group. To fulfill this responsibility, this group must produce all test data, check all test outputs, check all conversion audits and printouts, and determine the effects of any program or procedural errors. They are supported in this by the project staff which must eliminate all errors from its areas of responsibility.

The operations group reviews the testing and conversion activities to ensure that the Operations areas will be able to schedule, operate, modify, and correct the system after it becomes operational. They, therefore, concentrate on the systems costs, schedules, and quality as they affect future operations.

This assignment of responsibilities provides the same benefits as does the responsibility assignment during detail design and programming. In addition, it:

1. Eliminates any natural bias (from testing review) that the project staff might have.

2. Ensures that the users are satisfied with the functions of the system before it is put into operation.
3. Can be combined with training activities to decrease the total effort expended.

An initiation meeting and the procedures outlined in this section and in Chapters Six and Seven, will ensure that the testing and conversion responsibilities are understood and fulfilled.

Manual Systems—Study and Writing

Within the manual systems function, the study and writing tasks consist of the determination and writing of the new manual procedures that are required to support the computer system. Chapters One and Seven describe these tasks in more detail.

The project manager retains the primary responsibility for the study and writing tasks. He must plan, organize, direct and control the activities of the manual systems staff which actually performs the work.

The user manager is assigned the secondary responsibility for the study and writing tasks. His activities include the coordination of the manual systems staff's activities with the normal operational activities of the user department's personnel and the personal management of the review performed by the user group.

The development manager retains overall responsibility for the writing and study tasks and coordinates these activities with the activities of the review groups. In doing so, he must personally review the procedures as they are written.

The user group is primarily responsible for reviewing the procedures applying to the user groups as they are written. They must determine whether the procedures are understandable and whether they will produce efficient efforts. When possible, this group also assists the manual systems staff in the writing of the procedures.

The operations group reviews the procedures applying to the EDP Operations areas as they are written. This group should assist in the writing and must approve the clarity and efficiency of the procedures.

The benefits described in the preceding section on test and conversion are also derived from assigning similar responsibilities to the project manager, user group and operations group during manual systems study and writing. However, assignments of accomplishment responsibilities to the user manager and development manager provides:

1. The beginning of a normal transition of responsibilities from the Development area to the user area by:
   a. Directly involving the user manager.
   b. Retaining the overall direction of the development manager.
   c. Assigning the costs to the Development area.
2. Motivation for the user group by exposing their efforts directly to the user manager.
3. Emphasizing the importance of the procedures to the user area.

The procedures for achieving these benefits are described in more detail in Chapters Seven and Nine. In addition, the development manager should work closely with the user manager to ensure his understanding, interest, and involvement in his new responsibilities.

Manual Systems—Training and Conditioning

During training and conditioning the affected user and Operations personnel are trained in the use of the new procedures and are prepared for initiation of the new system. These activities are described further in Chapters One and Seven.

The only change in responsibilities from the study and writing tasks is the assignment of the primary responsibility for accomplishment and the overall responsibility to the user manager and the assignment of the secondary responsibility for accomplishment to the project manager. This reversal of roles:

1. Gives the user manager the responsibility of ensuring that his people are trained.
2. Allows the project manager to direct the manual systems group under the guidance of the user manager.
3. Increases the pace of the transition of responsibility from the Development area to the user area.
4. Provides all necessary support to the user area.
5. Transfers the cost burden to the user area.

No additional procedures, other than those described in Chapter Six and Eight, should be required.

OPERATIONS

Operations refers to the day-to-day functioning of the new computer system and all personnel and procedures required for the correct and efficient functioning of the system. Usually, the Operations efforts are divided between two basic functions:

1. User Operations
2. Computer Operations

In this section, a third function:

3. Expected Benefits

has been added so that the responsibility for the realization of expected benefits can also be described.

More detailed descriptions of the activities of the user areas and the computer operations areas can be found in Chapters One and Ten. Because of the basic belief that new projects should not affect normal responsibility relationships in operating areas, the primary and working responsibilities are assigned to the managers and staffs of these areas. The following sections of this chapter describe the additional responsibilities that should be assigned and the benefits that result from these assignments.

User Operations

In addition to the normal user manager, user staff relationship, the project manager is assigned the responsibility for accomplishing project objectives. To fulfill this, he must review all control reports, investigate whenever payback and payoff vary significantly from estimates, and determine how to reinstate control.

The development manager is assigned a review responsibility for the same reason. He also must review the control reports and must direct the project manager's investigation of discrepancies.

These additional responsibilities:

1. Ensure that the user operations are changed as required by the implementation of the system.
2. Provide continuing assistance in achieving goals.
3. Do not affect the prestige or authority of the user manager.

To achieve these benefits:

1. The development manager must accept the continuing nature of his responsibility and the project manager's responsibility.
2. The user manager must appreciate the assistance provided.
3. Accounting must continue to isolate new system costs and income in the user area(s).
4. Top management must agree to the preceding conditions and must coordinate the efforts of the affected groups.

Specific procedures for control are described in greater detail in Chapter Ten.

Computer Operations

The responsibilities for accomplishing the project objectives in the computer operations areas are assigned to the operations manager, operations staff, and project manager in the same manner as in user operations. However, because the user manager retains overall responsibility and is usually charged for computer services performed for his area, both he and the development manager review the control reports to ensure that the system is functioning normally in the computer areas.

The benefits of these assignments are the same as in user operations. In addition, the user manager reviews the controls and can ensure that computer operations is correctly servicing his area.

To achieve these benefits, top management, the operations manager and accounting must understand their individual and collective responsibilities. Specific procedures are described in greater detail in Chapter Ten.

Expected Benefits

In addition to all their other responsibilities, the user manager, project manager, top management, the development manager, and the EDP manager are also responsible (in various ways) for ensuring that all expected benefits are achieved.

Because the benefits from savings and increased income are reflected by improved cost/performance ratios in his areas (and therefore reflect credit upon him), the user manager is assigned the primary responsibility for reviewing and achieving these benefits. To fulfill this responsibility he must review the control reports and analyses provided by accounting and must direct accounting or the project manager to conduct new analyses or implement new methods, whenever they are needed, to determine the cause of variance from expectations.

As most tangible benefits from a project are monetary (see Chapters Four and Six), accounting must provide the majority of the working tools to assess variance from expectations. Usually normal cost distribution techniques are sufficient but, occasionally, other analyses are required.

The project manager, because of his detailed knowledge of the system and its controls, is responsible for supporting the user manager and for detecting and correcting variances in expectations.

Top management, by maintaining a continuing interest until payback and payoff are assured, accepts the primary responsibility for review. Therefore, review reports are submitted by accounting which define the overall success of the project and assess the manner in which each person or group is fulfilling his responsibilities.

The development manager reviews the control reports on the operation of the project and develops summaries of the overall performance of all new projects developed by his area. These analyses provide a basis for justifying the worth of his area.

The EDP manager must also review the control reports on the operation of the project to finally determine the efficiency and accuracy of the study effort.

If these responsibilities are all fulfilled, the project will produce all expected benefits and will usually yield a few unexpected beneficial results.

The procedures outlined above are described in greater detail in Chapter Ten.

SUMMARY

This chapter has described the changes in responsibility relationships from project initiation through operation. Figure 2-1, Responsibility Assignment Matrix, summarizes the recommended responsibility relationships.

If the recommended relationships cannot be implemented, the responsibilities must be assigned so that:

1. All responsibilities are defined and assigned.
2. The assignments reflect the changing nature of the project.
3. The prestige, knowledge, experience, and functions of each person are considered when making assignments.
4. Organizational realities are considered.
5. Responsibility assignments are made to improve and control the progress of the project and not simply as courtesy measures.

Violation of these rules will either cause conflict among the parties or will seriously impede the progress of the project.

EDP PROJECT RESPONSIBILITY ASSIGNMENTS

FUNCTION	ACCOMPLISHMENT			REVIEW			OVERALL
Activity of Achievement	Primary	Secondary	Working	Primary	Secondary	Tertiary	EDP Manager
STUDY							
1. Perfunctory Request Evaluation & Followup	EDP Manager	--		Requester	--	--	EDP Manager
2. Initial Survey	EDP Manager	--	Analyst	Dev. Manager	Requester	--	EDP Manager
3. Feasibility							
a. Conceptual Design	Study Manager	Dev. Manager	Study Team	User Group	EDP Tech.Rev.Team	User Group	EDP Manager
b. Analysis	Dev. Manager	Study Manager	Analysts	EDP Tech.Rev.Team	User Group	EDP Manager	EDP Manager
c. Project Justification	EDP Manager	Dev. Manager	Study Manager	Top Management	User Group	EDP Tech.Rev.Team	EDP Manager
4. Request Authorization	EDP Manager	--	--	Top Management	User Group	--	EDP Manager
DEVELOPMENT							
5. Detail Design	Proj. Manager	Dev. Manager	Project Staff	Operations Group	User Group	--	Dev. Manager
6. Programming	Proj. Manager	Dev. Manager	Project Staff	Operations Group	User Group	--	Dev. Manager
7. Testing	Proj. Manager	Dev. Manager	Project Staff	User Group	Operations Group	Project Staff	Dev. Manager
8. Conversion	Proj. Manager	Dev. Manager	Project Staff	User Group	Operations Group	--	User Manager
9. Manual Systems							
a. Study	Proj. Manager	User Manager	Manual Sys.Group	User Group	Operations Group	Dev. Manager	Dev. Manager
b. Writing	Proj. Manager	User Manager	Manual Sys.Group	User Group	Operations Group	Dev. Manager	Dev. Manager
c. Training	User Manager	Proj. Manager	Manual Sys.Group	User Group	Operations Group	--	User Manager
d. Conditioning	User Manager	Proj. Manager	Manual Sys.Group	User Group	Operations Group	--	User Manager
OPERATIONS							
10. User Operations	User Manager	Proj. Manager	User Staff	Dev. Manager	--	--	User Manager
11. Computer Operations	Op. Manager	Proj. Manager	Operations Staff	User Manager	Dev. Manager	--	User Manager
12. Expected Benefits	User Manager	Proj. Manager	Accounting	Top Management	Dev. Manager	EDP Manager	User Manager

Figure 2-1. Responsibility Assignment Matrix

3

Originating the Project and Conducting Basic Studies

Everything has to start somewhere. EDP projects start with an idea. Someone, somewhere, gets an idea that EDP could do a certain business activity (like payroll, production scheduling, or the issuance of the absenteeism report) more efficiently (faster, cheaper or just plain easier) or better (providing more income, more accuracy, more timely information, or a competitive edge). After the idea has been generated, it will be wasted unless the EDP manager is informed. The idea must be forwarded to the EDP manager before any action can be initiated. For this reason and because the easiest thing to do is to forget the idea, it is not surprising that the following comments are typical in almost every business:

> None of the people here ever come up with any real good ideas for improving the ways this company does business.
>
> The supervisors in this company are afraid of any ideas their people have and tend to squash them.
>
> The Suggestion Plan takes too long.
>
> EDP won't do anything about our ideas anyway.
>
> If you really want something done in EDP call Pete, he's only a programmer but he'll do it.

As a member of management, the EDP manager must accept the responsibility for fostering new ideas and for providing a mechanism for quickly and thoroughly evaluating them. As the manager of a service area, he must jealously guard EDP's reputation for providing help and for being interested in helping. As the manager of EDP, he lacks true control over his people and their activities if he allows them to operate on their own. Therefore, regardless of his role, the EDP manager must develop and control a system for obtaining and evaluating ideas about new EDP projects.

If new ideas are to be encouraged, the method for requesting new projects must:

1. Provide an understandable, informative and standard request medium.
2. Quickly provide feedback on the project's acceptability to the person who requests the new project.
3. Ensure that the requesters will, in some manner, benefit personally if their ideas are implemented.
4. Lead directly into initial (study) stages of implementation.

The remainder of this chapter presents:

1. A method for requesting new projects that encourages new ideas (project requests).
2. A method of evaluating the requests quickly (initial study).
3. The beginning of the second level of evaluation (feasibility study).
4. Media for informing project requesters of the progress of the project request.

These elements, taken together, provide thorough, centralized, practical control over project origination.

HANDLING PROJECT REQUESTS

Project requests, as described in this book, are simple, practical methods and media for communicating ideas, evaluating ideas, and communicating the results of the evaluations. These methods and media include:

1. The project request form.
2. Preliminary request evaluation.
3. Request follow-up.

The project request form describes a recommended form; how the requester gets and submits it, informal project requests, and mandatory project requests. The preliminary request evaluation describes the actions of the EDP manager upon receipt of such a form, the review of the contents of the form and the EDP manager's possible actions. The request follow-up indicates the media to be utilized in informing the requester of the results of the preliminary request evaluation.

Project Request Form

The philosophy underlying this section is fourfold:

1. Many ideas for worthwhile projects exist at all levels within a company.
2. Rarely do the ideas held by the lower (clerical and first line supervisory) level personnel get transmitted to the person or area that can best evaluate them.
3. The lack of transmittal of ideas from lower level personnel is caused by a lack of knowledge as to how to transmit ideas and by discouragement of transmittal after little or no review by superiors.
4. It is worthwhile to thoroughly review a large number of ideas even though only a few are actually implemented because the rejected ideas will provide knowledge that will assist in the implementation of other projects and because good will and interest will be generated for EDP.

This philosophy is based upon the analysis and implementation of a large number of EDP projects. During these projects, it became increasingly apparent that the majority of worthwhile ideas for new systems and for improving existing systems were suggested by lower level personnel.

Format and contents. Figure 3-1 illustrates the format and contents recommended for project request forms. The format is recommended because it is written in terms that are familiar and can be readily understood by clerical personnel, production personnel and first line supervisors. This is important because people who are confused by formats and/or language are reluctant to submit ideas.

Most project request forms are written by EDP personnel who have little understanding of the people who will be completing these forms. Therefore, most project request forms are written in unfamiliar terms that confuse or frighten those who are expected to complete them. For example, many EDP personnel would expect information on the source of a project's benefits to be included under the project description and do not solicit this information. When information on this subject is solicited, the question is usually stated as "Source of Benefits." While this saves space and would be understood by most EDP and management personnel, the question "Where will the savings income or other benefits come from?" would be understood by almost all personnel even though the grammar is not excellent.

Because all personnel can understand the form they do not have to ask their superiors or friends how to complete the form. This combined with the one addressee (EDP manager) not only eliminates the requester's hesitancy to display his ignorance, but also eliminates discouragement by superiors after little or no review.

The contents of the recommended project request form are:

1. Addressee
2. Project name (optional)
3. Project description
4. Benefits
5. Source of benefits
6. Basic project completion date and priority information
7. Identification of requester.

This request form illustrates the combination of contents and format. As can be seen, savings and income benefits are emphasized in a manner that will cause the requester to consider them seriously and are presented in a natural and straightforward manner. Likewise, information on completion date and project priority are elicited in a manner that merits the consideration of the requester but does not cause him to worry if he can't complete this information.

Accessibility. Project request forms should be directly available to every person in the company. Therefore, supplies of these forms should be maintained in places such as:

1. All general interest information areas (bulletin boards).
2. Lounges and cafeterias.

TO: EDP Manager

SUBJECT: Project Request Form

PROJECT NAME: ____
(optional)

What activities does the project replace or perform?

____

____

____

____

____ (Use back if necessary)

Will this project save the company money?_____ About how much $__________ per year / per month / per week

Will this project produce additional income?_____ About how much $__________ per year / per month / per week

What other ways will this project help the company?

____

____

____

____

____ (Use back if necessary)

Where will the savings, income or other benefits come from?

____

____

____ (Use back if necessary)

Does the project have to be done by a certain date?_____ What date? ____________

Is there anything that you know of that would be of more help to your area? ________

What? ____

Name______________________________ Employee # ______________

Position ____________________ Superior's name ______________

Your signature ______________________ Date submitted ____________

==

Date received by EDP Manager ____________

Figure 3-1. Project Request Form

3. Locker rooms.
4. The personnel reception area.
5. All EDP clerical and secretarial areas.
6. Each department.

If planned correctly, it should be impossible for any person to work for an entire day without passing a supply of these forms at least once.

The order of the places where the forms should be demonstrates what is meant by "directly available." No person should be required to go to a superior to obtain these forms either as policy or because of not knowing where to find the forms. At the time of hiring, all personnel should be informed about the use and the availability of the forms. Thereafter, they should be reminded periodically through company papers, information bulletins or brochures, posters, or any other normal communication media.

The direct and general availability of these forms is an additional reason why their language and format must be completely understandable. Any obscure language would require accompanying instructions or, as previously indicated, people would have to consult others to complete the form.

Submission. As indicated by the recommended request form, the original of the form is sent directly to the EDP manager. No other copy is required although the requester may keep one for his own records and may give a copy to his superior.

This direct submission to the EDP manager precludes intervention and discouragement by the requester's superiors or any other intermediary. This policy will undoubtedly increase the number of requests that must be reviewed and also places the control of this review entirely in the hands of the EDP manager. In this way, he is assured that:

1. He has a chance to review all new ideas that could affect his operations.
2. Rejection of a new idea is done in a manner that does not reflect adversely on EDP and that does not (or in some cases does) inhibit the requester from submitting other new ideas.
3. Everyone who submits a new idea gets some immediate recognition from EDP.
4. Those who submit good ideas get a good deal of recognition from EDP and that the requester's management is fully informed of the worth of the ideas.

These assurances are vital if the project request system is to continually fulfill the goals of encouraging the submission of new ideas.

Informal requests. In any company, many people will prefer to request new projects informally rather than complete the formal Project Request Form. Informal requests will usually be oral or through a short memo.

Many informal requests will be made to EDP personnel though not necessarily to the EDP manager. In these cases, all EDP personnel must be trained and motivated to immediately obtain and complete a formal Project Request Form to be submitted to the EDP project manager. Any deviation from this procedure will eventually lead to a breakdown in the entire project request system because:

1. No one other than the EDP manager is empowered to review project requests.
2. The information provided for the EDP manager's review must be standardized to economize his time.
3. Exceptions permitted within EDP breed greater laxity and an even larger number of exceptions outside EDP.
4. Control over requests is lost.

Supervisory or management personnel outside EDP also should be trained and motivated to instruct anyone making an informal request on the completion and submittal of the formal Project Request Form. This is necessary for the same basic reasons as were stated for EDP personnel. In addition, this policy will save time for the supervisors and managers.

Periodically, all personnel should be informed of the benefits both to the company and themselves from the project request system. At the same time, they can be reminded of the procedures, the location of the forms and, finally, the fact that they should encourage their friends who have ideas to utilize the provided forms. In this way, informal requests of peers will be redirected into formal requests.

Mandatory requests. Mandatory requests for project work are those that, because of the position (or political power) of the requester, cannot be rejected. Theoretically, requests should never be mandatory. Practically, if the president of the company is determined to have a project done, it is mandatory.

If, however, the EDP manager is the only person who can review and accept project requests, he automatically becomes the only person who can deem a project mandatory. This policy provides all other EDP personnel with a viable reason and method for not accepting mandatory projects. For example, the person would say:

> I'm sorry, I'd like to do that for you, but Mr. X, the EDP manager, is the only one who can accept project requests. I'll call him immediately and tell him what you want. It will help me to get his approval, however, if you could tell me . . .

and would then obtain enough information to complete and personally submit a Project Request Form. If the requester does not want to give additional information, the person in EDP fills out the form as best he can and takes it to the EDP manager.

The EDP manager, faced with a mandatory request, can:

1. Ensure that a proper Project Request Form is submitted (even if he has to complete it himself).
2. Review the information.
3. Determine if it is truly mandatory.
4. Point out all of the problems that will be caused, if he does not believe it to be mandatory.
5. Immediately proceed, if necessary.

Despite some loss of control, this permits the EDP manager to regulate the request process even though he does not have complete control over the project acceptance.

Preliminary Request Evaluation

The preliminary request evaluation is conducted by the EDP manager (or in some cases by his appointee). It consists of logging the date of receipt on the project request form and a review of the information contained in the form to ensure that it has been completed correctly and clearly. If the form is incomplete or confusing, the EDP manager directly contacts the requester and either clarifies the matter or arranges a meeting to do so. This contact should be made within one day of receipt of the Project Request Form.

During the contact and/or meeting, in addition to obtaining the information, the EDP manager must see to it that the requester is comfortable, and that he understands both that his idea is appreciated and why the information is required. He should know that the lack of understanding stems from the EDP manager's lack of understanding of the requester's area of expertise. One truly successful meeting can generate three new requests, while an unsuccessful one will discourage at least ten.

When the EDP manager has a complete and understandable project request, he then makes a preliminary evaluation of the information. Its entire purpose is to screen out the requests that do not merit attention either because they do not appear to be significant enough to be worked on or because the idea does not really pertain to EDP.

The EDP manager has three alternatives. Depending on his evaluation he can decide to:

1. Begin or schedule an initial study.
2. Reject the request.
3. Turn the request over to another, more appropriate, area or department.

In some cases, as previously noted under the section on Mandatory Requests, the EDP manager may also decide to skip certain steps and begin to implement the project.

The Preliminary Request Evaluation should never take more than ten minutes after the information has been completed. All Project Request Forms should be reviewed within one day of receipt, or completion of the information.

Request Follow-Up

Once the EDP manager has decided what action to take on the project request, he should send to the requester a Preliminary Review Memorandum (Figure 3-2), typed (either individually or via an auto-typewriter console depending on volume) and personally signed by the EDP manager.

The personalization of the Preliminary Review Memorandum and the prompt response will impress the requester with the consideration that has been given to his idea and the efficiency with which it was handled. This will encourage him (and his friends) to submit other ideas.

As the Memorandum is sent out, the EDP manager's secretary should note on his calendar a date one week in the future (set a one-week flag) on which the manager should call and discuss the decision. Specifically, he should ensure:

TO:________(1)_____________ - ________(2)________ Department

FROM: M. D. Wadsworth, EDP Manager

CONCERNING: New Project Entitled ____________(3)____________

Thank you very much for sending me the information about the possibility of beginning a project to ____________(4)____________

____

I thoroughly reviewed the information that you provided and can assure you that it increased my understanding of your area. Based on the information that you provided, we have decided to ____________(5)____________

____

Before this decision is considered final, however, I would like to talk to you and explain, more thoroughly, this decision. Please call me on Extension 697 and we'll either discuss the decision or set a time to discuss the decision.

Sincerely,

M. D. Wadsworth

M. D. Wadsworth
EDP Manager

MDW/jm
MDW/ jm
cc: Files

===

Fill in:

(1) Name of Requester - from Project Request Form

(2) Department of Requester - from Project Request Form

(3) Project Name - from Project Request Form

(4) Project Description - condensed from Project Request Form

(5) Alternatives - a."begin an Initial Study of the project requirements."
b."reject your request because its benefits do not warrant working on it at this time."
c."turn this request over to ___(a)___ because it seems that this project is more nearly their responsibility."

(a) Department Name to whom Project Request is being referred.

Figure 3-2. Preliminary Review Memorandum

1. That there are not additional benefits–rejections.
2. To whom the request should be referred–referrals.
3. That he has fully conveyed his appreciation to the requester–initial study.
4. That the requester agrees with his decision–all cases.

This action, more than any other, will encourage the submission of further ideas.

INITIAL STUDY

The initial study is conducted to substantiate the requester's concepts of the benefits to be derived and to make an initial, very rough estimate of the scope of the project. It begins with the EDP manager's decision that the project request warrants further investigation.

Preparation

Once this decision is made, the EDP manager asks the manager of Systems Development who will be assigned to conduct an initial survey and when it will be done. At this point, the EDP manager also:

1. Has the completed Project Request Form copied and sent to the analyst.
2. Determines how the survey should be conducted.
3. Estimates how much time should be expended on the survey as well as the final completion date.

Meanwhile, the manager-Systems Development meets with the selected analyst and reviews:

1. The purpose of the initial survey.
2. The Project Request Form.
3. The fact that the analyst will work directly for the EDP manager on this study.
4. The importance of initial surveys.
5. The Initial Survey Report Form (see Figure 3-3).

Finally, when the selected analyst is free to begin the initial survey, he meets with the EDP manager in order to:

1. Review the Project Request Form.
2. Discuss how the survey is to be conducted.
3. Impress the analyst with the need for haste, tact, and accuracy.
4. Agree upon the amount of time required for the survey and the completion date.
5. Let the EDP manager judge the acceptability of the analyst.

Conduct

The initial survey is composed of data analysis and interviewing. The total time spent on these two activities should not exceed five hours. Four fifteen-minute interviews and four hours of data analysis should be more than sufficient for the purposes of the initial survey.

To: EDP Manager
cc: Requester, Analyst, Manager-Development Systems

____________ PROJECT

INITIAL SURVEY REPORT

Analyst: ______________________________ Date Assigned: _______________

Man Hours Expended: _______ Completion Date: _________ Est. _________ Act.

Estimated Savings: $__________ Av. $__________ Min. $__________ Max.

Estimated Income: $__________ Av. $__________ Min. $__________ Max.

Other Benefits: ____

____

____ (Use back if necessary)

New System Functions: ____

____

____ (Use back if necessary)

New System Files: ____

____

Special Features: ____

____

Flow Chart: Initial (Show on back of this form if possible)

Cost Estimates:

Development- $__________ Av. $__________ Min. $__________ Max.

Operations- $__________ Av. $__________ Min. $__________ Max.

==

Sources of Information: Requester- ________________________________

Others- ____

Comments: ____

____

Figure 3-3. Initial Survey Report Form

The elapsed time for an initial survey should be about one week, depending upon the availability of the interviewees. Within one week, all required data should be gathered and analyzed, all interviews should be conducted, and the Initial Survey Report Form should be completed. The analyst who wishes to create a good impression can complete an initial survey in one day by using alternative sources of information if the primary sources are unavailable on a timely basis.

Many readers will believe that the times quoted are quite low. However, it should be understood that these times are based upon experience, not theory, and that a good deal of latitude (50% difference–minimum to maximum) is allowed in savings, income, and cost estimates. These wide variances are allowable because the initial survey, if accepted after review by the EDP manager, will lead to a much more complete feasibility study before top management is requested to authorize project inception.

Results

Further details about the types of information that the analyst must gather during the initial survey are illustrated by the Initial Survey Report Form (Figure 3-3). These details include estimates of savings (average, minimum and maximum), income, development costs, and operations costs. In addition the analyst must specify other benefits, new system functions, new system files, special features, and the sources of his information. Comments and an initial flow chart are optional but desirable.

When the Initial Survey Report is completed it is distributed to the EDP manager, the requester, the manager-development systems and the analyst who conducted the survey. The information contained therein can only

1. support the EDP manager's decision that the program will provide significant benefits; or
2. contradict this decision.

In either case, the EDP manager has been given an estimate of benefits and costs from an analyst whose background and experience qualify him to make such estimations. Prior to this, the EDP manager's decision to proceed was based upon estimations made by the requester–a person who could be exceedingly optimistic or pessimistic in his estimates.

Primary Benefit

The primary benefit of the initial survey is the confidence that the EDP manager can place in the estimates of savings, income, and cost. In addition, the EDP manager has more information upon which to base a decision and he has had a chance to personally evaluate the work of one of his analysts.

For the expenditure of about one day of an analyst's time, the EDP manager has gained a firm basis for deciding whether and when to proceed into the feasibility study. If one initial survey in ten correctly eliminates a feasibility study, the time saved will more than offset the time spent on initial surveys.

The decision to proceed. Using the information provided, the EDP manager must now decide whether and when to proceed into a feasibility study. This decision can be restated as:

1. Does the project apparently have sufficient potential to warrant further study?
2. What ranking (or priority) among similar projects is justified by the apparent payoff?
3. Should any political or other factors influence this ranking?
4. When will the personnel (and other resources) be available to begin a project with that ranking?

To help answer these questions, analytical tools for the evaluation of projects are included in Chapter Four. These techniques can also be applied to the results of the initial survey.

Initial Survey Follow-Up

If the EDP manager decides that additional study of the project does not seem to be warranted based upon the information provided by the initial survey, he should call the requester, the analyst and the manager-Development Systems to inform them of his decision and to arrange a meeting for discussion. During this meeting, all parties should discuss and understand that the information in the Initial Survey Report is substantially correct. They should also agree that the facts do not warrant further study of the project, that the idea was very good, and that the submission of the idea is greatly appreciated. If agreement is not reached, the analyst and requester must restudy the situation until it is reached.

If the EDP manager decides to proceed with a feasibility study, he must contact the manager-Development Systems and they must decide upon an acceptable timetable for this study. At this point, the EDP manager informs both the requester and the analyst of his decision and of the approximate starting date for the feasibility study. If the original analyst will not be managing or working on the feasibility study, the EDP manager must inform him of the reasons behind this decision.

FEASIBILITY STUDY

The feasibility study is conducted to provide a sound and detailed basis for project authorization. This basis includes:

1. Definition of system objectives.
2. Definition of all inputs to the system.
3. Definition of all outputs from the system.
4. Definition of the data base used by the system.
5. Preparation of a conceptual design of the system.
6. Estimation of final benefits and costs.
7. Definition and evaluation of alternative solutions.

Depending upon the size and complexity of the system, the effort required to complete a feasibility study can vary from six man-days to two man-years. However, when given a particular feasibility study, the EDP manager should be able to estimate the time required within a three to four man-weeks range based upon the information provided by the initial survey.

Since this book is concerned primarily with EDP project management controls and only secondarily with the techniques of systems analysis, the remainder of this chapter contains only a brief outline of how feasibility studies are conducted, the extent to which the system's objectives and scope, inputs, outputs and data base are defined, the contents and detail contained in a conceptual design and the controls and reports required for project requests, initial surveys and feasibility studies. Chapter Four provides additional details about the methods that should be used to estimate final project benefits and costs and describes the conclusion of the feasibility study.

Conduct

The feasibility study is conducted in much the same manner as the initial study. It consists mainly of data (or information) gathering, data review, interviewing, analysis of system elements, and the conceptual design or flow charting of the new system.

The reader is assumed to be familiar with the method of conducting feasibility studies in operation within his company. However, regardless of the methods of data gathering, types of data review, patterns of interviewing, specific analyses utilized, or the level of flow charting that may be employed, certain basic information must be provided. Each of the following sub-sections describes one element of the basic information relevant to the overall control of an EDP project.

Objectives. The objectives of the project, detailed in the Project Justification that is prepared at the end of the feasibility study, provide the yardsticks or controls against which the success of the entire project will be measured. For this reason, when stated, these objectives must be:

1. Complete.
2. Specific.
3. Attainable.
4. Measurable.

To illustrate:

> In the area of savings, the Initial Survey Report might indicate that savings would average $120,000 per year with a maximum of $140,000 per year and a minimum of $70,000 per year. The Project Justification would detail source of the savings by types (salary, equipment, materials), department, and time period.

The establishment of firm objectives early in the project is mandatory. If they are complete, specific, attainable, and measurable, all future requests for change, alternative techniques of design or programming, and questions about project scope can be evaluated in relation to them. Without firm objectives it is virtually impossible to determine whether a project has truly been completed.

The establishment of firm objectives also provides other benefits. The EDP manager and the manager-Systems Development can now evaluate their personnel (and themselves) by comparing the objectives with the results that are achieved. For the poor manager this concept will be frightening. For the good manager it will provide a long-awaited opportunity to demonstrate his (and his people's) true worth. In addition, when their role is understood within the company, firm objectives finally eliminate the misconceptions of users and/or management about the expected results and/or costs associated with the project. For any project manager who has been confronted with a misconception about the expected results midway through a project, this one benefit will provide sufficient reason for ensuring that the project objectives are complete, specific, attainable and measurable.

The preceding commentary does not mean, however, that, once stated, project objectives cannot be changed. Practically speaking, as a project progresses additional knowledge is gained by all participants (users, EDP personnel, and management). This makes changes in objectives a worthwhile and common occurrence. However, these changes may well cause basic alterations in all aspects of the project and could, therefore, necessitate a re-justification of the entire project. Illustrations of how requests for changes can be handled are included in Chapter Eleven.

Inputs. Inputs are defined as the data entered into the system to update (improve, add to, delete from, or change) its stored informational content, and are also defined as the control data that are entered to change (or select) options within programs or to vary the outputs of the system. The media for entry of these data are varied: punched cards, direct (on-line) and key-tape input, scannable documents (MICR and OCR), computer tapes and disks, and punched paper tape.

Inputs are important because they control the contents and quality of the system's stored information. "If it's not in the input, it's not in the data base," and "Garbage In results in Garbage Out" (GIRGO) are well-known phrases in the EDP industry.

For the purposes of the feasibility study, however, the following information should be known about each new input:

1. Source data.
2. Contents (but not layout or media).
3. Volume and periodicity.
4. Ultimate utilization within the system.

This information about the system's inputs should be summarized in a standardized format for better understanding.

Outputs. System outputs consist of the information (reports, raw data, and results of calculations), inputs to other systems (tapes, disks, cards) and products (bills, ledgers, forms, letters, etc.) that result from the operation of the system. As with inputs, the media involved are many and include printed forms and labels, computer tapes, disks, video display, teletype, and audio response.

Outputs are important because they are the reason for developing and operating the system. While they are its products, they are not its benefits. The utilization of these outputs and the efficiency of their production provide the basis for the benefits. This distinction must be made clear to EDP personnel who all too often confuse the product with the benefits resulting from its production.

For the feasibility study, the following should be known about each output:

1. Media.
2. Contents (but not layout).
3. Utilization of the outputs.
4. Users and their departments.

Again, particularly for systems with extremely large numbers of outputs, standardized formats for collecting (and reporting) this information are a definite aid when analyzing outputs.

Data base. The data base consists of all stored data required to operate the system. Typical elements in the data base are information master files, rate files, and other recirculating files (such as error files, incomplete new business, etc.). These files are stored on a variety of media, including computer tape, disk and drum, punched cards, punched paper tape, microfilm, and computer core.

Since the data base is the repository for the totality of the system's information, its importance cannot be overrated. Loss, destruction or damage to any portion of the data base can cause extremely serious problems unless the portion can be (quickly and correctly) reconstructed. Consider, for example, a company that suddenly lost or damaged all its records on accounts receivable.

The information about the data base that is most important during the feasibility study is:

1. The number of files in the data base.
2. Their contents, volume, and cycle of update.
3. Their present media and proposed media.
4. Their utilization in the system.

This information is required for the conceptual design and is additionally important because it provides the first knowledge about the scope of the conversion (translation of files from present to proposed media) effort that will be required.

Conceptual design. The conceptual design of a system describes all elements within the system and their flow (or inter-relationship). The elements of a system are the:

1. Inputs.
2. Outputs.
3. Data base.
4. Programs and functions.
5. Temporary data sets.

As can be seen above, the completion of conceptual design is dependent upon definition of the inputs, outputs and data base that were previously described. In addition, the conceptual design illustrates how the functions of the system are allocated to the various programs that comprise the system, and also indicates the utilization of temporary data sets (files which are not part of the data base) to provide transition between programs.

The usual method of illustrating a conceptual design is through a macro-flow chart. The amount of detail to be included is dependent upon the purpose for which it is being used and the knowledge of the group that will review the design. Figure 3-4 illustrates a very basic macro-flow chart which would be used to describe the system early in the feasibility study, while Figure 3-5 illustrates a quite detailed macro-flow chart which would be used later in the study as the basis for estimating the development schedule and operations schedules.

When a conceptual design has been completed and agreed upon, it becomes, in and of itself, a control for the system. All future activities included in the detail design and programming functions are simple expansions and translations of the conceptual design. These future activities take form from and exist entirely within the framework of the conceptual design. A good (thorough, logical, and efficient) conceptual design can simplify all future activities, while a poor one can cause untold problems and drastically increase project costs. For this reason, completion of the conceptual design is a significant control point in the project.

CONTROLS AND REPORTS

During project origination, from project request through conceptual design, the EDP manager should control the quantity, quality, and efficiency of project requests, initial surveys, and feasibility studies. In addition to the controls and reports already mentioned, the EDP manager should:

1. Maintain a log of requests and surveys.
2. Summarize the log in periodic reports and graphs.
3. Conduct an in-depth conceptual design review.

Figure 3-6 illustrates a typical Request and Survey Log. This log can be maintained by the EDP manager's secretary. As project requests, preliminary notifications, initial study reports, project justifications and other changes in project status are received by and/or sent by the EDP manager, his secretary can update the log with the required information as to dates, dispensation and causes.

Figure 3-7 illustrates a typical periodic report and indicates the information that would also be maintained in graph form. The EDP manager's secretary can maintain this report and the resultant graphs. All information on this graph is summarized directly from the Request and Survey Log. This report and the graphs provide the EDP manager and his superior with easily understood, pictorial information about:

1. The submission of new ideas.
2. EDP's performance in processing requests and conducting studies.

The EDP manager can, upon seeing this information, note and investigate any wide variation from the norm, make the changes necessary, demonstrate improved per-

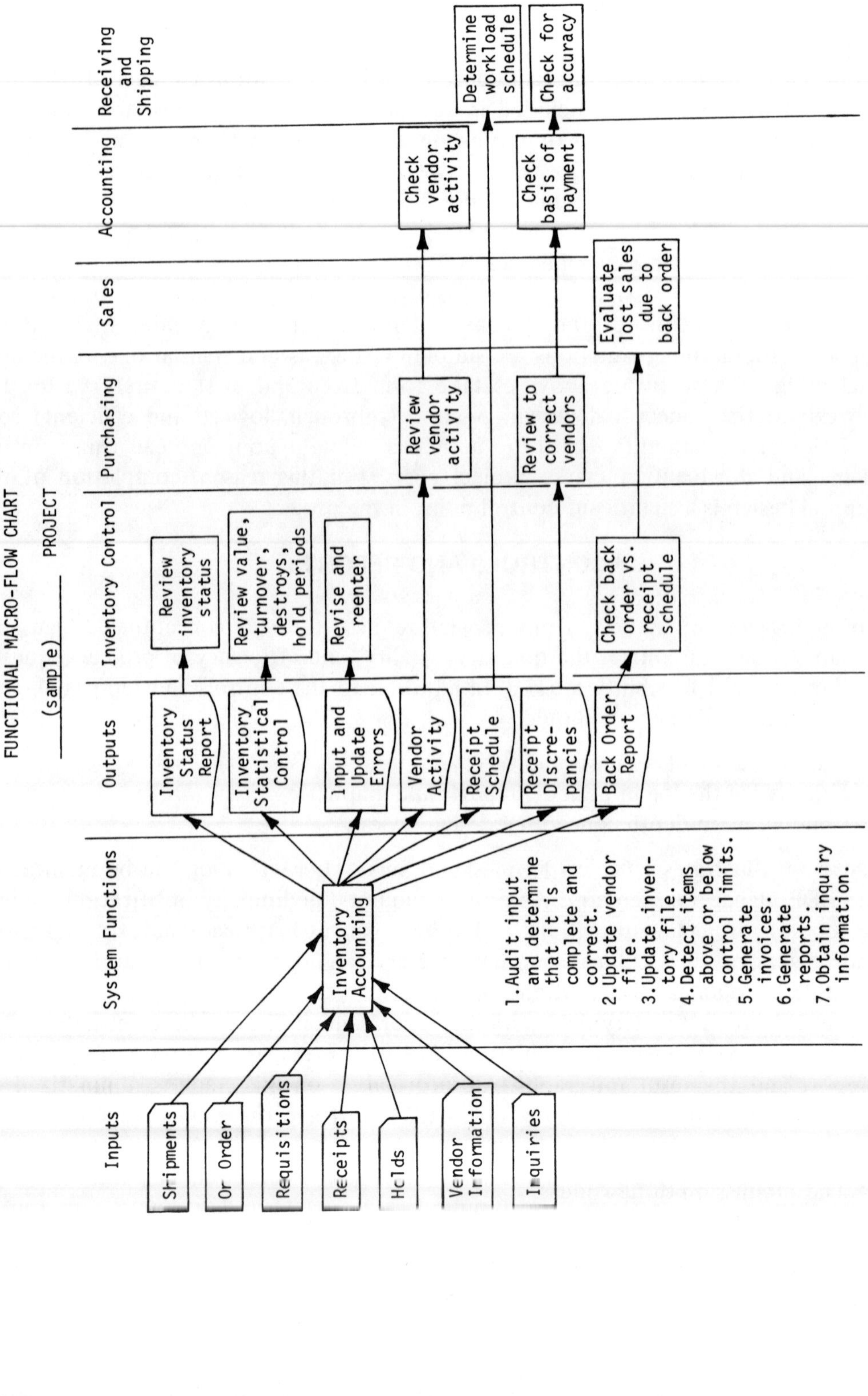

Figure 3-4. Functional Macro-Flow Chart

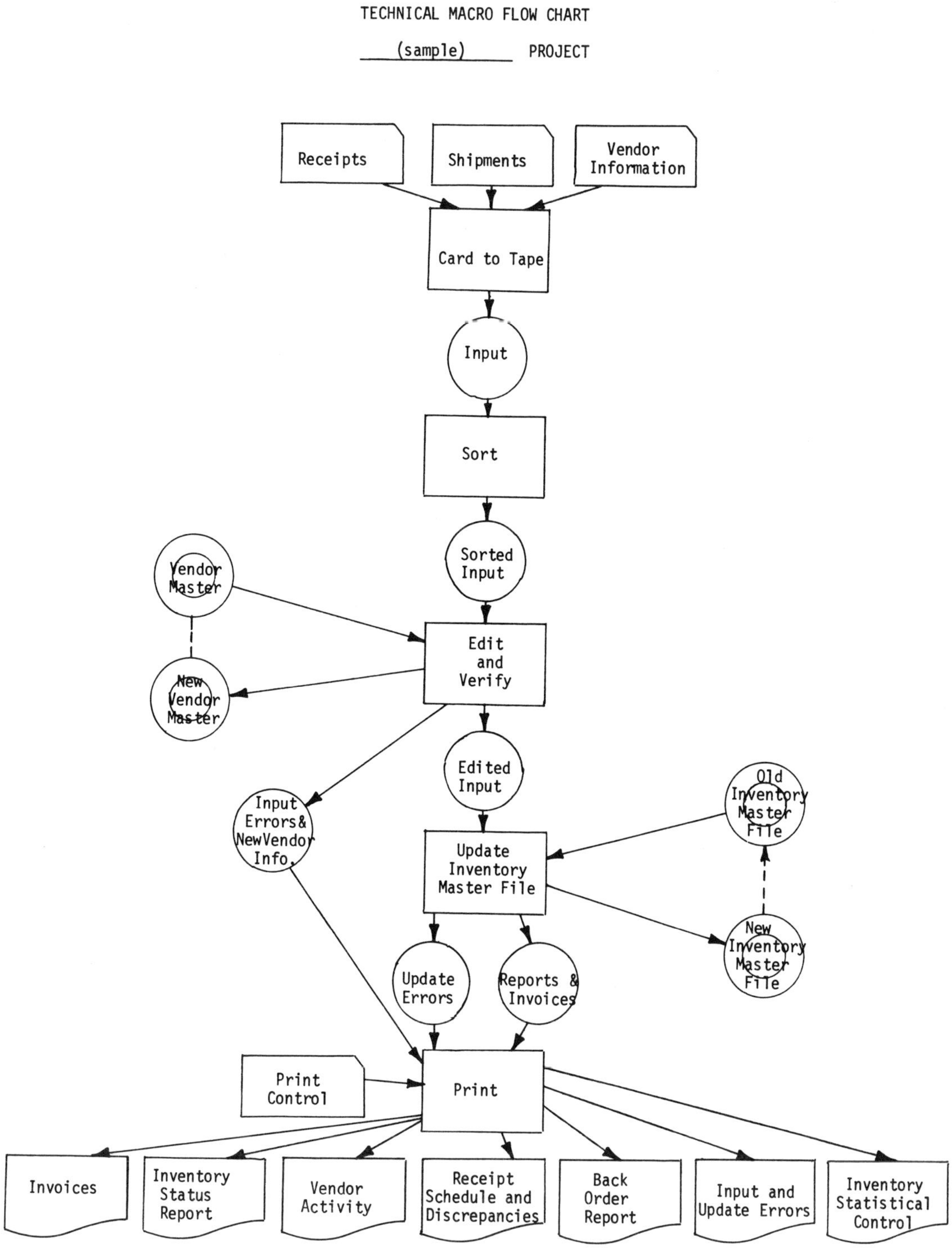

Figure 3-5. Technical Macro-Flow Chart

REQUEST AND SURVEY LOG

Receipt Date	Proj. ID	Project Name or Title	Requester	Employee Number	Dept.	Dates and Dispensation									Causes for Referral or Rejection
						Request Submitted	Notification	Prelim. Review Complete	Initial Study Begun	Init. Study Ended	Accept or Reject	Feas. Study Begun	Concept. Design Ready	Concept. Design Reviewed	

Figure 3-6. Request and Survey Log

TO: Senior Vice President

FROM: EDP Manager

SUBJECT: Weekly Project Request and Study - Week of September 11, 1970

Project Requests	Quantity Handled	Quantity	Cumulative Quantity
Requests on hand - last week		6	
Number requests received *		28*	395*
Referrals this week	6		(84)
Rejects this week	15		(201)
Initial Studies begun	6		(103)
Requests handled	27	(27)	(388)
Requests on hand		7*	7
Initial Studies			
Initial Studies in process - last week		9	
Initial Studies begun		6	103*
Rejects	8		(70)
Feasibility Studies begun	5		(31)
Studies completed	13	(13)	(101)
Initial Studies in process		2*	2
Feasibility Studies			
Feasibility Studies in process - last week		5	
Feasibility Studies begun		5	31*
Projects rejected	1		(7)
Authorization given	3		(18)
Feasibility Studies completed	4	(4)	(25)
Feasibility Studies in progress *		6	6*

AVERAGE DAYS: Submittal to Receipt *1.3 Receipt to Notification *1.7 Notification to Initial Study *3.5 Initial Study - Beginning to End *4.1 Feasibility Study Beginning to End *61.7

Note: * Indicates that this value is illustrated by a line graph portraying This Year vs. Last Year information. Copies of these graphs may be obtained from my secretary.

Figure 3-7. Typical Periodic Report

formance (or reasons why performance was not improved), and inform his superior of these actions in a short supplemental memo that accompanies this report. These controls allow the EDP manager to be "on top" of potential problems and minimize the possibility that he will be confronted with a problem that he has not already recognized.

The in-depth review of the conceptual design is conducted in two stages. First, a meeting is arranged at which the user manager, user area supervisory personnel, feasibility study team, development manager and EDP manager discuss the conceptual design to determine (and obtain agreement) that the new system performs all the functions that are required. When agreement has been reached the user manager writes a concurrence memo to the EDP manager. Second, while agreement that the system performs correctly is being reached the technical aspects of the design are reviewed by an EDP technical review team under the joint direction of the development manager and the operations manager. When this team is satisfied that the design is technically sound a memo is written to the EDP manager indicating the team's concurrence (and any minority opinions), and their signatures are added.

When the system has been determined to be functionally and technically sound, the feasibility study can be completed. Details about its completion, the preparation of the project justification, and the methods for obtaining project authorization are contained in the next chapter.

4

Setting Priorities and Authorizing Projects

The conceptual design that was agreed upon during the first phase of the feasibiltiy study provides the basic control over the contents of the proposed system. However, before personnel and other resources are committed to succeeding project functions such as detail design and programming, the prudent EDP manager will solicit and obtain top management's authorization to begin the project. He will obtain this authorization because it provides proof that top management was informed of his plans and that they agreed that these plans were in the best interest of the company and complimented its long-range plans.

With top management's authorization, the EDP manager does not have to worry about the following types of questions:

> Why are you working on that project? Didn't anyone tell you that next month we're selling the entire division for which that system is being developed? Can't you tell what is important to get done now and what can wait?

Moreover, to efficiently recommend projects for authorization, the EDP manager must be at least superficially aware of the long-range and short-range plans of top management. If he is not usually provided with this type of information, the "need to know" required for setting project priorities is usually sufficient reason for him to receive it.

Once the need for authorization from top management is admitted, the only problem is obtaining it. Because of the vast differences in the top managements of various companies, their organization, and the personalities of the managers, no book can describe an infallible method of obtaining project authorization. The methodology is dependent upon the personality, awareness, tact, and diplomacy of the individual EDP manager who must perceive the economic and political climate and prepare his arguments so that the format, language, and timing will be most effective.

Although there is no infallible method, there is certain information that should be included in a request for project authorization. Without this information, top management cannot logically evaluate the worth of an EDP project. With this information the veil of mystery surrounding EDP is stripped away, and EDP projects can be evaluated on substantially the same basis as any other new capital investment project. The information that translates EDP projects into terms commonly understood by top management includes:

1. Resource requirements.
2. Costs.
3. Benefits.
4. Risk.

This information is common to all projects requiring capital budgeting. If your company can agree upon a standard format for presenting this information, all projects can be evaluated on the same basis. Furthermore, if there can be general agreement about the relative importance (to the company) of each factor, those requesting project authorization can better judge the acceptability of a project before making a request authorization, thereby saving their time and that of their superiors.

This chapter describes the analyses required to translate the conceptual design into the common information required by top management, a method (Weighted Point Evaluation Technique) for evaluating alternative plans and determining project priorities, how authorization for a new project should be requested, and what should be included in the authorization of a project.

ANALYSES

To complete the feasibility study, certain analyses are required to translate the conceptual design into the information about resource requirements, costs, benefits, and risk that are necessary for top management to logically grant project authorization. Because this information is the basis upon which authorization is granted, its basic elements also provide the bases for the primary controls on the project. Therefore, the analyses that are described in this chapter are, in certain instances, described in greater detail in subsequent chapters.

Resource Requirements

Before authorizing the inception of any project, top management should be fully aware of the resources that will be allocated to it. The two primary resources about which they should be informed are the amount of computer usage and the number and types of personnel. Top management must know the quantities of these resources that will be required both during the development effort and during the later operation of the system. In addition, should the project require significant amounts of computer or communications equipment, special materials, floor space, air conditioning or lighting, this information must also be included in the project justification.

Development. To determine the quantities of primary resources that are needed during the development effort, you must begin by analyzing the conceptual design to estimate the amount of time that will be required to perform each project task necessary to complete the programs and its segments within the system. In this book, this analysis is termed an estimate of development and is illustrated by Figure 5-1.

In general, the format for the estimate of development is prepared by subdividing the overall effort into a large number of project tasks. When it has been completed, each task is then estimated by considering it in relation to a particular person and asking, "How long will it take this person to complete this particular work?" If you know who will be performing the task, then consider him in relation to it. If you do not know, then determine the actual person in the group who best typifies the average skills in performing the particular task.

When the estimate of development has been completed, it becomes the basis for developing the project schedule which allocates specific tasks to specific individuals at specific points in time. The basic method used to illustrate the project schedule is a Gantt Chart (Figure 5-2) described in Chapter Five which contains more details about completion of the estimate of development and the project schedule.

The project schedule can be easily summarized into Personnel Requirements Listing as is shown in Figure 4-1. The Personnel Requirements Listing indicates the types of skills required, the types of personnel having those skills and the dates during which these personnel will be required. As the project is staffed, the names of the personnel replace the numbers in the left-hand column.

The program-test task and the test function within the estimate of development provide information about the amount of computer time that will be required. In fact, to complete these portions of the estimate of development, a general idea is required of the number of times that each programmer will require access to the computer, the approximate amount of time for each access, the amount of programmer's time required to prepare for the next access, and the anticipated delays in obtaining access. The number of accesses and extent of each provide an estimate of computer test time. Further information on test time estimation is contained in Chapter Six.

To complete the analysis of the resources required for development, you must review the conceptual design to determine the manual systems analysis, keypunch, administrative operations and user personnel that will be required. If it is warranted, these efforts should also be included in the estimate of development and project schedule. Finally, you must determine whether the project will have a significant impact on other resources such as: computer tapes and disks, floor space, forms and materials, and communications equipment.

Operations. To determine the primary resources that will be required when the system is operational, the conceptual design must first be translated into an estimate of computer operations and then into a production schedule. The estimate of computer operations provides the computer run time and the production schedule provides information about the number and types of people required to operate the system.

The estimate of computer operations (Figure 8-2) defines for each program the factor which will most probably determine the running time for that program (limiting factor). You can determine the limiting factor by checking the conceptual design for:

sample PROJECT

PERSONNEL REQUIREMENTS LISTING

Initials__________ __________Date

Person Number	Activities	Skills	Title	Start	Finish
1	SA 4 Conceptual Design SA 4 Detail Design SA 4 Programming SA 4 Testing	Interview Analyze Program Manage(light)	Programmer/ Analyst	6/1	10/16 (19 weeks)
2	SA 1 Conceptual Design SA 1 Detail Design SA 1 Programming SA 2 Same as above	Interview Analyze Program Utility Modification	Programmer/ Analyst	6/1	8/30 (13 weeks)
3	SA 3 Conceptual Design SA 3 Detail Design SA 3 Programming SA 3 Testing	Interview Analyze Program Manage(light)	Programmer/ Analyst	6/7	8/30 (12 weeks)
4	SA 5 Conceptual Design SA 5 Detail Design SA 5 Programming SA 5 Testing	Interview Analyze Program	Programmer/ Analyst	6/10	9/30 (16 weeks)
5	SA 4 Flow SA 4 Programming	Program Analysis(light)	Programmer	7/12	9/11 (9 weeks)
6	SA 3 Programming SA 4 Programming	Program Program	Programmer	8/5	9/7 (6 weeks)

SUMMARY

Programmer/ Analyst	19+13+12+16= 60 weeks
Programmer	9+6 = 15 weeks

Note: Manual systems analysis, keypunching, administrative and operations personnel would also be estimated. For simplicity, they are not included in this listing or in the Project Schedule.

Figure 4-1. Personnel Requirements Listing

1. The volume of data flowing to or from each peripheral device.
2. The complexity and amount of the program's data manipulation.

This information, coupled with a knowledge of the speeds of the devices, is the basis for determining the limiting factor and estimating production time. Set-up times and delay factors transform production time into elapsed time. You can usually obtain this information from computer operations personnel. If this information is not readily available, you can estimate it by reviewing the production set-up, and elapsed times of similar programs that are already operational. Given elapsed times, the assignment of actual times for running the programs is a matter of coordinating project requirements with the overall computer operations schedule.

The production schedule (Figure 8-3) provides a time-table for the flow of data through all the steps necessary for preparation, processing and dissemination. To establish such a schedule, determine the maximum allowable rate of data flow for each step and calculate the number of personnel required to achieve such a rate. Chapter Eight describes the establishment of a production schedule in much more detail.

Costs

When the resource requirements for development and operations have been determined, calculation of development and operations costs is relatively straightforward. Chapter Eight fully describes the cost bases and calculation.

Benefits

While projects can provide an infinite variety of benefits to a company, these benefits can usually be described by one or more of the following categories of benefits:

1. Decreased costs—through reductions in personnel, inventory levels, etc.
2. Increased income—through improved information, service and management.
3. Competitive edge—through improved service and general effectiveness.

If the benefits provided by a project cannot be described by one or more of these categories, it will be difficult, if not impossible, to adequately justify the project and obtain project authorization.

Decreased costs. Decreased costs have provided the primary justification for data processing projects since computers were first applied to business activities. This reliance on decreased costs has occurred because most of the computer projects to date have been concerned with the computerization of a manual business activity. In turn, the replacement of manual activities has probably prevailed because the benefits are apparent and the concept of replacement is easy to grasp. Chapter Eight describes, in detail, a method that can be used to determine amount and rate of payback when costs can be decreased.

Increased income. It is usually more difficult to convince top management of the concept that utilization of computers can actually increase the income of the company. In some cases where the new systems provide sales personnel with new or more current information on inventory, prospects, or new products, the concept can be understood but it is difficult to determine the specific amount of income that should result. In other cases, top management must be convinced that, by providing the ability to try or explore a vast number of alternative plans, the computer system will allow management to select a plan which actually increases income. It is necessary to convince top management because they are in the best position to estimate the actual increases of income. EDP personnel should demonstrate the systems' benefits to the people whose area will be affected and then let these people estimate the amount of increase in income.

Competitive edge. Competitive edge is provided by improving the service to the company's customers. While EDP systems can provide a wide variety of results that are known to improve the company's service, many times the effect of these improvements cannot be quantified in terms of dollars. These improvements are, for the lack of a better name, termed competitive edge. Any project, the improvements of which are entirely of the competitive edge type, tends to be a weakly supported project because the benefits are measurable but the effects of these benefits are not.

Risk

Every project has an elements of risk for the company. Many risks are readily apparent:

1. Resources may be squandered.
2. Costs can be higher.
3. Benefits may not be realized.

However, the major risk, inherent in every project, is that the project will somehow ruin or obstruct a critical portion of the company's on-going operation.

The risk associated with the project must be evaluated. For resources, cost, and benefits, this can be accomplished by using three-point estimates. That is, instead of preparing only one "average" set of analyses (project schedule and its attendant cost and benefit analyses), three sets of analyses are prepared:

1. An average or expected set.
2. A minimum of "if-things-go-extremely-well" set.
3. A maximum of "if-things-go-extremely-poorly" set.

Given these three sets of analyses, top management can understand the full extent of its commitment and can also understand the degree of confidence inherent in the "average" or target estimates.

It should be pointed out that, at present, very few companies use, understand, or require three-point estimates. Therefore, if you begin to use three-point estimates, you may well be providing your management with innovative and sophisticated information. You should, therefore, prepare your management so that they understand the power and utilization of this information. In addition to the extra exposure and experience involved, you will also gain the ability to realistically describe the project and your confidence in the target estimates. Forever more, you are relieved of the nagging feeling that "These estimates are as good as I can make them, but so many things can happen that I'm just not sure." It should also be noted that this method of estimation will also tend to remove a good deal of the "fudge" or contingency allowances that are presently added to target estimates to provide a margin of safety.

To evaluate major risks, the design must be reviewed to determine:

1. The criticality of the data base.
2. The criticality of the activities involved.
3. The most sensitive project functions (those where critical errors could occur).
4. Methods of ensuring that major errors are eliminated.

Each of these points must be clearly explained in the project justification. Obviously, a project justification will not be prepared if major error is not guarded against. Top management would, however, be informed of the possibility of major error and the techniques that will be used to eliminate it. Not only does this demonstrate pre-planning but, on occasion, additional, worthwhile safeguards are recommended by top management.

WEIGHTED POINT EVALUATION

When the necessary information on resource requirements, costs, benefits, and risk has been obtained, the priority of the new project with respect to other projects that are (undoubtedly) awaiting implementation must be determined. Project priorities describe the overall worth or importance of the project at a given point in time. Because the description of the overall worth is based upon the relative importance (to the company) of a variety of factors, any change in the business environment or top management's planning can be reflected by a change in the importance of any factor or the relative importance of the factors. Therefore, as time causes changes in the business environment or in top management's planning, the priorities of the projects awaiting implementation also change.

The following paragraphs present a straightforward method of assigning and revising project priorities. This method is based upon a technique for quantitatively describing a project's overall worth (the weighted point evaluation technique). However, this method is not a purely mechanical process. It requires management judgment to be truly effective.

As is shown in Figure 4-2, the weighted point evaluation technique consists of:

1. Defining the factors that determine project worth.
2. Determining the value or commentary that applies to each factor for this project.
3. Determining the weight (or point value in relation to all other factors) for each factor.
4. Assigning the points from predetermined tables that are comparable to that particular value.
5. Multiplying each factor's points times its worth to determine the score.
6. Adding the scores to obtain a total score.

Additional information on how to define the factors that determine project worth, assign points, and determine weights is contained in the Definition, Assignment and Weighting segments of the chapter.

The total score represents this project's overall worth in relation to the total scores of all other alternative plans or projects. The total scores of the various plans or sample PROJECT

WEIGHTED POINT EVALUATION

FACTORS	VALUE	WEIGHT	SCORE	TOTAL
I. Costs and Payback				
A. Average (target) estimates				
1. Total investment				
2. Time until payback begins				
3. Time until payback is complete				
4. First year return after payback				
5. Three year discounted cash flow				
6. Five year discounted cash flow				
7. Ten year discounted cash flow				
B. Maximum estimates				
1. Total investment				
2. Time until payback begins				
3. Time until payback is complete				
4. First year return after payback				
5. Three year discounted cash flow				
6. Five year discounted cash flow				
7. Ten year discounted cash flow				
C. Minimum estimates				
1. Total investment				
2. Time until payback begins				
3. Time until payback is complete				
4. First year return after payback				
5. Three year discounted cash flow				
6. Five year discounted cash flow				
7. Ten year discounted cash flow				
II. Risk				
A. Files				
B. Existing activities				
III. Other Benefits				
A. Response time				
B. Vendor information				
IV. Resource Allocation				
A. Analysts				
1. Number				
2. Total months				
B. Programmers				
1. Number				
2. Total months				
C. Other				
1. User supervisors				
2. Clerical				
D. Equipment				
1. 360/30 time				
2. 360/50 time				
V. Systems Considerations				
A. Type of system				
B. System parameters				
1. Flexibility				
2. File security				
3. Accessibility				
4. Understandability				
5. Interactivity (conversational				
C. Compliments MIS planning				
			TOTAL	

Note: This is a very short sample outline. Many more factors important to your specific company should be included.

Figure 4-2. Weighted Point Evaluation

projects will tend to cluster in groups. For example, ten projects might have total scores of:

$$\underbrace{975,\ 970,\ 967}_{A},\ \underbrace{880,\ 870}_{B},\ \underbrace{800}_{C},\ \underbrace{770,\ 769,\ 750}_{D},\ \underbrace{620}_{E}$$

The groupings of scores in the example are enclosed in brackets and identified by a capital letter (A-E).

Given these groups, you should review the projects to decide if you would intuitively assign project priorities in the same sequence as total scores. Discrepancies between intuition and total scores should be reviewed in detail. When the calculations are verified as accurate, you must determine whether to assign priorities in the same sequence as total scores, in the same sequence as intuition, or in a compromise sequence. This decision and the reasoning that supports it are to be based on your managerial judgment.

Generally, you will find that your intuition will almost always sequence projects in the same order as their groupings. That is, you will intuitively rate all projects in Group A as more important than those in Group B, those in Group B as more important than those in Group C, etc. Discrepancies indicate that you do not intuitively believe that the point assignments or the weighting of the factors are correct. This requires that you become convinced of their validity or that you work with your management to change these assignments and weightings.

Theoretically, this process of refining the bases for total scores and your understanding will ultimately result in one-to-one correspondence between total scores and intuition. Realistically, this process will almost always result in correct relationships among the groups but will definitely allow change within any group.

Definition and Weighting

Many companies have already defined the factors that should be considered in assigning project priorities. If those factors have not been defined, you should begin by preparing a list of the factors that you would expect to be significant and by determining who (in top management) should be consulted to authorize projects and determine their priorities. You can then arrange for a series of discussions to determine each individual's criteria and can use the resultant listings as a starting point during these discussions.

When the individual discussions have been completed, a group meeting should be held to review and agree upon the list of factors and their meanings. At this meeting, the relative importance of each factor (with respect to the other factors) should be discussed and the numerical weights should be determined.

The determination of numerical weights is not difficult if the group of decision makers is interested in the concept and if the list of factors has been agreed upon. To obtain the interest of the group, and determine weights, you should:

1. Review the purpose of the weighting system.
2. Inform the group that the weights can and will be changed when experience shows that the weights assigned today are no longer valid.

3. Assure the group members that they will finally determine project priorities but that the total scores will serve as a guide.
4. Begin by sequencing the major categories of factors (indicated by Roman numerals in Figure 4-2 in their order of importance—most important, next in importance, etc.)
5. Once sequenced, give weights to the major categories so that a category's weight is in proportion to its relative importance (i.e., a category that has twice the importance has twice the weight, a category that is slightly more important has a little more weight, etc.) To start, give an arbitrary weight of 400 to the most important category and then weight the other categories accordingly.
6. When weights have been determined for the major categories, each weight must be divided among its component segments in relation to their relative importance. Segments are indicated by capital letters (A,B,C,etc.) in Figure 4-2.
7. Finally, the weight for each segment must be divided among its component factors (1,2,3,etc. in Figure 4-2) in relation to their importance.

When all weights have been determined, they should be reviewed to ensure that the group agrees that the weight assigned to each factor indicates its importance with respect to any other factor.

Point Assignment

When the factors (and weights) have been agreed upon, you must prepare a point assignment table that relates the values or comments that can be attributed to a factor with the point value of each of these values or comments. Figure 4-3 illustrates a typical point assignment table.

When prepared, the point assignment table should also be reviewed by the group of top management decision makers that reviewed the factors and weighting. This review will ensure that the points are assigned in a logical manner.

Utilization

At the conclusion of the review, you will have obtained all of the tools necessary to establish the priority of the EDP projects and alternative plans that are awaiting implementation. As the factors for these projects are valued and scored, you (EDP management) and top management will learn more about these project's relative priorities and will also learn more about (and probably improve) the factor listing, the point assignment tables and the factor weights. As conditions change, these same tools (and especially the factor weights) will also change.

When project priorities have been established, the overall Manpower Schedule (see Figure 9-5) should be prepared or revised. This schedule describes the starting and completion dates for all authorized projects and projects recommended for authorization.

(sample) PROJECT

POINT ASSIGNMENT TABLE

Factor	Points 1	2	3	4	5
Total investment	>100	51-100	11-50	1-10	<1
Time until payback begins(months)	> 36	12-36	6-12	3-6	< 3
Time until payback is complete(months)	> 60	48-60	24-48	6-24	< 6
First year return after payback($1000s)	< 10	10-20	20-50	50-100	>100
Three year discounted cash flow-returns	< 25	25-50	50-100	100-200	>200
Five year discounted cash flow	< 40	40-75	75-150	150-300	>300
Ten year discounted cash flow	< 85	85-150	150-250	250-500	>500
File-risk	several critical	one critical	several major	one major	no major
Existing activity risk	several critical	one critical	several major	one major	no major
Other benefits	a nicety	of worth	important	very important	extremely important
Analysts - Number	>10	6-10	4-5	2-3	< 1
Total months	>20	11-20	5-10	2-4	< 2
Programmers - Number	>30	11-30	6-10	2-5	< 2
Total months	>60	30-60	16-30	6-15	< 6
User supervisory	> 2	NA	2	1	<0
Clerical	> 5	3-5	2	1	< 0
360/30 time (minutes/day)	>80	60-80	40-60	21-40	< 20
360/50 time (minutes/day)	>60	46-60	31-45	15-30	<15
Type of system	batch	NA	on-line	NA	timeshared
Flexibility	single purpose system	NA	multi-purpose system	NA	multi-system usage
File security	top secret	secret	confidential		open
Accessibility		NA	terminals	NA	from anywhere
Understandability	EDP only	much training	some needed	little	anyone can use
Interactivity	programs only	NA	training required	NA	conversion
Compliments MIS planning	outside of plan	could be in plan	part of plan	necessary in plan	keystone in plan

Date ____________

Figure 4-3. Point Assignment Table

OBTAINING PROJECT AUTHORIZATION

The purpose of requesting project authorization from top management is two-fold: (1) to demonstrate the results of the feasibility study; and (2) to ensure that top management agrees with your priorities and the proposed schedule for implementation. Therefore, if it can be established, a planning committee (or project review committee) which meets periodically to review all proposed capital expenditures on new projects will provide an excellent forum for granting EDP project authorization.

However, regardless of the form or methods that must be used within individual companies, there are certain steps that should be taken when requesting project authorization. These are:

1. Preparation of the project justification and the request for project authorization.
2. Submission of these documents to top management.
3. Control of authorized projects prior to implementation.

The remainder of this chapter presents techniques that can be employed during each of these steps to improve the efficiency of this process and the image of the EDP area.

Preparation—General

The project justification and the request for project authorization are the documents which culminate the efforts expended in the feasibility study. These documents are the entire basis for top management's knowledge of the effort that has been expended, the controls that have been developed, and the conclusions that have been reached. For this reason they must provide specific, understandable, and complete information. In addition, these documents are, in effect, the primary sales media for the EDP manager's recommendations. Therefore, they must also present their information in an interesting manner so that top management can follow the logic of the recommendations, and will concur in the recommendation.

The project justification is prepared to provide all of the information, logic, and recommendations in a language and format that is specific, understandable, and directed at the interests of top management. The request for project authorization synopsizes this information, requests top management's concurrence, and provides a vehicle for their notification of concurrence.

Preparation—Project Justification

As is indicated by the Project Justification Outline (Figure 4-4), this document is organized so that the information important to management is summarized and the basis for the recommendations, the benefits, and the conceptual design and supporting information are described in detail. This allows the reader to investigate the information as deeply as his inclination and time permit. The important information is presented first and the bases for this information are detailed thereafter.

When preparing the project justification, the language must be explicit and understandable to top management. One way to ensure this is to have a secretary read the document. If she can understand and describe the major points, the document is well written. If she cannot understand certain sections, they should be rewritten so that she can understand them.

The general form and content of a request for project authorization is illustrated by Figure 4-5. This document should contain the same information that is contained in Section I, SUMMARY, Project Justification. In addition, the request should provide each decision maker with an easy means of indicating that he concurs with the priority assigned to the project.

I. SUMMARY - Summarizes the recommendation for priority assignment, the starting date and conclusion date (for implementation) based on this priority, the Total Score from the Weighted Point Evaluation and the four most important factors in the decision.

II. RECOMMENDATIONS -

A. Implementation schedule

B. Priority assignment

1. Projects sequenced by Total Scores (Weighted Point Evaluation)
2. Weighted Point Evaluation of this project
3. Managerial judgment factors and comments

C. Summary

III. BENEFITS

A. Resources

B. Costs

C. Other benefits

D. Risk

IV. FUNCTIONS

A. Conceptual Design - basic

B. Inputs

C. Outputs

D. Data base

E. Conceptual Design - detailed

V. SUPPORTING DATA

A. Calculations and tables

B. Old system flow

C. Other details not included elsewhere

Figure 4-4. Project Justification Outline

TO: Top Management (Names) Date September 12, 19

FROM: M.D. Wadsworth, EDP Manager

SUBJECT: (sample) Project - Request for Project Authorization

Authorization to begin implementation of the (sample) Project on or about June 1, 19 is hereby requested. The primary bases for this request are:

1. Assignment of implementation priority of 3 based upon a Total Score of 947 which ranks 2 in all Total Scores and the short duration (2 months) vs. high payback ($30,000/year) provided by Zilch Project (Total Score 938) which is hereby recommended to be implemented before the Sample Project (Implementation Priority 2).
2. A cost reduction payback of $48,000/year after a two year break-even period and the expenditure of $97,000 to implement the system.
3. Additional benefits relating to improved vendor information and more accurate inventory records with little risk to files or procedures.
4. Relatively low resource requirements in terms of Analysts (3) and Programmers (5).

Additional details supporting this request are contained in the Project Justification for this project which bears the same date as does this request.

If you concur in this request, please sign this request and return a copy to me. Action on this request by October 1, 19 is desired.

CONCURRENCE: SUBMITTED BY:

J.J. Jones
Financial Vice President

M.D. Wadsworth
EDP Manager

Figure 4-5. Request for Project Authorization

Submission—Project Justification and Request for Project Authorization

Both the project justification and the request for project authorization should be logged out and distributed to every person in the top management decision making group. If these people are going to discuss the request in a meeting prior to concurrence, the documents should be submitted at least three days before the meeting date. This provides sufficient time for the documents to be read and for the answering of any questions.

If it can be arranged, personal presentation (at the meeting) of the summary and recommendations sections by the manager-Systems Development and the EDP manager will usually result in:

1. A deeper understanding of the recommendations.
2. Faster concurrence.
3. Better communication between EDP and top management.

If such a presentation is arranged, all EDP personnel who attend must prepare thoroughly for their parts in it.

Control of Authorized Projects

When the concurrences are returned to the EDP manager form top management, they should be logged in and made a part of the project file. The log of the dates and times of requests for project authorization that are sent and the concurrences received:

1. Ensures an answer from each person who received a request for project authorization.
2. Provides knowledge on the average response time for individuals and groups.
3. Provides the EDP manager with knowledge about the likes and dislikes of top management.

This information can be summarized in numerical and graphical form in much the same manner as were the control reports and graphs in Chapter Three (see Figure 3-7). Usually, however, this information need not be interpreted formally.

The receipt of all concurrence marks the end of project authorization and the beginning of the development effort. From this point forward, the EDP manager must monitor the overall manpower schedule by requesting authorization for new projects and by advising top management when he believes changes in the business climate, the company, or his area warrant revisions to:

1. Benefits from authorized projects.
2. The factors influencing priority assignment.
3. The point assignment table.
4. Factor weighting.
5. Management judgment.

To monitor these factors a copy of the request for project authorization and for every authorized and recommended project (whose implementation has not yet begun) should be assembled in a "Projects Pending" looseleaf notebook. This notebook should then be reviewed periodically (every two weeks) to determine whether and how any changes in the overall environment will affect the project's priorities. Likewise, when any significant change in the environment occurs, the Projects Pending notebook should be reviewed. As the determination of whether and how priorities will be affected is almost entirely subjective, each EDP manager will have to define any additional analyses that will assist him in making these determinations.

5

Developing the Project Schedule and Monitoring Its Progress

In the vast majority of companies, EDP is notorious for not completing projects on time. In many companies, this situation has occurred so frequently that even the project personnel regard the estimation of completion dates as an administrative task rather than a personal commitment. Even the EDP managers and project managers who understand the purpose of estimating completion dates remain relatively unconcerned about project slippage until their superiors begin to ask:

> Will that inventory project ever end? In June you promised to get Speedy or one of your other top people on the vital Order Entry project by August. In late July you told me there'd "been a small delay but surely by September." It's now Christmas and it looks like that inventory project is going to tie up your good people forever. When are you going to get started on Order Entry? What do I have to do to get action?

At this point, we mercifully draw the curtain. The primary reasons why anyone should ever be subjected to such a tirade are:

1. The project was never scheduled correctly.
2. Proper controls over the schedule were not developed or maintained.

This chapter describes:

1. A method of estimating project development time (estimate of development).
2. The translation of development time into a project schedule (Gantt Chart).
3. How to define the critical path and check to ensure that the schedule works (Modified CPM).
4. Periodic controls on the schedule.
5. Benchmark controls on the schedule.
6. Exception controls on the schedule.

ESTIMATE OF DEVELOPMENT

General

The estimate of development is a matrix composed of data processing project functions and tasks as the column headings and programs or program segments (modules) as the row headings (see Figure 5-1). When the appropriate row and column headings have been decided upon, the estimate of the amount of time required to perform each specific task for each specific program is written at the appropriate intersection of row and column.

As a Control Mechanism

To be utilized as a control mechanism, the estimate of development should have sufficient rows and columns so that:

1. If the project is of more than four weeks' duration, the intersections are estimated in terms of man days and no intersection contains more than ten days.
2. If the project is of less than four weeks' duration, the intersections are estimated in terms of man hours and no intersection contains more than 24 hours.

To keep the intersections below the ten-day (or 24-hour) minimum, either add more columns by using segments of a task as column headings rather than the task itself or add rows by using segments of a program as rows rather than the entire program. For example, a column heading "Detail Design–Output" might be expanded into "Detail Design–Control Log," "Detail Design–Invoice," "Detail Design–Vendor File"; or the print program might be expanded into "Main Line Logic," "Invoice Print," "Control Log Print," "Vendor File Print."

Coding System

The final matrix may be filled in with any special coding system that the estimator may devise. In Figure 5-1:

1. The intersections of columns that do not apply to specific programs are marked with an "X," and an "NA" is printed above the "X."
2. If the intersection is inappropriate because the task is being performed in a preceding (or succeeding) program, the "X" is noted with the program number where the task will be performed. For example, the output for SA 1 is used as input to SA 2; therefore, under "Conceptual Design–Input" for Program SA 2 you will find an "SA" indicating that the design of this common output/income will be the sole responsibility of the person designing SA 1. (He will, however, have to understand the basics of SA 2 to complete this design.)
3. Notes can be added for understanding. For example, "Modify a can" under "Detail Design–Flow" for Program SA 1, means "Use a canned program; modify it as necessary."

4. Dash marks (–) are used when segments of a program are estimated (the entire program row has a dash) or when a segmented program is estimated (each segment has a dash).
5. The difference between the amount of time that a person will actually work and the amount of time that will elapse (due to computer turn-around lags, etc.) is indicated by intersections containing dual numbers in the worked/elapsed format. For example, under "Programming–Test" for Program SA 1, the 2/4 indicates two days of actual programmer's time during a four-day period.
6. The Elapsed Time row and column totals assist in preparing the project schedule.
7. The Actual Time (worked) row and column totals assist in preparing development cost estimates.
8. All column headings are illustrative and should be developed for each specific project.
9. The column "Programming–Test" includes compile, debug, and test with programmer generated data. The column "Test–Program" includes test of the program with non-programmer generated test data.
10. Brackets indicate that an estimate has been made for a group of tasks or programs.
11. Estimates of less than one day have been ignored or included in the intersection that precedes it in its row.

Method of Estimation

There are a vast number of methods for estimating development times. These methods include formulas, tables, listings of ranges, and proprietary computer programs. If you already have a method of estimation that has proven reliable, use it. The following simple and proven method of estimation is recommended for beginning to estimate and for logically improving each subsequent estimate.

1. If you know exactly who will be working on the project, segment the project and mentally assign personnel to each program or module. Then, look at each task for each program or module and ask yourself, "How long will it take the assigned person to complete this task?" By applying your knowledge of the task, the program, and the person's abilities and work habits, you should be able to estimate the required time quite reliably.
2. If you do not know exactly who will be working on the project, you should be familiar with the group of people from which the project team will be selected. In this case, for each task, you must decide who, within the group, is about average in ability and work habits *for that task.* Then ask yourself how long it would take that person to complete the task. This process is repeated for each task for each program or module.
3. After all individual tasks have been estimated, compute the totals as indicated in Figure 5-1. Review all estimates and totals to ensure that they reflect the relative complexity of the tasks and programs and that they are reasonable. If possible, have a skilled (successful) estimator check your estimates.

(sample) PROJECT

ESTIMATE OF DEVELOPMENT

Page 1 of 2

Date

Initials MDW

Program		Conceptual Design					Estimate			Detail Design						Programming		
#	Name	I	O	MF	Flow	Total	Op	Dev	Total	I	O	MF	Flow	Doc	Total	Study	Flow	Code
SA1-	CARD/TAPE	9	5	NA	SA	14	SA	SA	SA	-	9	-	2	1	12	NA	NA	8
-M	MAIN	-	-			-				5	-	-	MODIFY	-	5			-
-V	VENDOR	-	-			-				3	-	-	A	-	3			-
-I	INVOICE	-	-			-				3	-	-	CAN	-	3			-
-S	SHIPMENT	-	-			-				2	-	-		-	2			-
SA2-	SORT	SA1	SA3	NA		0				SA1	SA3	NA	1 MODIFY A CAN	-	1	NA	NA	5
SA3-	VERIFY	3		5		8				5		7	-	-	12	NA	-	-
-M	MAIN	-		-		-				-		-	4	1	5		-	7
-C	OTHER	-	SA4	-		-				-	SA4	-	9	3	12		1	10
SA4-	UPDATE	2	4	7		13				5	6	8	-	6	25	-	-	-
-M	MAIN	-	-	-		-				-	-	-	13	-	13	-	-	15
-V	VENDOR	-	-	-		-				-	-	-	8	-	8	2	1	9
-I	INVOICE	-	-	-		-				-	-	-	7	-	7	2	1	8
-S	SHIPMENT	-	-	-		-				-	-	-	6	-	6	2	1	6
SA5-	PRINT	SA4	9	NA		9				SA4	-	NA	-	-	-	NA	NA	-
-D	DEALER		-			-					4		2	1	7			7
-I	INVOICE		-			-					4		3	1	8			7
-C	CONTROL		-			-					4		3	1	8			6
-M	MAIN		-			-					-		4	1	5			7
SYSTEM SA	ALL	-	-	-	2	2	1	2	3	-	-	-	-	3	3	-	-	-
TOTAL	MAN DAYS	14	18	12	2	46	1	2	3	23	27	15	62	18	145	6	4	95
TOTAL	ELAPSED DAYS	14	18	12	2	46	1	2	3	23	24	15	62	18	145	6	4	95

Figure 5-1. Estimate of Development

(sample) PROJECT

ESTIMATE OF DEVELOPMENT

Page 2 of 2

Date ________ Initials MDW

Programming					Testing					File	Grand	Manual Procedures				
Check	Test	Doc.	Total	Program	Linkage	System	Pilot	Parallel	Total	Convert	Total	Study	Write	Train	Switch	Total
1 - - - -	2/4	1	12/14	1/2	1/2		SA		1/2	NA	39/42 5, 3, 3, 2 } 52/55	15	20	10/20	5/21	50/76
1	1/2	1	8/9	-/1					1/3		10/13			NA		
- 2 3	5/9	2	7/11 9 14	1/2					1/2	1/2	29/35 14, 26 } 69/75	5	5	2/20	1/21	13/51
- 3 2 2 1	6/10	3	9/13 18 14 13 10	2/3	3/5				5/8	2/2	54/61 31, 22, 20, 16 } 143/150	20	20	10/20	5/21	55/81
3 - - - -	4/6	2	9/11 7 7 6 7	3/6					3/6	NA	21/26 14, 15, 14, 12 } 76/81	10	5	2/20	2/21	19/56
NA		4	4	2/3	NA	3/5	2/6	2/15	9/29		21/41			NA		
18 18	18 31	13 13	154 167	9 17	4 7	3 5	2 6	2 15	20 50	3 4	371 415	50 50	50 50	24 80	13 84	137 264

Figure 5-1. (cont.)

4. Repeat the entire process to obtain maximum and minimum estimates (three-point estimation).

Having tried a wide variety of mathematical and other methods for estimating the time required for project tasks, the author has found that the consideration of a particular person in relation to a particular task is most reliable because:

1. By subdividing the effort into a large number of tasks, random errors tend to cancel out.
2. There are only two major variables: the task and the person. Errors are caused by a lack of understanding of one or the other. Errors in task estimation are reduced by splitting the task into comprehensible elements. Errors in estimating personnel efficiency are reduced by continued contact and by documentation of actual performance.
3. Utilization of this standardized method will be self-improving if previous estimates are analyzed (at a later date) in respect to the actual performance. This analysis will illustrate your most common errors in estimating tasks and people. These errors can be guarded against in making further estimates.

Shortcomings

The estimate of development provides basic information about the times required to perform the tasks that make up the project. By applying the appropriate costs (see Chapter Eight), these estimates can be translated into total project cost. However, you do not know:

1. How many or what type of people will be used on the project.
2. When these people will be used.
3. When the salaries for this effort will be incurred.
4. How long the project will take.
5. The critical path or task interdependencies.

PROJECT SCHEDULE (GANTT CHART)

General

The project schedule is a Gantt Chart which indicates:

1. The sequence in which the project tasks will be performed.
2. How many people will be required to accomplish the tasks.
3. Specific assignments of tasks to people.
4. The dates each person will begin and end his work on the project and any periods when he will not be working full time on this project.
5. The beginning and concluding dates (benchmarks) for each task.

As a Control Mechanism

Once completed, the project schedule is one of the primary control documents utilized by the project manager during the development effort. It is a simple graphical portrayal of the simulated efforts of the project personnel as applied to the project tasks (see Figure 5-2). It is the basis for:

1. Analysis of periodic reports.
2. Comparison of benchmark reports.
3. Generation of exception reports.
4. Monitoring the majority of project personnel costs and determining when these costs will be incurred.

To achieve these ends, the project schedule must be clear and understandable. It must also provide a simple medium for the comparison of estimates (the project schedule) and actual results (the control reports). This medium is simply provided if the schedule is drawn so that there is room to chart each person's actual performance against the schedule. In Figure 5-2 this has been accomplished by leaving space for an "Actual" bar immediately above or below each person's "Forecast" (or estimated) bar.

Coding System

For each estimate of development (average, maximum and minimum), the project schedule is prepared by simply translating the times in the estimate of development into an overall bar graph where:

1. The X (bottom) axis portrays the number of working days and the Y (vertical) axis portrays the people.
2. Each segment of the bar represents a task and the graphical length of that bar is equal to the elapsed number of days (as measured on the X-axis) for that task in the estimate of development.
3. Each entire bar represents the tasks assigned to one person.
4. The tasks required for one program are grouped together to the greatest extent possible.
5. Tasks being worked on at the same time by different people appear over the same time period on the X-axis but on different lines on the Y-axis.
6. Tasks worked on concurrently by one person are shown by dividing that person's bar during the correct period. These must overlap during the period of concurrent work (time period on the X-axis).
7. There are as few gaps (no tasks during a time period) for individuals as possible.
8. There are as few personnel on the project as is possible.
9. The dates that personnel are required and released are reasonable.
10. The types of personnel required are reasonable.
11. The dates, tasks, programs, and personnel are clearly labeled.
12. Any end date for the project that was previously decided upon is met.
13. All personnel restrictions are observed.

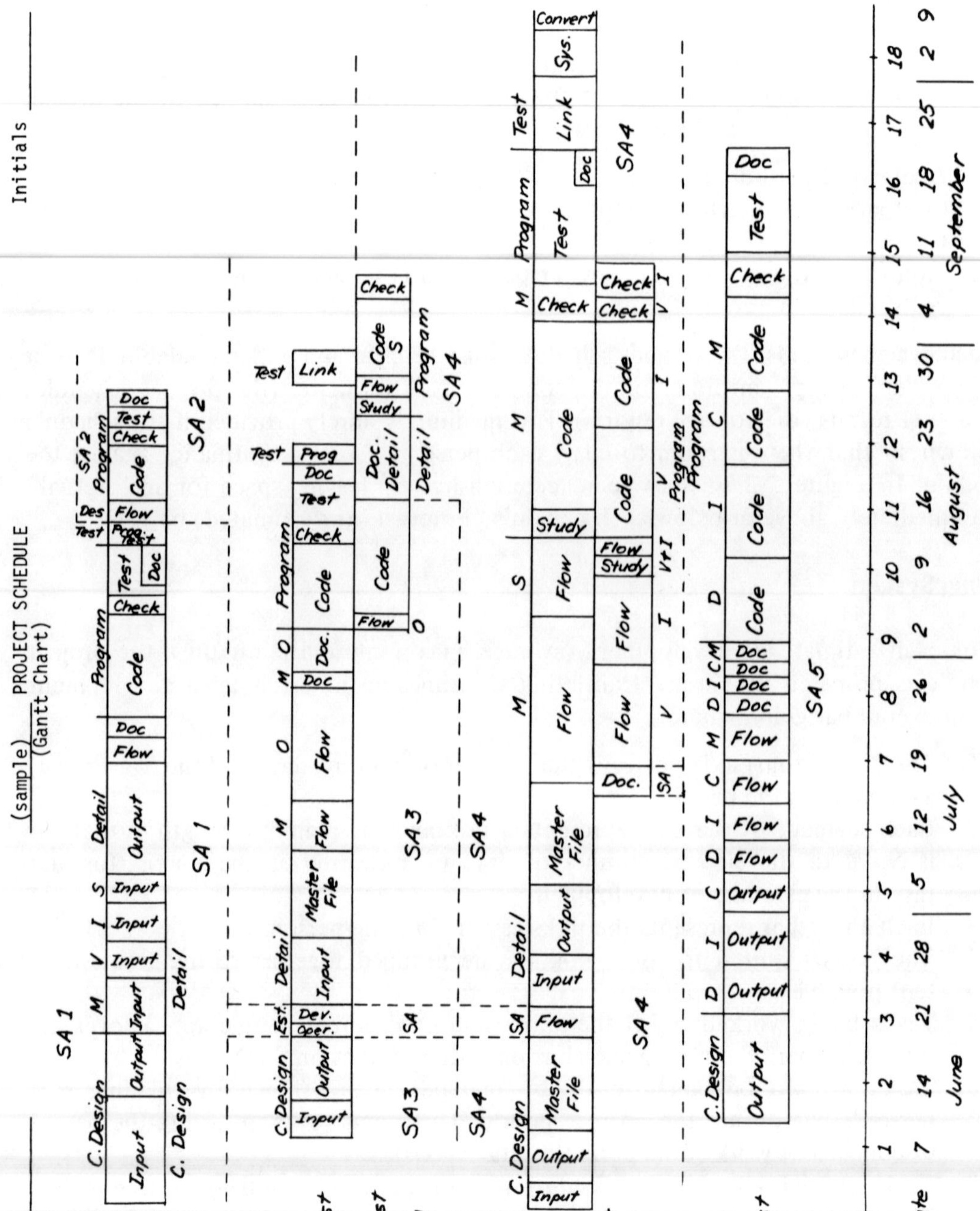

Figure 5-2. Sample Project Schedule

Shortcomings

The project schedule can easily be translated into personnel costs by applying actual or average costs (see Chapter Eight). In addition, because the timing of personnel requirements is defined, the salary costs per time period can be predetermined. However, with only a project schedule, you do not know:

1. Task interdependencies.
2. The critical path.

Until these elements are known, *no project manager can be sure that the project schedule will work* even if his estimates of individual tasks are 100% correct.

MODIFIED CPM

General

The Modified CPM is a graphical presentation of all interdependency relationships among the tasks within the project. An interdependency relationship between tasks exists when any task cannot be begun or completed until another task has been completed.

For example, in any program, the programming testing of any segment cannot begin until at least one segment of the programming coding and checking has been completed. In addition, the testing of a program cannot be completed until the checking has been completed. Between programs, for example, the testing-linkage cannot be begun until the testing-program for all the programs in the link are completed.

The critical path on a Modified CBM is the largest sum total of task times in any bar or any number of bar segments between which interdependencies exist. For example, in the illustration in Figure 5-3, the dotted arrow indicates an interdependency relationship (Task 5 cannot begin until Task 2 is complete). This makes the critical path Tasks 1, 2, 5 and 6 rather than Tasks 1, 2, and 3. Tasks 1, 2, 5 and 6 take five weeks. Tasks 1, 2 and 3 take between four and five weeks.

As a Control Mechanism

The main purpose of the Modified CPM is to ensure that there is no interdependency relationship which makes the project schedule impossible. The second purpose is to

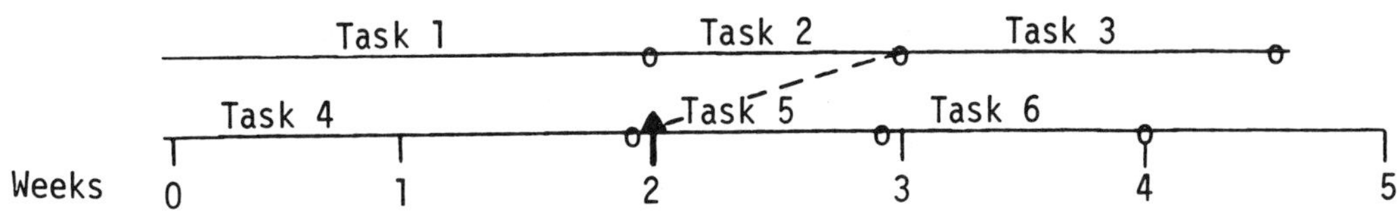

Figure 5-3. Simple Critical Path

ensure that the project manager knows exactly which tasks are on the critical path and also knows how close other tasks are to becoming critical.

Coding

To prepare a Modified CPM you must begin by listing all interdependencies. The easiest way to do this is to use the project schedule, point to each task, and ask, "Is the beginning of this task (Task A) dependent on the completion of any other task (Task B)? If Task A and Task B are in the same bar (the same person is responsible) and if Task B (the dependent task) is scheduled after Task A (the critical task), the interrelationship should be listed and annotated as "Schedule Relieved" interdependency. Otherwise all interdependencies are listed without annotation.

When all interdependencies have been listed, a modified CPM can be begun. To draw and analyze a Modified CPM, see Figure 5-4:

1. Copy the project schedule.
2. Draw each interdependency as a dotted arrow with the arrowhead pointing toward the beginning of the task that cannot be begun.
3. Check to ensure that the arrow does not slant backwards in time (left to right or arrowhead to left of tail). This is impossible. You must re-schedule.
4. All vertical arrows indicate events that must happen at the same time. This indicates possible but very critical scheduling. In addition, the bar segment prior to and including the critical task plus each bar segment after the beginning of the dependent task must be measured and added together to see if any combination is longer than (or equal to) an existing bar.
5. The longest bar or bar segment plus bar segment combination is the critical path.
6. Forward (right to left) slanting arrows indicate extra (or slack) time. The amount of (X-axis) time equivalent to these arrows is the amount of slippage that can be encountered during these tasks before they become critical.

Shortcomings

The Modified CPM is a complete schedule. The only problem is that it is extremely messy and confusing. Therefore, a Modified CPM should be done for each project schedule, but the project schedule should be used for control.

Beginning Controls

Because the project schedule is inherently tied to the total developmental costs, it is mandatory that the project manager maintain an exceedingly close control over any events which might significantly affect this schedule. He must, therefore, communicate the importance of this schedule to his project staff and must motivate them to inform him of any changes. In addition, because the project schedule is so critical to the overall successful implementation of the system, the project manager must utilize his initial meetings with the members of his staff to convince each of the im-

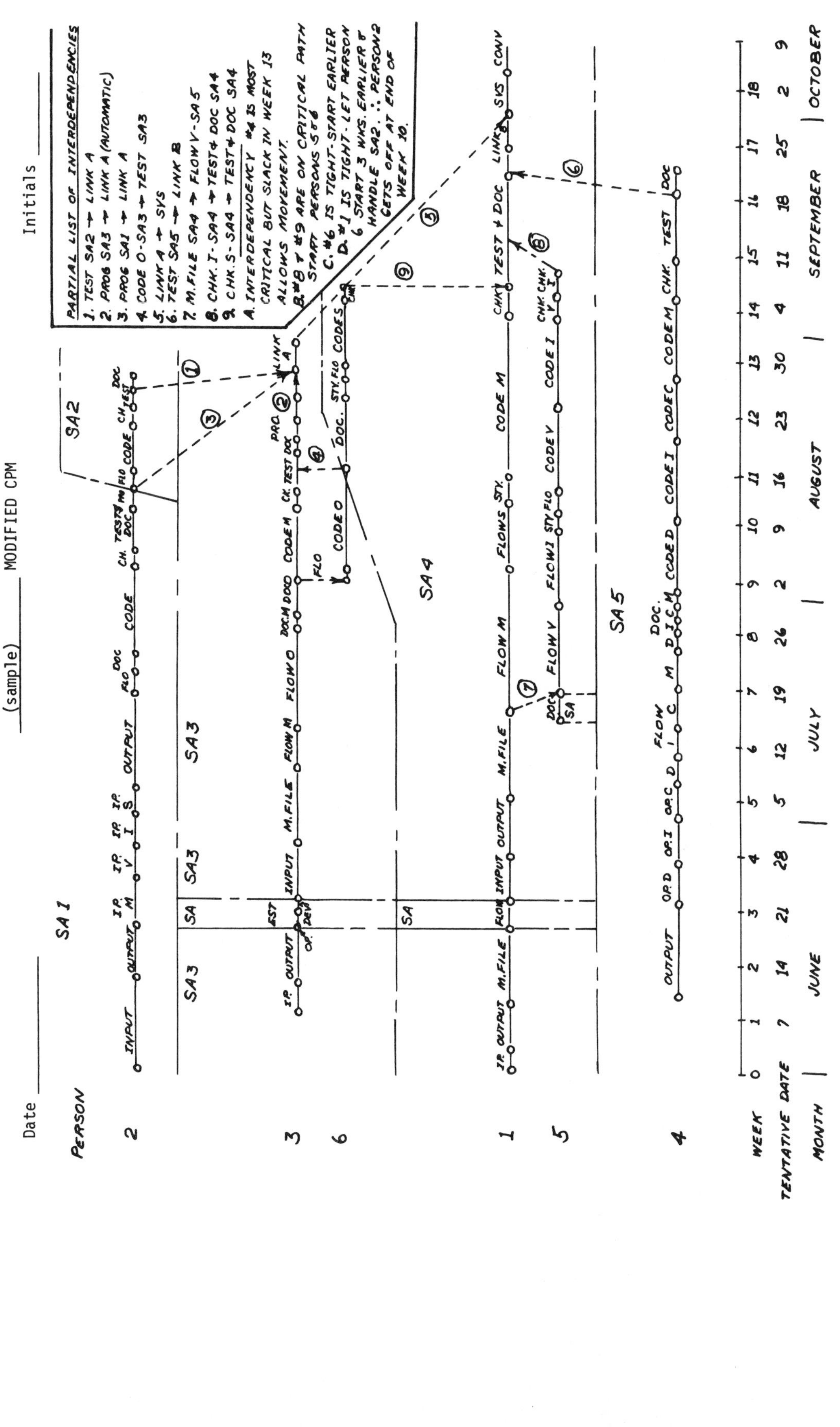

Figure 5-4. Modified CPM

portance of reporting all deviations from schedule (no matter how insignificant to the individual). During each interview, the project manager must emphasize the importance of the project schedules and must explain how the control reports are used and how they should be completed. The eight to ten minutes spent with each individual emphasizing these factors can save enormous time in chasing after reports and obtaining information.

PERIODIC CONTROL REPORT

Figure 5-5 illustrates a typical periodic control report containing information about the project schedule and the computer operations time. As can be seen, the report provides a quick synopsis of estimated versus actual efforts of the staff member, his confidence in completing the task in which he is engaged on (or prior to) deadline for that task, and his confidence in completing his overall project segment on schedule.

During the planning phase of the project, a report form should be developed for each staff member. Each report form should subdivide the staff member's project segment into the number of specific tasks shown on his portion of the project schedule. The number of tasks for any staff member will be in direct relation to the length of his overall project segment. As was explained previously, for projects of less than four weeks' duration (total elapsed time), the tasks should be estimated in hours and no task should exceed twenty-four hours' duration. Projects of more than four weeks' time should be estimated in man-days of effort and no task should exceed ten such days.

If the foregoing rules are generally adhered to, the completion of each individual's task becomes a benchmark and benchmark reports are submitted every two to three days during short projects and every week or two during longer projects.

The periodic reports should be submitted weekly if the tasks are established as recommended. In short projects, the project manager will receive one to three interim benchmark reports between periodic reports. In longer projects, the project manager will receive one or two periodic reports between benchmark reports. Therefore, in either case, the combination of periodic and benchmark reporting will provide the project manager with an up-to-date picture of the progress of the project. In addition, the two reports provide a basic validity checking media that the project manager can use to determine whether the reports correctly reflect the status of each segment of the project. Finally, the utilization of weekly periodic reports for all projects permits the project manager to establish a time (4:00 Friday afternoon is recommended) when all personnel devote their efforts to completing the periodic reports.

If 4:00 P.M. Friday is established as the time to complete the periodic reports, the forms can be distributed at that time, the personnel reminded to complete the forms, and the forms submitted to each individual's immediate supervisor by 4:30. This permits discussion between supervisors and subordinates before the end of work and the submission of all reports to the project manager by the end of work on Friday. The project manager, therefore, has the weekend to review the reports and to plan any actions necessary for the coming week.

WEEKLY PROGRESS REPORT

NAME: EXTENSION: HOME TELEPHONE: EMPLOYEE NO:

PROJECT: DATE: / / SUPERVISOR:

PROGRAM NUMBER: PROGRAM NAME:

LAST FUNCTION COMPLETED: FUNCTION BEING WORKED ON:

ESTIMATED PROD. TIME	ESTIMATED SET UP TIME	ESTIMATED DELAY	ESTIMATED TOTAL TIME	CONFIDENCE FACTOR

FUNCTION OR TASK	ESTIMATED			ACTUAL		
	DAYS	CUMULATIVE		DAYS	CUMULATIVE	
		Days	Dates		Days	Dates
DEFINE INPUTS TO PROGRAM						
LAYOUT INPUTS TO PROGRAM						
DEFINE OUTPUTS FROM PROGRAM						
LAYOUT OUTPUTS FROM PROGRAM						
DESIGN MASTER FILE						
WRITE PROGRAM NARRATIVE						
SEGMENT PROCESSING FUNCTIONS						
DEVELOP MODULE DEPENDANCY CHART						
FLOWCHART MAIN LOGIC						
ORGANIZE ASSISTING PROGRAMMERS						
CODE MAIN LOGIC						
KEYPUNCH MAIN LOGIC						
DESK CHECK						
DEBUG THE COMPILATION						
PROGRAM TEST						
DOCUMENT THE PROGRAMMING						

REMARKS OR COMMENTS:

CONFIDENCE IN MEETING SCHEDULE-PRESENT FUNCTION OR TASK ________*
CONFIDENCE IN MEETING SCHEDULE-REMAINDER OF TASKS ________*
CONFIDENCE IN MEETING SCHEDULE-FINAL COMPLETION DATE ________*

* If your confidence in meeting these schedules is not good, indicate an acceptable schedule by writing acceptable times in the remaining "ACTUAL DAYS" column. Enclose new estimates in brackets ( ).

INITIALS____________

Figure 5-5. Periodic Report

BENCHMARK CONTROL REPORT

As discussed in the preceding section, each member of the project team must notify his immediate superior when he completes a specific task. The completion of a specific task is usually referred to as a benchmark (or milestone); therefore, these reports are called benchmark (or milestone) reports. They provide the project manager with definite knowledge of the date and time that each benchmark was obtained and give the individual an opportunity to change the operational estimate or his confidence in these estimates.

Figure 5-6 illustrates a typical benchmark (or milestone) report form. A supply of these report forms should be given each individual at project inception. Upon completion of a specific task, the person should complete a benchmark report and submit it to his superior and the project manager. The purpose and conduct of discussions pertaining to benchmark reports is described in greater detail in Chapter Nine.

EXCEPTION CONTROL REPORT

Exception control reports are made immediately, whenever any staff member determines that something has occurred which will have significant effect on the project's schedule, costs, or quality. The report is made verbally to the person's immediate supervisor and to the project manager. The verbal report must be delivered with enough emphasis or emotion so that the recipients understand the severity of the problem. Once the verbal report is completed, the project manager, the supervisor, and the staff member should prepare a written exception report. The format of the exception report should vary with the ultimate utilization of the report. For example, a report for higher management would be more formal and in greater detail than would a note prepared for files. In any event, the report should contain:

1. program identification
2. a statement of the problem
3. a statement of the cause

TO____________________________________

PROGRAM NO.______PROGRAM NAME______________________________

ESTIMATED DATE______TIME_____
FUNCTION COMPLETED________________
ACTUAL DATE______TIME_____INITIALS_____

FACTOR___________PROD.TIME______SET UP TIME______DELAY_____TOTAL_____

NEXT FUNCTION STARTED_________________DATE____TIME_____CONFIDENCE_____

Figure 5-6. Benchmark or Milestone Report

4. the actions to be taken to eliminate or minimize the problem and to ensure that it will not recur.

These elements provide the basic information that will be necessary to reconstruct the reasons behind changes of agreed-upon project commitments at any future time.

CHANGES IN ESTIMATES

In almost all computer projects there will be a number of changes to the development schedule. As the project progresses:

from inception . . .
to conceptual design . . .
to detail design . . .
to programming . . .
to testing . . .
to conversion . . .
to operation –

the amount of information about the system and its basic elements increases significantly at each stage. This causes the estimates of the time required for succeeding tasks to vary and causes the confidence in these estimates to increase proportionately.

It is very important to document all changes of estimates connected with the development schedule because major changes or an accumulation of minor changes can seriously alter project completion times and development costs. In addition, the documented changes provide a record to which the project manager can refer when making future estimates of development. Without this information, the project manager cannot learn from his own errors. The documented changes show him the basis for the step-by-step transformation of his original, rough estimate into the actual project development schedule.

ANALYZING CHANGES

As each report is received by the project manager, he must analyze the contents of the report to determine whether it reflects a change in the project schedule. To accomplish this, the project manager must compare the actual performance with the expected (estimated) performance and must note any changes to estimates of future performance. Utilizing the periodic and benchmark report forms (Figures 5-5 and 5-6) recommended in this book, the task of determining changes is relatively simple. The project manager simply notes any changes that are indicated by differences in estimated and actual times on the periodic report or by the differences in estimated and actual completion dates on the benchmark report.

Once changes in the development schedule are noted, the impact of these changes must be determined. If the change has occurred in a critical path item on the schedule, the project manager can:

1. change the completion date of the project.
2. re-schedule the project to eliminate the effect of the change.
3. motivate the project personnel to work (harder or more efficiently) to eliminate the effect of the change.

If the change has occurred in a non-critical path item, the project manager must review the schedule interdependencies to ensure that the change has not caused the item to become a critical path item. In any event, the prudent project manager will have the project schedule redrawn whenever a change requires re-scheduling.

If re-scheduling is necessary, the project manager must determine its impact on the development costs and project quality, and must inform his management of the change in schedule and its effect on completion date, costs, and quality. The only time that a project manager can re-schedule and not inform his management is when the change in schedule does not significantly affect the project completion date, the cost of the project, the over-all utilization of the project personnel, or the quality of the project. Chapter Nine presents a periodic report form that the project manager can use to summarize the main elements of the project's status.

6

Ensuring Project Quality and Eliminating the Problems in Testing

Testing provides the most definitive control of the quality of the individual modules, programs, and systems before they become operational. It is, in effect, the culmination of all of the preceding development efforts. As such, the testing period should be a time of pleasure and fruition. Why then is the testing period on many projects a time of extreme tension, irritation, and general confusion? Why must experienced project managers learn to expect and to prepare answers for the following discourse?

> I don't mean to pry, but you said you'd started testing the inventory system three weeks ago. Since then the users have become extremely concerned that the errors they've found out about will not be eliminated. I know you'd never put in a jury-rigged system but the users are worried. You can level with me. How bad is it? Can we salvage anything?

Intelligent and experienced project managers never have to prepare answers for this type of discourse. They accomplish this by:

1. Initiating and administering a variety of quality controls during the preceding stages of the project.
2. Utilizing the various types of testing that are available.
3. Managing the testing effort efficiently.

This chapter describes a method of conducting the preceding activities that eliminates many of the usual problems during testing and that leads to formal acceptance of the project at the conclusion of testing.

QUALITY CONTROLS

The controls over the quality of a project are instituted to ensure that the system performs the required functions in an efficient manner. The overall system quality and an outline of the manner in which this quality will be achieved are described by the conceptual design developed during the feasibility study. The in-depth review of the conceptual design ensured that the design was both functionally and technically sound.

The detail design and programming functions expanded the detail of the conceptual design and then translated these details into a machine (understandable) language. During these functions, specific quality controls must be instituted and administered to ensure that the project, when complete, has not unknowingly deviated from the conceptual design. The basic controls utilized during these functions are:

1. Documentation.
2. Standards.
3. Benchmark reviews.
4. Testing.

None of these controls can ensure project quality by itself. It is the combination of these individual controls into an overall plan that eliminates problems and provides the basis for formal acceptance.

Proper initiation and administration of quality controls admittedly requires a good deal of time and effort. However, the alternative is to trust each individual staff member to determine and administer his own quality controls. This over-reliance on the individual results in systems where the quality of the programs and documentation varies widely and where the testing period is marked by long hours, confusion, irritation, and tension.

Documentation

There is an almost universal dislike among EDP personnel for documentation. The main reason for this dislike is that the documentation of a project function is usually performed at the end of the function and, therefore, does not really help to accomplish that function.

Properly administered, good documentation of a function will:

1. Occur progressively as each task within the function is completed.
2. Assist the person (who does the documentation) in accomplishing the function.
3. Demonstrate the quality of the work.
4. Provide the information required to find and eliminate errors.
5. Describe the status of the accomplished work.

The remainder of this section describes the general contents of the documentation and the methods recommended to initiate and administer documentation for the detail design and programming function.

Contents. Documentation of the detail design is based upon the documentation included in the project justification. To begin, each analyst should rewrite the information pertaining to his (assigned) program(s) into a program summary. This summary will include, as a minimum, the objective or purpose, the inputs, the outputs, the data base, and the segments of the conceptual design that pertain to that program. This rewrite will provide the analyst with all available information about the program and will also (hopefully) make him reflect on what he does not know.

Based on the knowledge provided by completing the program summary, the analyst will gather data and conduct interviews (or meetings) to supply any missing information about the program. As each piece of data is collected it must be annotated as to source, the pertinent information contained, and the area it affects. Each interview must also be documented as to interviewer, important information obtained, and areas of impact of the information. In addition, at the conclusion of all interviews and meetings it is recommended that the interviewer prepare an interviewee summary (Figure 6-1).

When all pertinent information has been collected, the analyst will develop final layouts of the program's inputs, outputs, and data base. Utilizing all preceding information, he will then segment the run into logical functions (modules), will develop the interrelationships among modules (modular dependencies), and will prepare detailed flowcharts or decision tables to describe the steps and sequences of steps required to accomplish each of the functions (detailed flowcharts). Every layout, module description, modular dependency chart, and detailed flowchart is part of the program's detail design documentation.

The documentation of the Programming Function begins with a summary of detail design that is written at the end of programming study. The summary of detail design is a one-page synopsis of the most important points within the detail design. If programming study is not done, this synopsis is an added activity in the programming flowcharting task. During programming flowcharting, the flowcharts showing the exact logic of each of the program segments are completed. These flowcharts are also elements of the documentation.

Programming documentation (through programming flowcharting) is translated into machine language during the coding task. The program listings resulting from each module of coding also become portions of the documentation.

(3X5 card)

General Impressions of: ______________________________
Interviewee

Department: ______________________________

Position: ______________________________

Age: ________ Physical Characteristics: ______________________

Interview Ease: Assisted Spoke freely Gave information Difficult

Interview Method: Indirect Democratic Authoritarian Friendly

General Comments: ______________________________

____

____

Interviewer: ______________________ Date: ______________

Figure 6-1. Interviewee Summary

Initiation. To obtain all detail design documentation on a timely and efficient basis, you must, during your initial meeting with each person, describe the purposes of documentation and emphasize how the recommended method of documentation will benefit the individual. If each person clearly understands all the benefits that documentation can provide, the usual efforts expended in obtaining documentation will be minimized.

The main benefit that any analyst receives from documenting his work is the clarity and logic that is required for him to document his thoughts. Many times, the analyst feels that he knows the solution but is surprised at how much the solution is improved when he describes it segment by segment during each task. Therefore, a primary requirement for any method of documentation is, *to clarify your thinking, document it immediately.* This means that as soon as any element of any task of the detail design is completed, it must be documented.

To the analyst, the next most important benefit of documentation is the opportunity for immediate review by a superior. This assures the analyst that he will not complete the entire design function only to discover that some obvious error in an early design task has made a substantial portion of his efforts worthless. To achieve this benefit, the method of documentation must "provide immediate management review."

Recommended method. The recommended method of documentation requires immediate documentation and provides immediate management review. It therefore provides a viable basis for motivating analysts to complete their documentation in a timely and efficient manner. This method consists of:

1. Ensuring at the outset of the project (via the project schedule) that each analyst fully understands his responsibility and its interface with other analysts' and programmers' responsibilities.
2. Requiring that each analyst submit one copy of a hand-written draft of his documentation of each element in the detail design as soon as he completes his analysis of that element.
3. Determination by the analyst of the distribution list for the finished documentation (beyond his "program documentation" copy and your "systems documentation" copy).
4. Immediate review of the documentation for clarity, content, conformance with standards (see Standards Section) and coordination with other analysts' work. Included is the review of the distribution list.
5. Submission to a central typing group for typing, copying, and distribution to the user group and operations group (see Chapter Two).
6. Assembly by the analyst into a loose-leaf "program documentation" manual and by you into a loose-leaf "systems documentation" manual.

In this way, the analyst completes the major portion of his documentation as each task progresses. Therefore, at the end of the detail design function, the analyst will only have to document any program interfaces that are not already clear.

In addition to the benefits to the analyst, this method of documentation engenders a simple and efficient information flow among analysts and provides a positive, continuing, quality control. This quality control also provides more detailed control over each analyst's progress than do benchmark reports. To obtain these benefits, you must:

1. Impress each analyst with the worth of the method of documentation at your initial meeting.
2. Make sure that each analyst fully understands his responsibility.
3. Review all rough documentation within one day of receipt.
4. Use your influence to obtain fast turnaround from the typing group and thorough review by the user and operations groups.
5. Establish a control log and control reports (similar to those described at the end of Chapter Three) to ensure fast response to the analyst.
6. Review the log weekly to determine if any analyst is getting behind schedule.

This method of documentation, in addition to providing these extra benefits, provides the information necessary to describe the current status of the project.

Interview file. The interviewee summaries of the company's personnel are submitted to the EDP manager's secretary and are assembled in a 3x5 card file. They are sequenced alphabetically by the name of the interviewee. The purpose of this file is to collect basic information about the people who have been interviewed as a basis for conducting more efficient interviews and meetings with these people in the future. By reviewing this information and by discussing the people to be interviewed with the past interviewers, an analyst can prepare himself. For the minute or two taken to complete the form, the benefits can be very substantial.

Standards

Prior to testing, standards are required for the detail design function and the programming function (including all documentation efforts). These standards are implemented and administered to:

1. Reduce and restrict (to management levels) the areas where errors can be made.
2. Provide a common and understandable means of communicating ideas and thoughts within the company.

To achieve these objectives, the standards must be developed for each project within each specific company and must be adhered to by all personnel. Therefore, the outline of standards and the methods of administering them presented in this chapter provide only a general overview. To be usable, this outline and these methods must be modified to fit the specific company and detail must be added.

If no standardization exists within your EDP areas, begin by standardizing practices on your projects. As the standardization proves beneficial, promote its utilization. Standards that grow through usage last and are followed. Standards that are imposed from above usually die of neglect.

Detail design. Design standards consist of:

1. nomenclature;
2. input, output, data base, and temporary data set formats;

3. modularization;
4. symbols and charting techniques utilized in the program flow charts.

Nomenclature, during detail design, refers to the basic methods used to identify systems, programs and files. EDP facilities that operate large numbers of systems must, of necessity, institute complicated coding standards so that the code for each system describes the system's:

1. name (shortened)
2. purpose
3. main user department.
4. relationship with larger systems

Then, within this definition:

1. Programs are identified as to their relationship to the system.
2. Files (data base) are identified as to their relationship to programs.
3. Input files, output files and temporary data sets are identified as to their relationship to the programs.

For example:

P	*SAMP*	*VERI*	*P*	*INV C*	*IEROR*	*SAMP*
Major System	Minor System or Program Ident	Program File or TempData Set,Ident	Program File or TDS, Indicator	User Depart-ments	Purpose	Name

might be used as the code for the edit and verify program of the sample system in the production system used by inventory control for input error correcting; while:

P *VERI* *VNMF* *F* *PURC* *VNACT* *SAMP*

would be the code for the vendor master file of the edit and verify program of the sample system in the production system used by purchasing to review vendor activity.

The coding standards in the example are only for illustration. Their only strong point is that they are easily translatable. In real life they would probably be cumbersome to use and maintain. Many computer manufacturers and software suppliers of maintenance programs have extensive written material on coding standards (nomenclature) recommended for use with their products. Utilization of the nomenclature that is recommended for your equipment or software will probably be most efficient for most companies because it can also be used as header information to identify internally (in the computer) the system's elements.

Input and Output Format Standards prescribe specific ways that all inputs and outputs must be described. The description includes contents, relationships, and layouts. Most computer manufacturers and several companies who market proprietary software provide coding sheets for standardizing input and output formats. Some large companies have adopted the coding required by the division of program compilers (of manufacturer's software) to provide Input Format Standards. This technique requires all coding to be keypunched and an 80-column print program, but it provides an easily changed medium that can be used during programming. Regardless of the techniques, standardization of input and output formats should provide clarity, understandability, and ease of completion.

Data Base (File) and Temporary Data Set Format Standards specify how, where, and with what layout the sorted and transient information required by the system will be kept. As with inputs and outputs, techniques for standardization range from the utilization of manufacturer-supplied forms to the purchase, lease or internal development of (small) specialized computer systems. The selection of a specific technique for your company should depend entirely on the degree of sophistication that is required. Highly sophisticated standardization techniques are impressive, but they can cost your company a great deal of money by over-restricting your personnel and by being complicated to use.

Modularization refers to the segmentation of a program into its component's logical sub-sets (or modules). Some program modules, (common modules) are required in almost every program (data division modules, housekeeping modules, initialization modules). Other program modules (functional modules) are required to accomplish the program's functions (main line logic modules, activity, or application modules). In common modules, the format, contents nomenclature and relationships among modules can be standardized. In functional modules, only some nomenclature and some relationships can be standardized. However, for any program, the method of describing all module inter-relationships (Modular Dependency Chart) should be standardized as to symbols, charting techniques and nomenclature.

The standardization of symbols and charting techniques is required for:

1. Systems (technical and functional) Macro-Flow Charts,
2. Modular Dependency Charts,
3. Detailed (Internal) Program Flow Charts or Decision Tables,

to ensure complete understanding of the logic, meanings, and relationships expressed in the charts. Small deviations from standards can, in many cases, cause large deviations from expected results. Selection of a template (of symbols for drawing flow charts) and a statement of how this template is to be used make up the bulk of the standardization process. The statement of template utilization should not be long or complex. Simple rules, easily understood, will usually be followed.

Programming. Basic standards for the programming function include: nomenclature, error routines and outputs, checkpoint and restart routines, audit routines, and the programming language itself. These standards enhance consistency, clarity, and understandability. Programming to standards that enhance consistency, clarity and understandability requires little additional time. It pays great dividends during review and is almost mandatory for efficient program error definition and elimination.

Nomenclature for the programming function refers to the identification of the various modules within the program and identification of the data, notes, storage areas, and logic contained in these modules. This identification must be consistent and should also be very clear and understandable.

Errors (conditions that prohibit further processing of a piece of data) of one type or another can occur in almost any program. Many times (as in edit and verification programs) all possible errors are fully pre-defined as is all subsequent processing. Standardization of error search, definition, and processing modules can greatly simplify future programming of similar programs. In other cases, the probability of occurrence can be predetermined (as in unmatched items in an update program or in unreadable records), but the subsequent procedures and displays are dependent upon the effect of the error upon the file(s) and other logic. In these cases, only error definition and search techniques should be standardized. In any case, error displays and error outputs for all types of errors should be standardized to the greatest possible degree. This will simplify correction and can also reduce programming time.

Checkpoint and restart routines provide a method of halting the operation of a program and, later, beginning operation again without reprocessing all of the data that had been processed prior to the halt. When using large volume files, these routines are required to save computer time. Many of the routines can be standardized modules which require a minimum degree of modification to be used. The determination of whether, how and when to employ these routines should be based upon written rules (standards).

Audit routines ensure that the program has correctly processed the information it received. These routines:

1. Count the number of input records received and the number of output records received.
2. Count "Dollars In" and "Dollars Out" for all cash fields.
3. Perform trial balancing functions on records and cash.
4. Statistically select records for display and manual verification.

Here also, many of the modules comprising these routines can be standardized. In all cases, the determination of when and where to use these routines should be a matter of standard (EDP) policy and not left to the individual programmer.

The programming language itself is the medium for translating the ideas contained in the programming flow charts into machine (understandable) language. Many sophisticated translation techniques are embodied in the commonly used programming languages (COBOL, FORTRAN, PL-1, etc.). However, the EDP area management or the prudent project manager will define a subset of these language techniques because some techniques save programming time but vastly extend testing time and are very complicated to change or modify. Therefore, the techniques which provide the best overall efficiency should be selected as the standard language. Once defined, the standard language must be used by all programmers.

Initiation. The initiation of standards is begun by defining (or selecting) the standards that are necessary and/or will be helpful in controlling the quality of the project. This definition is the most important element in the initiation and administration of standards. If the standards are too restrictive, too numerous, confusing, or contradictory, they will either be ignored or the efficiency of the conduct of the project will be severely decreased. If the standards are not restrictive enough, ambiguous, or contradictory, the quality of the project will suffer and the testing period will be filled with crises.

When selected, the standards should be explained to each staff member during his initial meeting with the project manager. The following points should be included:

1. What the standards for the project are.
2. How the standards are to be used.
3. Why the standards are necessary.
4. Which standards pertain (most) to each individual.
5. How utilization of the standards will benefit the individual.

Obviously, the emphasis in this meeting should be placed on the benefits to the individual from utilizing the selected standards. If the individual is convinced that he will benefit, he will work at utilizing the prescribed standards. If he cannot see their benefit they will usually not be employed unless a great deal of effort is provided by the project manager.

Administration. The only successful method of ensuring that standards are being followed is to continually review the project documentation. Usually this necessitates a dual review of the documentation; once for content and once for conformance to standards. Admittedly this review is time consuming. However, a lack of conformance to standards that is not discovered and returned for correction is an admission that you are not sufficiently interested in conforming to standards to perform thorough reviews. This admission, in much the same manner as a hole in a dike, perpetuates other more serious deviations from standards which, unless checked, eventually inundate the project with work of poor and inconsistent quality.

If you do thoroughly review documentation for conformance with standards, you will soon find that you will become much more selective when defining standards. This is good because it is easy to decide that a large number of complex and unnecessary standards are required (of others) unless you must review for conformance to standards. In addition, if your review discloses that a specific standard is not generally being followed, you can decide whether to try to impress the staff with the necessity of the standard or to change the standard.

The review for conformance to standards takes place at the same time as the reviews of documentation. It, therefore, must also be accomplished within one day of receipt. On large projects and with multi-project responsibilities you will find that you cannot personally accomplish the necessary reviews within one day. If, at this time, you decide to delegate your review responsibilities, you must also delegate the authority to modify or change standards. Naturally, as you are still responsible to higher management for project quality, you will review all changes before they are initiated. However, the primary authority for change must be delegated.

Benchmark Reviews

The completion of each major project task (e.g. coding) is a benchmark (see Chapter Four for further definition). As each benchmark is achieved, it is a signal to you that the documentation, which has been reviewed piece-by-piece, should be reviewed in its entirety. Similarly, when a project function (e.g. programming) is completed, a benchmark review of the entire function should be held.

To facilitate benchmark reviews, as you receive each piece of documentation, the "Systems Documentation" should be assembled in a loose leaf binder. Separators should indicate the programs, each of the functions within a program, and the tasks within each function. The "Program Documentation" should also be separated in the same manner. Utilization of a loose-leaf notebook permits change to any section and also permits removal of interim documentation when a benchmark is reached.

Benchmark reviews consist of scrutiny for consistency, completeness, and overall clarity. In addition, the list of interdependencies (Chapter Four) should be referenced and any interdependency relation with another program should be checked at this time.

Benchmark reviews should be accomplished independently by you and the person who has achieved the benchmark. Within two days after you receive the benchmark report (Chapter Four), you should meet with the person who achieved the benchmark and agree on any changes, additions, or deletions.

After the meeting, you should summarize your thoughts about the manner in which the benchmark was achieved (i.e. adherence to schedule, general quality, documentation, standards, attitudes, morale and general performance). These benchmark performance summaries are very helpful for goal setting, performance appraisals, and for motivational purposes. When all corrections to the documentation have been made, it should be copied and sent to the review groups for more detailed review. These reviews are discussed later in this chapter and in Chapter Two.

TYPES OF TESTING

Seven commonly accepted types of testing are:

1. Desk checking
2. Program (by programmer)
3. Program test
4. Linkage test
5. Systems test
6. Parallel test
7. Pilot test

There is a natural progression of the testing effort from one type of testing to another (in the sequence of the prior listing); however, not all types of testing are required in every project. In most projects, one or more of these types are not required and are eliminated. You must be aware of the differences between these types of testing, must determine the types that best fit your project, and must control the progress of the testing effort as it proceeds from type to type.

The remainder of this section will describe the functions of, and significant differences among, the various types of testing. Because detailed analysis of the techniques and methods used in the various types of testing would require a large amount of space and would probably lack interest for the reader experienced in EDP, the description of the types of testing will be brief and general.

Desk Checking

As was described earlier in the chapter, flowcharts and decision tables describing the internal logic of the program have been prepared and reviewed. When the coding sheets comprising each module of program coding are returned from Keypunch with the cards into which the coding (of the logic) has been punched, the programmer must:

1. check the cards against the coding to ensure 100% accurate keypunching.
2. review the logic of the coding.
3. check the coding for completeness, correctness, and clarity.

In many cases, before being returned to the programmer, the coding sheets and the punched cards will be sent from Keypunch to a computer operations area where an 80 column listing will be printed from the cards. The listing, the cards and the coding sheets are then returned to the programmer. The listing is a useful tool because it is easier to read than are the cards themselves and because the special symbols, printed via computer, are usually more programming-oriented than are the special symbols printed on the cards. This difference in symbols occurs because there may be several special symbols that can be printed (depending on the type of printer) from one code punched in the card.

All desk checking is a manual process. The programmer must physically check and review every character of every card. This detailed checking may be done by a person other than the programmer who did the coding. However, unless the reviewer is also a programmer, the completeness, correctness, clarity, and logic of the coding cannot be affirmed by the reviewer. Regardless of who does the checking, the responsibility for desk checking should remain with the programmer who did the coding because it is he who will be penalized for improper checking during the program (programmer) testing.

Although desk checking is manual and almost mandatory in every project, it is part of testing because it is quality control-oriented. Thorough desk checking can significantly reduce the computer and programmer time required during the remainder of the testing effort.

Program (Programmer)

The program (programmer) type of testing consists of:

1. assembly of modules into a total program.
2. adding the control cards necessary for machine operation.
3. assembling and compiling the program on the computer.
4. testing the program functions by the programmer.

At the conclusion of this testing, the programmer verifies that the program is operational and that it will function according to specifications.

This type of testing begins when the cards for the various modules are manually assembled into a total program (card deck) and an 80-column listing and a duplicate card deck are obtained. After these elements have been checked for accuracy, the tops of two card decks should be diagonally striped with a felt pen (to ensure that the sequence is not lost) and annotated with system identification, program identification, programmer and date.

The control cards that are required for the operation vary widely with manufacturers' equipment and software. Often the developmental programmer will require the assistance of an expert in manufacturers' software to prepare these cards. However, all programmers should know how to prepare normal or commonly used control cards. When prepared, the cards are added to one of the card decks and the resultant program deck is sent to computer operations for processing.

During computer processing, the language used by the programmer is again translated into electronic machine language and all of the instructions in the program are assembled into the proper sequence. This assembly and compilation operation also uncovers any errors in the control cards or in the card deck that prevent the program from completing the assembly and compilation.

Unfortunately, these errors (all too frequently) do occur. At this point processing is usually halted and a vast amount of information (diagnostics) that indicates the area and type of error is generated. In some cases, the processing can and does continue; in others, further processing is prohibited. In any case, the programmer should receive his program deck and all diagnostics. He must now find and eliminate all errors until the computer can complete an assembly and compilation that is free of significant errors. When it is error free, the program is operational.

Finally, the programmer must obtain or prepare the test data (input, files, etc.) necessary to assure himself that the program is functionally correct. He must then submit the program and the test data for operation and must check the outputs to ensure that the program did, in fact, function correctly. This testing also uncovers a relatively large number of errors in the program that must be corrected. When all errors have been corrected, the program is again tested to ensure that it is operational and functionally correct, a process repeated until the programmer is completely satisfied with the results.

Because any error in system logic, design, test data, program logic, coding, control cards, or keypunching can cause severe error conditions during the program (programmer) type of testing and because the cause of any specific error condition is usually not immediately identifiable, program (programmer) testing is very time consuming. However, thorough program (programmer) testing is worthwhile because it virtually eliminates major problems during the remainder of the testing effort.

Program Test

Program testing is a more exhaustive or thorough test of the program functions. It consists of the processing of additional test data (that has been prepared by the user group) through the program and the checking of the outputs to ensure that the program is correctly performing all of its functions. This type of testing is eliminated in many projects because the program (programmer) testing is considered to have been sufficiently thorough to ensure correct program function.

Linkage Test

When the output of one program is the input of another program in the same system, the programs are linked. Linkage test refers to the testing of two, three or more linked programs, and consists of processing test data through the entire linkage and checking the various outputs to ensure that the linkage is functioning correctly. The primary use of the linkage test is to reduce the areas where errors can occur during the systems test. It, therefore, is conducted after program tests have been performed on the programs in the linkage and before the systems test is performed.

Systems Test

Systems test is performed to ensure that the computer system functions correctly. Test data is processed through the computer system and all system outputs are thoroughly checked. The test data used in systems testing should simulate all of the actual inputs and data base to the greatest possible degree. During linkage test and especially during program test, the test data is usually designed specifically as a simulation of the input and data base for the linkage (and program) and, therefore, will not correctly reflect the actual inputs and data base. This precludes destruction of production data if the system had, for any reason, caused these changes in inputs and data base.

Parallel Test

The purpose of the parallel test is to ensure that the entire system functions correctly with actual inputs and data base. It consists of duplicating all input that is received and processing one set through the new computer system and the new manual procedures necessary to operate the new computer system while the old system is being operated normally by utilizing the other set of input. The new and old systems are operated in parallel and all outputs and data base are checked until the correct functioning of the new system is ensured; at this time, the old system is discontinued.

Pilot Test

Pilot test is also used to ensure that the entire system functions correctly with live or actual input and a data base. It is a simulation of actual operation of the computer system and also of the manual processing required to operate the computer system. Pilot test simulation is used rather than parallel test duplication:

1. to reduce cost.
2. because resources are not available to conduct parallel listing.
3. to reduce the time period required.

To accomplish pilot test, the following methods are common:

1. Use a selected and representative subset (geographical areas) for data base and input.
2. Randomly select a subset of input and only check the output from the selected input.
3. Collect a large number of sets of inputs (four weeks of daily) to periodic processing; process them sequentially in a short (one day) period; and only check the final day's outputs.

While pilot test can be (statistically) as thorough as parallel test, most people will not have the same confidence in the results. However, even if it is not as thorough, pilot test is a very acceptable alternative because of cost, resource, or time restrictions.

MANAGING THE TESTING EFFORT

The testing effort requires special attention. The planning organization, direction, and control of the testing effort can determine the final quality of the project and can also drastically affect the time required for this effort. This section presents methods of managing the testing effort that, when augmented by testing methods already proven successful in your company, can eliminate many of the problems that would otherwise occur during testing.

Planning

Planning of the testing effort begins with the selection of the types of testing that are required and can be used on each specific project. When selecting the types of testing for your project, you must:

1. estimate the resources required (personnel, computertime, etc.)
2. estimate the time required.
3. estimate the cost involved.
4. decide how critical it is for each specific program to function correctly.
5. determine whether and how alternative types of testing can provide acceptable results.

Alternative plans for the testing effort can be evaluated either informally or more formally through a method such as the Weighted Point Evaluation Technique described in Chapter Four.

After selection of the types of testing, the schedule for the testing effort must be incorporated into the overall project schedule (see Figure 5-2). This should be accomplished as part of the feasibility study effort. Figure 6-2 illustrates a method of estimating testing computer requirements. All decisions about the testing effort and the bases for these decisions should be documented in the "Project Justification."

(sample) PROJECT

TESTING SCHEDULE AND REQUIREMENTS

M. Wade Analyst — 360/50 Equipment — Date ______

Prog. or Mod.	Person or Seg. #	Type of Test	Total Run Time	Est. # Tests	Test Time - Each Shot 1	2	3	4	5	6	Total	Week Ending Date-Each Shot 1	2	3	4	5	6
SA 1	2	Assemble/Compile	507	2	7	10					17	8/9	8/16				
"	"	Program Test	"	3	50	50					100	8/16	8/16				
SA2	2	Assemble/Compile	27	3	5	10	15				30	8/23	8/23	8/23			
	"	Program Test	"	2	15	15					30	8/23	8/23				
SA3	3	Assemble/Compile	"	4	6	15	30	45			96	8/2	8/9	8/9	8/9		
	"	Program Test	"	3	45	45	45				135	8/9	8/9	8/16			
	6	Assemble/Compile	17	2	8	30					38	8/9	8/16				
	"	Program Test	"	3	30	30	30				90	8/16	8/16				
SA4	1	Assemble/Compile	"	2	10	10					20	9/4	9/11				
	"	Program Test	"	6	10	10	10	10	10	10	60	9/11	9/11	9/18	9/18	9/25	
	5	Assemble/Compile	"	4	10	10	10	10			40	9/4	9/4	9/11	9/11		
	"	Program Test	"	6	10	10	10	10	10	10	60	9/11	9/18	9/18	9/25	9/25	
		NOT ALL TESTING SHOWN															
SA 1,2, & 3	2 & 3	Linkage	551	3	42	50	50				142	9/25	10/2	10/2			
All	1,2,3,4 & 5	System	647	4	112	160	160	160			592	10/2	10/2	10/9	10/9		
Parallel	1-5	Parallel	647	1/day	647						Not Included	10/15					
TOTAL											1449						

SUMMARY: Total Computer Utilization 1860 min. Parallel Requires 647 min per day Begins 10/15
Weekly Test Requirements: W/E 8/2 Amt 6; W/E 8/9 Amt 240; W/E 8/16 Amt 160; W/E 8/23 Amt 60;
W/E 8/30 Amt 130; W/E 9/4 Amt 160; W/E 9/11 Amt 150; W/E 9/18 Amt 92; W/E 9/25 Amt 180
W/E 10/2 Amt 372; W/E 10/2 Amt 320

Figure 6-2. Testing Schedule and Requirements

Organizing

After the project has been authorized, the decisions (and bases for the decisions) relating to types of testing and the testing schedule should be reviewed to ascertain the:

1. amount and types of test data that will be required.
2. extent and method of checking outputs and data base that will be required.
3. starting date for program, linkage, and systems tests.
4. number and types of people.

After consideration of this information, the composition and organization of the user and operations review groups should be determined (see Chapter Two). When organizing and staffing these groups, every effort should be expended to make the user group responsible for test data preparation and checking (output and data base) test results. The User Group must be given any assistance necessary to assist them and instruct them in the correct and efficient methods of preparing test data and checking test results, but it must have the final responsibility for these functions so that:

1. It (the user group) is involved in the project and fully aware of project quality.
2. It can be trained in any new procedures while it benefits the testing effort.
3. It has confidence that the testing was performed in a thorough and comprehensive manner.
4. It is willing to accept responsibility for system operation at the conclusion of testing.
5. The programmers and analysts can concentrate on, and be responsible for, determining and correcting the causes of errors that are detected by the users.

Because the organization of the review groups is so dependent upon the specific skills of the individuals and upon the project requirements, no single organization can be recommended. However, it has been ascertained that user and EDP personnel seem to provide the best results when they work separately prior to project test and are combined into test teams with specific and separate responsibilities during and after program test.

Direction

To achieve the best results during the testing effort, each person must fully understand his responsibility and its relation to those of others. Specifically, every person must know exactly where to obtain expert assistance and be motivated to utilize it. Too often, EDP personnel spend a great deal of time trying to discover and eliminate the causes of errors when expert assistance (in such areas as the utilization of manufacturer's software, interpretation of diagnostic information, and how to obtain additional diagnostics) would have immediately pinpointed the solution.

Control

To control the testing effort you must control each individual type of testing that is being used. Therefore, each type of testing must have:

1. resources allocated to it;
2. a schedule for completion;
3. limitations placed on computer usage and overall cost;
4. a method of determining whether more of any type of testing is required.

The controls on resources, schedule and cost during testing can be almost exactly the same as the development effort's project controls.

To determine whether more of any type of testing is required, specific elements must be reviewed and certain factors must be verified. Figure 6-3 summarizes the review elements and verification factors for each type of testing.

Because of the amount of information that must be reviewed during program (programmer) testing and the technical nature of that information, a considerable amount of assistance will be required from the review groups to actually perform these reviews during the entire testing effort.

In many cases, because of the great assistance required, it is necessary to delegate the responsibility for testing by appointing a head of the testing group. In these cases, the programmer is primarily responsible for desk checking and program (programmer) testing his program, while the head of the testing group is responsible for all subsequent reviews of these and all other types of testing.

Regardless of who is primarily responsible, copies of the output of each compile, assembly, and test must be placed in the "Program Documentation" (by the programmer) and the "Systems Documentation" (by the project manager). Additional copies must also be sent to each person responsible for reviewing that particular element.

Type of Testing	Review Elements	Verification Factors
Desk Checking	Cards Listing Coding Sheets	Exact correspondence among review elements Obvious errors in logic or coding Conformance to standards
Program (Programmer)	Computer Listing Test Input Data Base Input Test Output	Errors in assembly and compilation Conformance to standards Completeness of Input and Data Base Correctness of Output
Program Test Linkage Test Systems Test	Test Input Test Output Data Base Listing	Completeness of Input Correctness of Data Base Correctness of Outputs
Parallel Test Pilot Test	Old System Outputs & Data Base New System Outputs & Data Base	Differences Old vs. New Systems Discrepancies from expectations

Figure 6-3. Review Elements and Verification Factors

After each review, the reviewer should briefly summarize his findings and send copies of the summary to the programmer(s), the manager of the user group, the head of the operations group, and the project manager. A general outline of the format of the testing review summary is illustrated by Figure 6-4. Copies of this summary and the benchmark review summaries become the final portions of the "Program Documentation" and the "Systems Documentation.

TO:________________________________ ____________DATE

FROM:________________________________

SUBJECT:______________Project-Testing Review Summary

Today as part of the __________(a)__________ type of testing, I have completed a review of __________(b)__________ a portion of the __________(c)__________.

This review indicates that the system is functioning in a _______(d)_______ manner.

The following error conditions were discovered________________

____

____

____

____

____

(a) Type of testing
(b) Name of the specific document
(c) Review element
(d) Acceptable or unacceptable

Figure 6-4. Testing Review Summary

SYSTEM ACCEPTANCE

To gain acceptance of the system, the manager of the user area, the project manager, the EDP operations manager, the development manager and the EDP manager must agree that the system:

1. performs the required functions.
2. is relatively machine efficient.
3. can be maintained.

If the user group is responsible for test data preparation and the checking of test results, its management must affirm correct performance when the system test is successfully completed. Failure to affirm, at this point, indicates doubt about the quality of the test data or the checking but not the system. The supervisor of computer operations can, after a review of the operations logs for the systems test, tentatively affirm the relative machine efficiency of the system. Actually, the machine operators or shift chiefs should have notified the supervisor, the programmer, and the operations manager of any problems in this area during program test or linkage test.

The operations manager will receive a copy of the final program compilation listings. The review of these listings is usually accomplished by systems modifications personnel. It will uncover areas that do not conform to standards and/or are unclear. Prior to systems test these areas must either be changed or be explained to the satisfaction of the operations manager.

This indicates that, if the recommended methods are followed, tentative system acceptance can be obtained from all responsible personnel at the end of the systems test. Pilot and parallel testing are only required to ensure that the user group has thoroughly and correctly fulfilled its responsibilities.

7

Converting Files, Programs, and People

Conversion is the interim process that is required to transform a fully tested system into an operational system. Before a system can be operated, the data base (all required files), the program preparation, and the people and procedures required by the system must be completely operational. The data base must be complete, correct, and in the proper format. The programs must have the proper backup, must be entered into the program library, and must be properly documented. The people must have been trained in the proper procedures and must be ready to begin using them.

Although the conversion effort requirements are straight-forward and logical, their importance cannot be over-emphasized. The most efficient computer system is worthless if the data base is not usable, and many computer systems have been destroyed by user personnel who were not correctly trained and motivated. Therefore, to avoid the following questions, the foresighted project manager will ensure that the conversion effort is thoroughly and capably managed.

> If the system was ready six weeks ago, why haven't you put it in yet? Why weren't the master files corrected weeks ago? Why don't the users know what's happening? Don't you ever plan ahead?

The main problem in planning and in thoroughly and capably managing the conversion effort is the extreme accuracy that is required. During conversion, even more than during the detail design and programming functions, 100% accuracy on all details is essential. The remainder of this chapter will describe the functions, problems, and control of the conversion effort.

DATA BASE

The data base of a system comprises the master (including error) files utilized by that system. The data base, therefore, contains the totality of the system's stored data or information. The system continually updates this information so that it is always current and can be retrieved, compared, selected, manipulated, transmitted, and displayed in the output formats required. Obviously, the most critical functions of any computer system are the maintenance and subsequent utilization of the data base.

Because of its importance to the system, conversion of any part of the data base must be done in a thorough and extremely accurate manner. Its accuracy must be preserved and/or improved.

Functions

The feasibility study provides the first information about the scope of the conversion effort. The conceptual design describes:

1. the number of files in the data base
2. their contents, volume and cycle of update
3. their present (storage) media and proposed media
4. their utilization in the new and old systems.

The methods for converting each of the files in the data base must be determined using this information. For any file, the conversion effort may include one or more of the following types of file conversion:

1. No change.
2. Changing the information, format, or media of an existing file.
3. Combining the information on the existing file with the information in another file.
4. Creation of a completely new file.

Knowing the types of conversion required, the volumes of data in the files involved, and the time period in which the files must be converted is essential to develop a step-by-step method for effecting each of the required types of conversions. These methods can vary in complexity from simply correcting and reprinting printed tables to the development of highly complex computer systems.

When the methods to be used have been determined, an overall conversion plan must be developed. It should define the schedule, cost, and resource requirements with respect to:

1. methods of conversion
2. equipment
3. manufacturer's software
4. systems analysis and programming effort
5. testing, standards, and documentation
6. training

Depending on the methods of conversion and the scope of the conversion effort, the plan may be contained in a simple one-page document or may require the equivalent of an entire "project justification." Regardless of its size and complexity, the conversion plan must be relatively well developed before the "project justification" for the system can be completed. If it is not, the total cost of the project may double or even triple when the required conversion costs are added. Any significant additions to costs after a project has been authorized are correctly viewed by top management as poor project planning.

When the (data base) conversion has been planned, it must be organized, directed, and controlled. The methods for accomplishing these activities are substantially the same as the methods described in this book for developing any computer system. There are, however, specific problem areas that are more frequently encountered during data base conversions. These problem areas and the special controls required to minimize or eliminate these problems are described in the remainder of this section.

Overcoming Problems

In many companies, the first problem peculiar to the conversion effort becomes apparent during the feasibility study when, because of the incomplete or incomprehensible documentation of previously implemented systems, the number, contents, format, media, and/or utilization of present system files cannot easily be determined. This problem is compounded when it is discovered that, in many cases, the existing computer master files are continually changed in format and content without notification or documentation. Finally, it is decided that the files will have to be printed to find out their contents and format. Moreover, the logic behind the methods used to indicate records and blocks is very complex and must be reconstructed entirely from existing program listings and manufacturer's documentation. When, by means of exhaustive analysis and programming, all computer master files related to the system have been identified and their contents and formats have been determined and frozen from change, one basic conversion problem has been surmounted.

The second basic conversion problem is the identification of all manual information that is being used as part of the data base. All too often, internal (system) program functions are unclear until "Jack's Conversion Table" or "Jill's Vendor Table" provides the translation and transformation of data that have been missing. Because the users are so familiar with the procedure, it never seems worthy of mention to the analyst. Conversely, many analysts do not recheck the information that they have or ask for additional information until it is known to exist.

The knowledge of files and file contents is essential because it permits determination of information use and storage media. These factors, in turn, permit determination of the types of conversions that will be required and the development of an overall conversion plan.

One of the largest problems within most conversion plans is the time period within which the conversion must be completed. This restriction is especially evident whenever the files to be converted are already a part of the data base of an ongoing computer system. In many of these cases, the final file conversions must take place when the file is not being utilized. Therefore, files which are used on a daily cycle will usually be converted on either a weekend or overnight. For files utilized on weekly, monthly, or yearly cycles the problem is greatly minimized. For fulltime, on-line files, the conversion requires shutdown of the system and the duration of the conversion period is much more critical.

Another large problem is the one-time-only nature of data base conversion. When it is attempted, the conversion must be accomplished correctly. Any errors must be immediately detected, the beginning of operations halted and the conversion attempted again after the cause of errors has been eliminated.

The most critical problem in data base conversion is the need for 100% accuracy. While the extent of errors induced by a conversion may not justify a re-running, any unforeseen errors indicate an acceptance of poor quality work.

A summary of conversion problems indicates that, after solving the initial problems in obtaining the information necessary to plan a conversion, you will be faced with the need for converting the data base 100% accurately, in one attempt, in an extremely short time. These problems must be considered and eliminated during the planning stage because, during actual conversion, a variety of unforeseen problems will undoubtedly occur. Solving these problems usually requires the total attention of the conversion team and, therefore, no time is available to consider the solutions to larger, predeterminable problems.

Establishing Controls

Data base conversion efforts contain many of the same functions as system development projects. Therefore, all of the controls presented in the other chapters of this book should also be reviewed when developing a control plan for a large-scale data base conversion effort.

The controls that follow can be used in system development projects, but they have their greatest impact when applied to data base conversions. They are:

1. input/output matrix
2. detailed conversion schedule
3. alternative plans
4. record and money audit routines
5. conversion testing

When judiciously combined with system development project controls, the conversion effort controls provide the information required to modify and regulate the conversion activities prior to (and during) the conversion period.

Input/output matrix. This should be developed during conversion planning. It traces the step-by-step generation and utilization of every element in every field in the data base. Figure 7-1 illustrates an input/output matrix for a portion of the sample project.

The elements, fields, and files in this figure refer to the sequence in which they are laid out (i.e., in the Vendor Master File (VNMF), the first field (1) is the vendor number which consists of two elements (a), an eight digit vendor number (b), a one digit check digit and the second field (2) is the Vendor Name which consists of only

Analyst ______________

______ PROJECT

INPUT/OUTPUT MATRIX

Data Base Sequence

Data Base			Source				Output				
File ID	Field ID	Element ID	Program or Department	Process*	Input or File	Field in Input or File	Program or Department	Process*	Output	Field in Output	Element in Field
VENMF	Vendor #(1)	Base 8 digits(a)	1.Edit & Verify(SA3)	Assign or Manip.			1A Update (SA 4)	Manip Pass	New Inv. MF	Vendor #	1st 8 digits
VENMF	Vendor #	Base 8 digits	2.Sort(SA2)	Manip.			2A,1B Print (SA5)				1st 8 digits
VENMF	Vendor #	Base 8 digits	3.Card to Tape(SA1)	Pass	Receipts & Vendor Inf.Cards	Vendor #			Vendor Activity	Vendor #	1st 8 digits
VENMF	Vendor #	Base 8 digits	4.Manual/ Keypunch		NewVendor Request Receipts Form	None Vendor #		Manip Pass or Manip	Receipt & Schedule Discrep. Input & Update Error	Vendor # Vendor #	1st 8 digits 1st 8 digits
VENMF	Vendor #	Check Digit(b)	1.Edit & Verify(SA3)	Assign or Manip.			1A Update (SA4)	Manip	New Inv. MF	Vendor #	Check Digit
VENMF	Vendor #	Check Digit	2.Sort(SA2)	Manip.			2B,1B Print (SA5)	Same as Base 8 Digits of Field			Check Digit
VENMF	Vendor #	Check Digit	3.Card to Tape(SA1)	Pass	Receipts	Vendor #					
VENMF	Vendor #	Check Digit	4.Manual/ Keypunch		Receipt Form	Vendor # Digit 9					
VENMF	Vendor Name(2)	All(-)	1.Edit & Verify(SA3)	Assign or Manip.			1A Update (SA4)	Pass	Vendor Name Errors	Vendor Name	
VENMF	Vendor Name	All(-)	2.Sort(SA2)	Pass			1A,2B Print (SA5)	Pass	Vendor Activity	Vendor Name	
VENMF	Vendor Name	All(-)	3.Card/Tape (SA1)	Pass	Receipts & Vendor Inf.Cards	Vendor Name		Pass	Receipt & Schedule Discrep.	Vendor Name	
VENMF	Vendor Name	All(-)	4.Manual/ Keypunch		Receipts Form / NewVendor Request	Vendor Name / Vendor Name		Pass	Input & Error Report	Vendor Name	

Comments

*NOTE: Process coding might be:

Pass-Program passes this data element without change.
Manip-Program manipulates this data element but does not change it.
ChngTo-Program changes data element to (new element)
ChngFrom-Program changes data element from (old element) .
Comb (#)-Program combines this data element with (other data element). The other data element will bear the same number.
Assign-Program adds this element.
Dele-Program deletes this element.

Figure 7-1. Input-Output Matrix

one element). The programs in this figure begin with the one which creates (or updates) the particular file and then work backward to the physical input and forward to the physical outputs.

By assigning simple nomenclature to programs, inputs, outputs, files, fields, and elements as they are designed this information can be punched into cards. The punched cards can then be sorted (and listed):

1. In file, field, element sequence, as is the input/output matrix, to ensure that all elements of the data base can be generated from the physical inputs and to determine the areas of impact if the data base were to be changed (data base sequence).
2. In input, field, output, and field sequence to ensure that all input fields are utilized by the system (input sequence).
3. In output, field, element sequence to ensure that all output fields can be generated (output sequence).

In large systems, the utilization of these punched card listings will greatly simplify the work involved in ensuring that information can be generated and utilized. In addition, with punched cards, the maintenance of these listings is greatly simplified. These listings are of enormous benefit (if properly maintained) during all detail design, programming, testing, and application system modification efforts. They provide simple checklists of places where changes may be required when any element of the data base, inputs, or outputs must be changed.

These three input/output matrices, when prepared for the conversion effort, provide the basis for determining whether any required file or input element has been overlooked during analysis. If so, some element in the data base will not have a logical trace from its file to a physical input. This can be determined by visually scanning the "input" column and finding a "file element" whose trace does not conclude with a physical input.

Detailed conversion schedule. All of the activities prior to the final conversion period should be controlled by using the techniques described in other chapters. These activities in large scale conversions approximate a project within a project. Therefore, the system development controls can easily be selectively applied.

The conversion period itself, because of its short duration, must usually be scheduled in great detail. The method for scheduling this effort is very similar to that used for the systems development effort. However, the time increments should be ten or fifteen minutes rather than the daily increments shown in Figure 5-2. All else is the same and (as in the project schedule) each person's activities are indicated by horizontal bar segments, none of which is (to the greatest degree possible) longer than two time increments (twenty to thirty minutes).

The detailed conversion schedule should indicate the times:

1. when the present files will be available for conversion.
2. necessary for all computer processing activities.
3. for transporting files, outputs, inputs, etc.
4. required for all checking of outputs and other manual processing.

When all elements of the conversion have been included and the conversion schedule has been completed, it should be validated by the preparation of a Modified CPM (Figure 5-4). Then the schedule can be used as the basis for (conversion) costing as described in Chapter Eight.

After an original conversion schedule has been developed and validated, its various time estimates must be continually improved as more and more information is obtained about computer processing times and manual processing times. Controls on the detailed conversion schedule should provide sufficient basis for changing any plans or estimates connected with the conversion effort.

Alternative plans. In any project with a tight schedule, any problem is a serious problem. Therefore, during the actual conversion period all problems become serious.

To ensure that he can devote the time necessary to correct the unforeseen problems, the foresighted project manager will review the detailed conversion schedule and predetermine the (critical path) areas where errors or delays would prevent successful conversion. Having identified the critical areas, he will prepare alternative plans to eliminate the effects of problems in these areas. These alternative plans usually provide backup for equipment, files, programs, critical personnel (including the project manager) and any transportation. In addition, other personnel are usually trained and placed on alert so that, should the work in any area begin to fall significantly behind schedule, they are available and can provide the necessary assistance.

Alternative plans are the controls ensuring that predeterminable errors will not prevent successful project completion. As time permits, alternative plans should be developed for critical error conditions in each of the alternative plans. Although this process can be repeated indefinitely, quite soon it becomes an unprofitable exercise in logic because of the low probability of the specific errors actually occurring.

Regardless of the number and detail of the alternative plans, the foresighted project manager must ensure that the basic plan and all alternatives are known and understood by the critical personnel. Too many excellent plans have never been used because they were not known or understood by the personnel that could implement them. The degree of delegation of authority for initiating alternative plans is greatly dependent upon the reliability of the personnel involved. However, key personnel must understand basic plans and alternative plans so that they can inform the project manager when change is (in their opinion) required.

Record and money audit routines. These routines provide assurance that the number of records and the cumulative dollar value in any money field that is taken into (input) any program is maintained (equals) and included in the output records of that program. These fundamental accuracy checks should be in every program but are a requirement in any conversion program. Some additional audits that may be used include:

1. Debits in = debits out.
2. Credits in = credits out.
3. (Debits in = credits in) = (debits out = credits out).
4. Debits in + credits in = debits out + credits out.
5. Records in − records combined + records split = records out.
6. $ In − $ deleted + $ added internally = $ out.

To accomplish these audits, basic program modules are prepared which accumulate and display the totals indicated. These program modules are selectively incorporated into each of the (conversion) programs and the program is written so that the necessary data is supplied to these modules for accumulation and display. In many cases, display of totals is necessary at various (checkpoint, geographical, physical file, etc.) logical breaks in the file as well as at program end. Discrepancies in expected totals usually halt the program and require operator intervention for restart. All halts and restart procedures must be clearly documented so that, during conversion, the operator will know how to proceed in all instances.

These record and money audit routines provide (partial) assurance of the accuracy of each of the conversion programs. For manual (conversion) operations, similar totals can be logged and maintained manually. However, this may be a very time-consuming activity and should only be initiated if there is no other way of pinpointing errors.

The results from the manual and computer audit routines demonstrate the accuracy of certain portions of the conversion. Their primary benefit, however, occurs during testing of the conversion programs. At this time these routines quickly pinpoint areas where errors are occurring. This greatly simplifies the error determination and elimination procedure. To gain even further assistance, most good programmers design and include special purpose audits that assist them in each of their complex programs.

Conversion testing. Testing during data bank conversion provides the ultimate control over the accuracy and the quality of the conversion effort. It is conducted in the manner described in Chapter Six but, because of the accuracy required, must usually be even more exhaustive than is the testing of development systems. For any major conversion system, all types of testing will probably be employed. Special emphasis should be placed on pilot test and parallel test because they provide the most intensive tests of accuracy under actual conditions.

Although thorough pilot test and parallel test are required, every record in every file need not be checked. If the files are small enough, complete checkout is advised but if the files are too large to make 100% checkout feasible the following techniques can be employed:

1. Pilot test using selected (geographical, physical, or other) subsets of the file.
2. Pilot test using a random sampling of the entire file.
3. Parallel test of the entire file but checkout of selected subsets and a random sampling of the remainder of the file.

With good planning, any or all of these techniques can be employed to drastically reduce the checkout effort without decreasing its accuracy.

PROGRAM PREPARATION

Program preparation is the process of converting fully tested (system development and conversion) programs into operational programs. This minor but important process consists of the following three steps:

1. The preparation of program backup.
2. Completion of documentation.
3. Delivery of programs and documentation.

These steps, when performed correctly, ensure that the programs are completely ready for operation when required.

Preparation of backup programs is accomplished by duplicating and identifying the program decks. This preparation should be done program-by-program when the system is fully tested. The original decks are then ready to be delivered to operations and the duplicate decks are ready for submission to the supervisor of Operational Programming. If computer operations or any other group requires additional program decks, they are also prepared for delivery at this time.

Completion of documentation includes:

1. Review of all program documentation.
2. Removal of all temporary interim documentation.
3. Preparation and inclusion of any additional documentation.

The programmer reviews the program documentation to ensure that it is complete, accurate and understandable. He then prepares a one-to-two page summary, includes it in the documentation and delivers the completed "Program Documentation" to the project manager (or his delegate) for documentation review. The project manager then reviews it for completeness, conformity with standards, clarity, and assessment of the overall performance of the programmers (and analysts).

When he has completed his review, the project manager removes all the interim documentation, which includes the documents required during the programming and test functions and those necessary to assess the programmer's efforts. Some of the documents that can usually be removed are:

1. Interim program listings.
2. All test results, with the exception of the final test result.
3. Diagnostic outputs.

All other data not required for understanding should also be removed at this time, any confusing points should be noted, and the programmer should be informed.

The programmer must now rewrite, or add to, any unclear areas in the "Program Documentation" and must review his changes with the project manager and the review teams. If any points are still unclear the programmer and project manager should work together to clarify the writing.

While this is being done, the "Systems Documentation" and "Operations Documentation" for that program are reviewed in a similar manner. After all reviews are done, the project documentation is complete. Programs and all project documentation should then be delivered to the operations manager who will cursorily review them and handle distribution as follows:

1. The programs to supervisor-file library.
2. The "Program Documentation" and "System Documentation" to supervisor of operational programming.

3. The "Operations Documentation" to the supervisor of computer operations.

Within a reasonable time period, all elements of the programs and documentation must be reviewed by the operations group, all questions must be answered, and the operations manager must issue a final operation acceptance of the system. The format for this acceptance can be almost exactly the same as a Testing Review Summary (Figure 6-4).

Before (or possibly after) accepting the system, the responsible operations personnel should:

1. catalogue and/or file all programs.
2. enter the operation times for the system into the overall operations schedules.
3. review all documentation to ensure that it is understandable.

In addition, many operations groups will wish to re-run the system in its entirety to double-check processing times, job control, and machine efficiencies. If all previous control reviews have been completed in a thorough fashion this re-run is unnecessary.

PEOPLE AND PROCEDURES

New systems almost always require the people who support these systems to use new procedures. Because people do not adapt to change as easily as do computers, the conditioning (conversion) period for people usually requires a great deal of effort and attention to detail.

The people who support the system may be generally described by the following functional groups:

1. data preparation and output dissemination
2. computer operations
3. file library and scheduling
4. quality control
5. manufacturer's systems modification
6. application systems modification.

The people in each of these groups must understand what they are expected to do and how they are expected to do it. Conveyance of this understanding generally requires the writing of new procedures, training of the group in the understanding and utilization of these procedures, and the conditioning of the group so that it uses the procedures when required. The degree of success with which the understanding of groups' new roles is conveyed determines, to a very large extent, the efficiency and acceptance of actual system. Until these people are fully conditioned and ready to operate the system, no conversion or system implementation can be affected.

By integrating the conditioning effort with the system development effort, both can be conducted much more efficiently. The remainder of this section describes how the conditioning and system development efforts are integrated in each functional group.

Data Preparation and Information Dissemination

Data preparation and information dissemination groups are of two primary types: clerical and data entry. The clerical sections make up the bulk of the user groups and perform all necessary manual preparation and dissemination activities. The data entry sections perform the keypunching, key-tape typing, or other activities necessary to transform raw data into machine-readable data. A further description of the various activities involved is contained in Chapter One.

The conditioning of all sections of the data preparation and information dissemination groups follows the same basic timetable relative to the systems development functions.

1. During the conceptual design function the people in the groups are interviewed and interested in the concept of the project.
2. During the detail design function, the present annual procedures are studied in detail and the user group is formed from selected personnel of the data preparation dissemination groups.
3. During the programming function, the detail design is reviewed and new procedures are written and reviewed by the members of the user group under the guidance of the manual system group.
4. During the testing function, all personnel in the user group are trained through class room instruction, preparation of test data, and review of new system outputs. The personnel in the user group act as cadre and supervisors during training.
5. During the conversion function, final conditioning is conducted. All obsolete forms, materials and manuals are replaced. Necessary changes in personnel, layout and equippage are finished. Schedules for cutover to the new system are distributed and reviewed.
6. Operation begins, and the members of the user group act as liaison and consult on problems as they arise.

This general method of conditioning provides a number of significant benefits and controls for the project. Among the most important of these are:

1. The involvement of clerical (user) and data entry personnel that is begun during conceptual design and that increases as the project progresses.
2. The establishment of a non-EDP-oriented user group which (with any necessary assistance from the manual systems group) monitors the practicality of the design and produces (the bulk of) the new procedures.
3. The early involvement of the training cadre so that they know why as well as what activities must be done.
4. The utilization of the groups' personnel during testing. This provides training and accomplishes necessary testing activities at the same time.
5. The development of the user group into internal consultants which minimizes the EDP follow-up required and maximizes improvements from the groups in the future.

These specific benefits may well be overshadowed by the knowledge, friendship and confidence that can be generated between EDP and these groups during the conditioning effort. This training and morale is extremely useful in future projects.

Computer Operations

The supervisor of computer operations becomes aware of the general system requirements during his review of the conceptual design. This awareness is emphasized by his review of the detailed design, by the test time requirements, and by his operators' comments during programming.

During testing, the actual conditioning of computer operations personnel is accomplished. It progresses step-by-step as each type of testing is initiated until, by conversion, the operators are fully conditioned and can easily operate the system. The steps in this conditioning are:

1. During program (programmer) testing the operating instructions are written by the programmer and used by the operators. Problems are noted by the operators and corrected by the programmer.
2. During program test, each programmer completes his portion of the Operations Manual. These are again used by the operators to run the program tests and are revised, as necessary, by the programmers.
3. During linkage test, the appropriate sections of the Operations Manual are combined, used by operators, and revised.
4. During systems test, the draft Operations Manual is used during all operations. In addition, it is reviewed by the technical review group, the supervisor of computer operations, and all shift chiefs. Necessary corrections are noted and made.
5. When acceptable to the manager of computer operations, the Operations Manual is completed in final form, copied and distributed per his instructions.

Conditioning of computer operations personnel, using these methods, is very straightforward. Development supplies the instructions and operations requests changes, rewording, and modification until the instructions are clear and efficient. The major benefits of this method of conditioning are:

1. The programmers learn how to communicate with operations.
2. Operations learns how to communicate with programming.
3. The responsibility for learning is placed upon the operators.

This method also ensures that future turnover in (operations or programming) personnel should not affect the operation of the system.

File Library and Scheduling

The conditioning required for the file library and scheduling groups is minimal. The tasks, activities and procedures of these groups do not usually vary when new systems are implemented. They must only be prepared for and deal with new systems.

To prepare for new systems, the supervisors of these groups and the technical review group should review the "Project Justification" and detail design documentation as they are available. Then, during the programming, testing, and conversion functions, these groups will perform their activities so that the files and computer time necessary for these functions are available.

The file library and scheduling groups are very important to the success of the project, for throughout its duration, these groups must maintain good communications with the project staff so that the required facilities are ready when needed. However, no formal conditioning is required for these groups because their duties are expanded rather than changed.

Quality Control

The conditioning of quality control personnel is conducted on the same schedule as the conditioning of the data preparation and information dissemination group. The quality control group is, however, entirely responsible for its own conditioning which begins when the technical review groups and the supervisor of quality control review the conceptual design to determine the overall quality requirements. Then:

1. During the detail design and programming functions, the quality control group defines and writes the procedures required to determine the quality of the system's inputs and outputs. These procedures are communicated to the technical review group and the user group for inclusion during testing.
2. During testing, the quality control group combines with the user group to perform and monitor the quality and accuracy checking. Any changes required in the procedures for checking or monitoring input/output quality are communicated to, reviewed by, and written by quality control personnel.
3. During conversion, specific assignments and schedules are established for actual operation.

This method of conditioning the quality control group:

1. Simplifies the job of the user group and technical review group by providing quality checking procedures.
2. Gives actual practice in these procedures to quality control personnel before the system is installed.

In addition, because they are completely responsible for developing the procedures, the Quality Control personnel can accept complete responsibility for the quality checking of system inputs and outputs from the first day of system operation.

Manufacturer's Systems Modification

The manufacturer's systems modification (MSM) group assists the systems development programmers by providing specialized knowledge so that the control cards can be prepared for all program decks. To accomplish this purpose, the MSM group must:

1. Review the detailed design to determine whether new manufacturer's software/application software interface is required.
2. Work with the manufacturer's systems representative on new interface requirements.
3. Advise the programmers as they become ready for program (programmer) test.

This low level of involvement frees the time of the MSM personnel so that they can concentrate on being fully informed about the manufacturer's software.

Applications Systems Modification

Upon completion of its conditioning, the application system modification (ASM) group must be able to make any required changes in any program in the system. While one method of accomplishing this would be to turn the development staff into the modification staff, the volume of change and the talents required in modification usually preclude this allocation of personnel.

Successful conditioning of ASM personnel requires their close cooperation with systems development programmers. This cooperation is fostered by the following methods:

1. The supervisor of ASM reviews the conceptual design and tentatively assigns ASM personnel to learn the system.
2. During detail design and programming, the ASM personnel, as a small portion of their regular duties, contact the system development programmers and arrange to review the design as it progresses. The system development programmers are informed that they are responsible for providing training to ASM personnel and that they will have to provide necessary maintenance until a qualified replacement is trained. ASM personnel are informed that their job is learning, and that future assignments, raises, and promotions are based, in part, on their ability and aggressiveness in learning. In addition, during this period the technical review group or ASM personnel may request changes from, or supply solutions to the systems development programmers.
3. Beginning with program test, assigned ASM personnel join the technical review group on the project. As testing increases, ASM personnel should review all changes and should perform increasing amounts of the actual changes until, during systems test, pilot test, and parallel test, the ASM personnel are making all changes and systems development programmers are simply overseeing and approving them. However, during this period, each systems development programmer retains the responsibility for his programs.
4. As portions of programs are found to be unclear to ASM personnel, the systems development programmer must either improve the documentation or rewrite the program so that the area is clear and understandable.
5. Upon the completion of testing ASM personnel are expected to be ready to maintain the system.

This method of conditioning:

1. Correctly places the responsibilities for training and learning.
2. Adds another review mechanism to the detail design and programming efforts.
3. Allows all personnel to operate efficiently in their areas of expertise and interest.

This method also provides a vehicle for increasing understanding and morale between ASM and development personnel.

8

Determining Costs, Cash Flow and Payback

Costs are the third major factor that must be controlled. Only if the projects costs, quality, and schedules are agreed upon and under control is the project itself then under control.

Projects whose costs are not under control provide the basis for many of the disagreements that are all too common between Accounting and EDP. These are typified by exchanges similar to the following:

Accountant:	How much is that inventory project going to cost anyway? We've already sunk a large amount of money into that project and there's no end in sight. Don't you EDP people know the value of a dollar?
EDP:	Of course we know the value of a dollar. This project will save plenty of dollars if you nit-pickers don't destroy it before it even gets off the ground. You guys aren't willing to spend the money to do a thing right and then you get mad when we have to do it over again. There's no satisfying you.

These disagreements can be avoided and project costs simply controlled, however, if EDP and Accounting will work together to apply common accounting techniques to EDP projects. This chapter explains how cost accounting, cash flow and payback period techniques can be applied to EDP projects. Combined, these techniques provide the basis for controlling project costs.

COST ACCOUNTING

For any EDP project, costs are generated by the utilization of people, equipment, and materials. In certain cases specific portions of these elements are only utilized on one project (or area) and their associated costs can be assigned directly to that project (direct charges). In other cases portions are used by more than one project and their costs must be apportioned to the various projects within which they are utilized (indirect charges). Then there are some portions of these elements that are used by the project but are not apportioned to the project (absorbed charges) because of their small size or difficulty in determination.

This section on cost accounting describes the application of direct, indirect, and absorbed charges to:

1. Develop development cost estimates.
2. Develop operations cost estimates.
3. Establish and maintain development cost controls.
4. Establish and maintain operations cost controls.

This description is intended only as a starting point. Thorough cost accounting for EDP projects requires a great deal of additional anlaysis, definition, calculation, and procedures. However, to accomplish this, EDP and Accounting personnel should use this description as a point of departure to determine when and how the improvements, innovations, and other specific deviations required by their company should be implemented.

Development Cost Estimates

The estimation of development costs is based upon:

1. the Estimate of Development (Figure 5-1)
2. the Project Schedule (Figure 5-2)
3. the Personnel Requirements Listing (Figure 4-1)

These basic schedules indicate the type and number of people who are required and the specific tasks in which they will be engaged.

Salary. With this basic information, the salary portion of a development cost estimation (Figure 8-1) can easily be completed by applying direct or indirect charges.

1. If the people who will be working on the project are known, the cost equals the portion of each individual's estimated salary that is equivalent to the number of days that he will work on the project.
2. If specific individuals are not known but the group from which the project personnel will be drawn has been identified, then the equivalent portion(s) times the average salary for the group should be used.
3. If there is no knowledge of the individuals or the group, the equivalent portion(s) times the average salaries for the type(s) of people (job titles) should be used.
4. Where costs are absorbed, they are not included in the development cost estimate.

In all cases, salary estimates should include any normal types of raises (cost of living, merit, etc.) that the individuals and/or groups would be expected to receive during the duration of the project.

(sample) PROJECT

DEVELOPMENT COST ESTIMATION

By P. Williams Date ______________

Component Title	Yearly Salary 225days	Allo-cation Method	Minimum Days	Minimum Cost	Maximum Days	Maximum Cost	Average Days	Average Cost
Salaries:								
Manager, Project	$15,000	Person	100	$ 6,700	125	$ 8,300	112	$ 7,500
Programmer Analyst(4)	12,000		275	14,700	350	18,700	300	16,000
Programmer(2)	9,000	Avg. of	60	2,400	125	5,000	75	3,000
Manual Systems(3)	9,000	Group	125	5,000	225	9,000	150	6,000
Keypunching(4)	6,000		200	5,300	300	8,000	225	6,000
Operators-Computer	7,000	StdCost	-	-	-	-	-	-
Clerical-Quality(6)	5,000	Avg.	200	5,500	225	5,000	225	5,000
Clerical-User(6)	5,000	of	225	5,000	400	9,000	300	6,600
Supervisory-User(2)	8,000	Group	112	4,000	112	4,000	112	4,000
TOTAL SALARIES				$48,600		$67,000		$54,100
Fringe Benefits	-	20% of Salaries	-	$ 9,700	-	$13,400	-	$10,800
	Rate		Mach. Hrs.		Mach. Hrs.		Mach. Hrs.	
Equipment:								
360/50-	$100/hr.	StdCost						
SA 1	"	"	1	$100	5	$500	2	$200
SA 2	"	"	1	100	3	300	1	100
SA 3	"	"	2	200	10	1000	6	600
SA 4	"	"	3	300	15	1500	7	700
SA 5	"	"	2	200	8	800	5	500
System	"	"	7	700	40	4000	10	1000
TOTAL EQUIPMENT				$1,600		$8,100		$3,100
			Quan.		Quan.		Quan.	
Materials								
Disk Packs	$150ea.	Direct	3	$450	4	$600	3	$450
Invoice Forms	$2.50/K	Direct	100K	250	200K	500	100K	250
Misc.	-	-	-	300	-	600	-	300
TOTAL MATERIALS				$1,000		$1,700		$1,000
GRAND TOTALS				$60,900		$90,200		$69,000

Figure 8-1. Development Cost Estimation

Fringe. Fringe includes all benefits received in addition to basic salary as a condition of employment. Included in fringe are company-paid hospitalization, company-paid life insurance, bonuses, profit sharing, contributions, stock option contributions, and (where they have not been already excluded in calculating salary) holidays and vacations. Fringe costs can be estimated element by element for each group or individual, or they can be estimated in total as a general percentage of total salaries if there are no significant differences among the groups or individuals. It is important to include this portion of personnel costs as it may increase the salary portions of the development costs by as much as forty-five per cent.

Equipment. Equipment costs must be estimated for each computer or electronic accounting machine configuration that will be used for project testing or conversion. To obtain these, the number of hours of utilization (per program) is multiplied by a cost for each hour of operation. The estimate of the number of hours of utilization is based upon:

1. The amount of time required to operate the program. The basis for this estimate is the estimate of computer operations (Figure 8-2).
2. The number of times that the program will be submitted to operations during testing. This estimation should be based entirely on past experiences and the programmer's experience in testing similar programs. It is a function of the programmer's ability, the complexity of the program, and the cooperation and efficiency of computer operations (Figure 6-2).

The cost for each hour of operation for a specific configuration may be calculated by dividing the total (yearly) cost of operation by the number of hours that it will be operated during the year. This standard cost method includes the following cost elements in the total cost of operating the equipment:

1. Equipment rental or depreciation including interest.
2. Equipment maintenance and other servicing costs.
3. Operator salaries for all personnel assigned to the configuration.
4. All common materials (disks, tapes, standard paper, etc.)
5. An indirect charge for all overhead salaries such as supervision, scheduling, clerical, administration, and quality control which cannot be directly allocated to systems or configurations.

The number of hours that the configuration will be operated during the year is another projection that is based upon utilization in previous years and upon expected growth and new systems.

Materials. Only significant increases in volumes and/or special materials required for the specific project need to be included when estimating the materials costs. In most cases, they are minimal. The materials costs are, because of their nature, direct charges and can be estimated by multiplying the estimated volume by the cost per unit.

(sample) PROJECT

ESTIMATE OF COMPUTER OPERATIONS

360/50 Computer

Date ____________ Analyst M. Wade

Program #	Program Name	Determining Factor	Speed	Volume	Production Time	Setup Time	Delay Factor	Elapsed Time
SA1	Card to Tape	Card Read	300 CPM	110,000 cards*	367 min.	13 min.	1.33	507 min.
SA 2	Sort	Tape	750 IPS	5,000,000 char = 6250" at 800BPI Block 400 = 12,500 IRG 12,500 IRG = 3,125" 6250" + 3125" = 9375" 781' = $\frac{1}{3}$ tape $\frac{1}{3}$ tape = 5 min.	5 min.	5 min.	1.33	13 min
SA3	Verify	Tape	750 IPS	2,500,000 = $\frac{1}{6}$ tape $\frac{1}{6}$ tape = 3 min.	3 min.	5 min	1.33	11 min.
SA4	Update	Compute	×	×	Double × Tape (10 min)	5 min	1.33	20 min.
SA5a	Invoice Print	Printer	1100 LPM	112,000 Lines	102 min.	10 min.	1.2	134 min.
SA5b	Dealer Print	Printer	"	10,800 Lines	10 min.	5 min.	1.1	17 min.
SA5c	Control Print	Printer	"	12,000 Lines	11 min.	5 min.	1.1	18 min.
		WEEKLY TOTAL TIME			508 min.	48 min.		720 min.

* Calculation of Card Volume:

	Transactions/Wk.	Average Cards/Transaction	Card Volume
Receipts	5,000	9	45,000
Shipments	10,000	6	60,000
New Vendors	200	10	2,000
Changes	600	2	1,200
Error Corrections	900	3	1,800
Totals	16,700		110,000

Figure 8-2. Estimate of Computer Operations

Three-point estimates of cost. The estimate of development costs should be developed as a three-point estimate. That is, it should contain estimates for the minimum and maximum costs as well as for the average costs. Generally these estimated costs respectively represent the costs for the project:

1. If everything words well (Minimum).
2. If all predictable problems occur (Maximum).
3. If things happen normally (Average).

To thoroughly prepare three-point cost estimates, all of the bases for these estimates, such as schedules, personnel requirements, computer operations estimates, and number of tests should also be developed as three-point estimates.

Utilization of three-point estimations throughout the project provides an understandable method of communicating your confidence in the average estimate and also forces you to consider where and how problems might occur. This early analysis of problem areas permits the establishment of thoroughly planned alternative courses of action to minimize the effects of the more probable problems. These pre-planned alternatives allow you to maintain complete control when expected problems occur and eliminate most of the seat-of-the-pants, fire-fighting type decisions that characterize the management of many EDP projects.

Operations Cost Estimate

Estimating the costs of operation begins with the Estimate of Computer Operations (Figure 8-2). Based upon the amount of computer time required for each run, a production schedule (Figure 8-3) is developed by:

1. Setting the schedule for computer operations.
2. Thinking forward and determining the cut-off times for the various input preparation areas.
3. Thinking backward and determining cutoffs for the various information dissemination areas.

When a production schedule has been developed that accepts the inputs and produces the outputs so that all user (timing) requirements are satisfied, the feasibility of processing according to this schedule must be verified.

The verification of the production schedule's feasibility is accomplished in two ways: by determining or estimating the number of people, or man-hours of work, that will be required to process the volume of work within the time limits imposed for each department, and by reviewing these requirements with the respective department heads to ensure that the personnel can be made available when needed. The estimation of the number of people or man-hours required in each department is made by dividing the volume of work that is processed each day, week, or month by the department's average production rate for a comparable type of work. This verification of the schedule's feasibility is important since it also provides conformation of the necessary estimates of the numbers and types of production personnel.

(sample) PROJECT

PRODUCTION SCHEDULE

Week Ending (estimate)

	Intake From	Monday	Tuesday	Wednesday	Thursday	Friday	Saturday	Sunday
Shipment Codes	08:00-16:00	A	C	E	G	I	A	A
	16:00-17:30	B	D	F	H	A	A	A
Receipts Codes	08:00-16:00	Q	S	U	W	Y	Q	Q
	16:00-17:30	R	T	V	X	Q	Q	Q

PRIORITY CODES

Department	Cutoff	Monday	Tuesday	Wednesday	Thursday	Friday	Saturday	Sunday
Shipping	16:30	A	C	E	G	I	-	-
	18:00	B	D	F	H	J	-	-
Receiving	16:30	Q	S	U	W	Y	-	-
	18:00	R	T	V	X	Z	-	-
Keypunch	17:00	A,Q	B,C,R,S	D,E,T,U	F,G,V,W	H,I,X,Y	-	-
360/50: SA1	19:00-19:40	A,Q	B,C,R,S	D,E,T,U	F,G,V,W	H,I,X,Y	-	-
SA2	19:40-19:50							
SA3	19:50-20:00							
SA5(errors)	20:00-20:30							
Quality Control	22:00							
Keypunch (errors)	24:00	↓	↓	↓	↓	↓		
360/50 (with error):								
SA1	01:00-01:30	H,I,X,Y	A,Q	B,C,R,S	D,E,T,U	F,G,V,W	-	-
SA2	01:30-01:40							
SA3	01:40-01:50							
SA4	01:50-02:00							
SA5: Dealer	05:10-05:45							
Invoices	05:00-05:10							
Control	05:45-06:00							
Quality Control	06:00-08:00							
Bursting: Invoice	07:00-07:30							
Dealer	07:30-07:40							
Control	07:40-07:50							
Distribution:								
Dealer	08:00							
Control	08:00							
Received by Inserting	08:00							
Invoices in Mail	16:00	↓	↓	↓	↓	↓		

Example: All paperwork on shipments that is generated from 08:00 to 16:00 on Monday is coded "A". The last transmittal of this material leaves the Shipping Department by 16:30 so that Keypunch can finish all "A" shipments by 17:00 on Monday. Monday night, from 19:00 to 20:30, the first running of the Sample System is accomplished. Quality Control then corrects all errors and returns them for Keypunch by 22:00. Keypunch repunches all errors by 24:00 and the final run of the Sample System for "A" shipments is made from 01:00 through 06:00 on Tuesday. "A" invoices are burst, inserted and in the mail by 16:00 Tuesday.

Figure 8-3. Production Schedule

Base period. Unlike the development efforts, the operations efforts are expected to continue indefinitely. Therefore, a base period (week, two weeks, or month) must be selected and all operations costs should initially be estimated for this period. For control purposes, calculations are simplified if the base period is identical to the company's payroll period.

Salaries. The calculation of the salaries portion of operations costs is very simple if the number and types of people have already been estimated. For each type of people, the salary for a given base period equals the number of people (or man-hours) used during that base period multiplied by the average cost per person (or man-hour).

Salary changes such as cost-of-living, merit increases, and seniority increases for the personnel who operate the system should also be estimated. These factors, if they are not expected to be offset by personnel turnover and additions to staff, can be accommodated by making proportional increases in the average cost per person. Operations cost estimates can be displayed in the same format as the development cost estimates (Figure 8-1).

Fringe. The fringe portion of operations costs is calculated as a percentage of total salaries as was the development cost fringe, and can be displayed in the same format as the development cost estimate.

Equipment. After the estimate of computer operations and the production schedule have been completed, the equipment portion of operations cost can be calculated by multiplying the total operation time (in the base period) by the standard cost for the equipment configuration. The total operations time is the sum total of each program's elapsed time multiplied by the number of times it is run during the base period. The standard cost is calculated in the same manner as was the equipment portion of the development cost.

The equipment portion of the operations cost can be displayed in the same format as was the equipment portion of the development cost estimate. Any periodic runs (monthly, six-month, yearly, etc.) that cannot be accounted for in this format should be indicated in footnotes of additions to the operations cost estimate.

Three-point estimate. The salary, fringe, and equipment operations cost estimate should also be developed as the three-point estimate that encompasses minimum, maximum and average costs. As with development cost estimates, the three-point estimate provides a better description of the expectations of system performance and also forces early consideration of operational problems. As was indicated in Chapters Two and Three, all estimates are thoroughly reviewed and approved by the project manager and the technical and user groups.

Development Cost Controls

From project authorization through conversion, the control of development costs is a major responsibility of the project manager. Unlike the control of schedule and quality, the control of development costs is usually also a responsibility of some segment of the Accounting area. A common understanding of the differences in these responsibilities provides the basis for an efficient working relationship between the project staff and the Accounting area.

As is described more fully in Chapter Two, the project manager is primarily responsible for control over development costs. He can directly influence these expenditures through his utilization of the project resources. Accounting, on the other hand, is responsible for determining what and where actual expenditures have been made for the project, and is also responsible for developing a method for reporting these expenditures. As a part of this responsibility, Accounting must inform the project manager and top management of any significant deviations from expected costs.

The remainder of this section on development cost controls describes the preparations that must be made so that development costs are collected and reported efficiently and understandably.

Preparation. Before the development cost estimate can be effectively used as a control medium, it must be segmented into individual estimates for each base period. This can be done by applying the cost estimation calculations that were used for the overall development cost estimates to the personnel, fringe, equipment and materials for each base period as indicated by the project schedule and estimate of development. As in the operations cost estimates, the base period that is chosen should be identical to the company's payroll period.

When the development cost estimate has been segmented into its individual base period costs, each base period will contain estimates of the average cost (the minimum or the maximum cost) for each component of salaries, fringe, equipment and materials (see Figure 8-1). The significant components in the detailed development cost estimate (Figure 8-4), which are:

1. grand total
2. total salaries
3. total fringe
4. total equipment
5. total materials
6. any individual major cost component

should then be summarized and the cumulative costs should be calculated, summarized, and graphed as in Figure 8-5. Except for actual figures, these completed forms provide a major cost control media for the project manager.

Project expenditure data. Most companies have established a system for collecting and distributing expenditures to the projects, departments, and areas for whom the work was performed. Within such a system, to ensure that all project expenditure data are collected, summarized, and reported efficiently, the following general activities should be performed:

1. The assignment of a project (cost) distribution code.
2. The collection of basic information.
3. The calculation of expenditures.
4. The reporting of expenditures.

(sample) PROJECT

DETAILED DEVELOPMENT COST ESTIMATE

By ____________ Average Cost Basis * Date ________

COMPONENT	PERIOD June 1- June 14	June 15- June28	June29- July12	July13- July26	July27- Aug.9	Aug.10- Aug.23	Aug.24 Sept.4	Sept.5- Sept.18	Sept.19 Oct.2	Oct.3- Oct.16	TOTAL
Salaries											
Manager-Project	750	750	750	750	750	750	750	750	750	750	750
Programmer Analysts	1000	1000	1500	1500	2000	2000	2000	2000	2000	1000	16000
Programmer	0	0	0	250	750	900	900	200	0	0	3000
Manual Systems	0	0	0	250	750	1000	1000	1000	1000	1000	6000
Keypunching	0	0	0	0	250	2000	2000	1000	500	250	6000
Clerical-Quality	0	0	0	0	0	300	800	1000	1400	1500	5000
Clerical-User	0	0	0	0	0	200	200	1200	2000	3200	6600
Supervisory- User	0	0	500	500	500	500	500	500	500	500	4000
TOTAL SALARIES	1750	1750	2750	3250	5000	7650	8150	7450	8150	8200	54100
Fringe:	350	350	550	650	1000	1530	1630	1490	1630	1640	10820
Equipment											
SA1	0	0	0	0	0	200	0	0	0	0	200
SA2	0	0	0	0	0	100	0	0	0	0	100
SA3	0	0	0	0	0	300	300	0	0	0	600
SA4	0	0	0	0	0	0	0	500	200	0	700
SA5	0	0	0	0	0	0	0	400	100	0	500
System	0	0	0	0	0	0	0	0	0	1000	1000
TOTAL EQUIPMENT	0	0	0	0	0	600	300	900	300	1000	3100
Materials:											
Disks	0	0	0	0	0	250	200	0	0	0	450
Invoices	0	0	0	0	0	0	100	150	0	0	250
Misc.	0	0	0	0	0	0	300	0	0	0	300
TOTAL MATERIALS	0	0	0	0	0	250	600	150	0	0	1000
GRAND TOTAL	2100	2100	3300	3900	6000	10030	10680	9990	10080	10840	69020

*Note: A Similar Detailed Development Cost Estimates should also be prepared for the Maximum Cost Basis and Minimum Cost Basis

Figure 8-4. Detailed Development Cost Estimate

_________ PROJECT

TOTAL DEVELOPMENT COST SUMMARY

		Period Costs				Cumulative Costs			
Period	Dates	Minimum	Average	Actual	Maximum	Minimum	Average	Actual	Maximum
1	June 1-June 14	1500	2100	2500	3000	1500	2100	2100	3000
2	June 15-June 28	2000	2100	2500	3000	3000	4200	5000	6000
3	June 29-July 12	2000	3300	3000	4000	5000	1500	8000	10000
4	July 13-July 26	3000	3900	4000	6000	8000	11400	12000	16000
5	July 27-Aug 9	4900	6000		7500	12900	17400		23500
6	Aug 10-Aug 23	9000	10030		11000	14900	27430		34500
7	Aug 24-Sept 4	10000	10680		11000	31900	37110		45500
8	Sept 5-Sept 18	9000	9990		11000	40900	48100		56500
9	Sept 19-Oct 2	10000	10080		14700	50900	58180		71200
10	Oct 3-Oct 16	10000	10840		13000	60900	69020		84200
11	Oct 17-Oct 30				6000				90200

CUMULATIVE COSTS - GRAND TOTAL

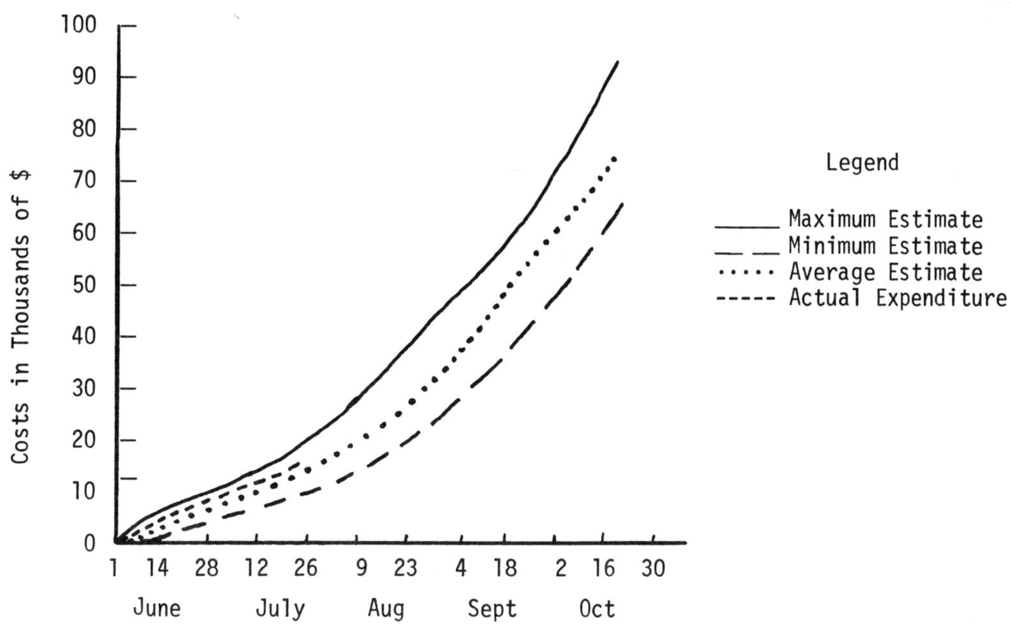

Figure 8-5. Total Development Cost Summary and Cumulative Graph

The project distribution code should, by its structure, indicate the division, department, and/or section (area) that should be charged, and the specific project. Additional coding should indicate the area that did the work, the type of person (job title), or equipment, and the specific activity or type of work done. These codes should be assigned by the Accounting area so that they conform to the company's other cost accounting codes and so that this data can be processed along with the regular cost data.

Collection of this information involves the training of all project, user, and computer operations personnel to utilize the project code properly. For labor and equipment this training describes how and when to log hours of work to the new project code. For materials, the training indicates the utilization of the project distribution code on the materials request. In addition, the training describes how and where to send the completed logs and requisitions. If they do not already exist, these collection points must be established to:

1. ensure that the information is prepared;
2. monitor the completeness of the information;
3. maintain summaries of the information.

Collection points are usually established within each department and service the entire department. This activity should be organized so that one person can collect, monitor, and summarize the information from as many as fifty people in the department in less than eight hours.

Calculation of expenditure consists of the multiplication of the hours worked on the project by the correct salary or standard cost rate for each component and the summation of all expenditures (by component) for the specific project code. Usually a portion of the payroll system (and/or department) performs these calculations.

Reporting consists of the preparation and distribution of reports that inform the project manager, the user manager, and top management of the project expenditures. For easy comparison, their format should be the same as that for the cost estimates. If cost distribution reports are already being produced in your company, the detailed development cost estimate and summary cost estimates should be prepared in the same way as the existing cost distribution reports.

Controlling development costs. Given the estimates of the project's costs and the project expenditure data, control of project costs in maintained by:

1. comparing significant actual vs. estimated costs;
2. determining potential problem areas;
3. planning to eliminate or minimize problems.

The various summary cost estimation forms (see Figure 8-5) should provide the basic media for comparing actual and estimated costs. Actual project expenditures should be entered in the appropriate column as they are incurred and should be compared with the average, minimum, and maximum cost estimates.

Problems in cost develop when the actual expenditures for a period are less than the minimum cost estimate, larger than the maximum cost estimate, or when the cumulative actual cost does not approximate the cumulative average cost estimate.

These potential problems are very easy to determine if the format of the summary portion of Figure 8-5 is used and if the cumulative figures are graphed.

After determining, by a review of the cost summaries and graphs, whether there are potential cost problems, the project manager must integrate this information with his knowledge of the project's performance with respect to schedule and quality. For example, a project that is in perfect control with respect to cost (actual costs equal average cost estimate) but two weeks behind schedule, has serious scheduling and cost problems. Chapter Nine presents a method for integrating and reporting cost, schedule and quality information.

Good cost control methods can only indicate the presence and source of problems. They cannot substitute for the innovative and organizational skills of the manager. They can only provide direction so that the manager can use his skills where they will have the most effect.

Operations Cost Controls

Because the operations cost estimate is already prepared using the base period as a basis with notations concerning any changes, the bulk of the preparation has been completed. In general, all that is necessary is:

1. the calculation and graphing of cumulative figures;
2. any necessary changes from project distribution codes to operations distribution codes.

When these activities have been accomplished, the methods and techniques employed in the control of operations costs for a project are much the same as in the control of development costs. However, to ensure proper control, the primary responsibility for achieving the expected results from the system should be assigned to one individual. If this responsibility is included in those of several (operating) department managers, each manager will only consider his own area and no one will consider the overall operation. However, if it is given to one individual after the basic controls have been established, he can usually perform all necessary planning, organization, motivation, and control for any operational system as a portion of his overall responsibilities (see Chapter Two).

To accomplish his operational responsibilities, the manager will require:

1. A budget similar to the detailed development cost estimate and based on the operations cost estimate.
2. A set of summary controls which include the summary budget figures and graphs.
3. Periodic receipt of actual expenditure information.

All of this information is received during the development effort and should be continued during actual system operation. Then, by updating the summary controls, the manager can detect deviations from expected costs, can determine their source, and can plan accordingly.

Summary

The previously described cost accounting techniques and controls provide the project manager with the information that he requires to determine potential problems and their source. However, by itself, cost accounting does not provide top management with the information that it requires to approve a project or monitor its progress. Two techniques for supplying top management with cost information are described in the remainder of this chapter.

CASH FLOW

A cash flow analysis of a project illustrates the total amount of money that the company will have to spend to implement and operate the project of a period-by-period basis (see Figure 8-6). A cash flow analysis is composed of:

1. The development cost estimate summaries.
2. The operations cost estimate summaries.
3. The estimated cost of operations during development.
4. Additional profits or income generated after implementation.

The development and control of the first two elements have been described in detail in the preceding portions of this chapter. The estimated cost of operations during development is simply the budget for the user department's normal operation with any additions or deductions necessary to reflect the impact of the development effort. The additional profits are composed of more sales (generated by the system) of present or new products times their expected profit margin.

For complete information, cash flow analyses will be completed for average costs, minimum costs, and maximum costs. When all elements have been estimated, combined and reported, top management will be able to determine whether the cash flow required for this project is acceptable. Cash flow analysis facilitates comparison of project expenditures and project savings (or profits) with the costs (and/or profits) of current operations.

Figure 8-7, Cost Variance Report, illustrates a medium for informing top management of the following:

1. Cost variance (actual vs. estimated-average) for this period.
2. Cumulative cost variance through this period.
3. The estimated costs for the remainder of the project.
4. A projection of the costs for the remainder of the project based on the estimate of the remainder of the costs and the cumulative variances thus far.
5. The estimate of the maximum remaining costs.

This information provides top management with the overall knowledge of project expenditures. If significant deviations from expected costs occur and the project manager does not convince top management that the causes of these are justified and that the project is in control, then top management can initiate the actions necessary to restore control.

CASH FLOW ANALYSIS

Initials ______________ (sample) PROJECT Date ___________

Average Cost Basis

Period Ending	6/14	6/28	7/12	7/26	8/9	8/23	9/4	9/18	10/2	10/16	10/30	11/13	11/27	12/11	12/25	1/8	1/22
PROJECT COSTS:																	
Salaries&Fringe	2100	2100	3300	3900	6000	9180	9780	8940	9780	9840	1000	0	0	0	0	0	0
Equipment	0	0	0	0	0	600	300	900	300	1000	0	0	0	0	0	0	0
Materials	0	0	0	0	0	250	600	150	0	0	0	0	0	0	0	0	0
Other	0	0	0	0	0	0	0	0	0	0	0	0	0	0	0	0	0
TOTAL PROJECT	2100	2100	3300	3900	6000	10030	10680	9990	10080	10840	1000	0	0	0	0	0	0
OPERATIONS COSTS:																	
Salaries	32000	32000	32000	31000	30000	30000	31000	30000	30000	29000	4000	4000	4000	4000	4000	4200	4200
Equipment	500	500	500	500	500	500	500	500	500	500	4500	4500	4500	4500	4500	4100	4100
Materials	600	600	600	600	600	600	600	600	600	600	1300	1300	1300	1300	1300	1300	1300
Other	100	100	100	100	100	100	100	100	100	100	200	200	200	200	200	200	200
TOTAL OPERATIONS	33200	33200	33200	32200	31200	31200	32200	31200	31200	30200	10000	10000	10000	10000	10000	9800	9800
TOTAL COSTS	35300	35300	36500	36100	37200	41230	42880	41190	41280	41040	11000	10000	10000	10000	10000	9800	9800
PROFITS FROM:																	
Increased Sales	0	0	0	0	0	0	0	0	0	0	0	0	0	0	0	(1000)	(1000
New Products	0	0	0	0	0	0	0	0	0	0	0	0	0	0	0	0	0
Other	0	0	0	0	0	0	0	0	0	0	0	0	0	0	0	0	0
TOTAL INCOME	0	0	0	0	0	0	0	0	0	0	0	0	0	0	0	(1000)	(1000
GRAND TOTAL	35300	35300	36500	36100	37200	41230	42880	41190	41280	41040	11000	10000	10000	10000	10000	8800	8800
Cumulative	35300	70600	107100	143200	180400	221630	263910	305100	346300	387340	398340	408340	418340	428340	438340	447240	455040

Figure 8-6. Cash Flow Analysis

(sample) PROJECT

COST VARIANCE REPORT

Period Ending: July 26, 1970	This Period			Cumulative			Remaining to 12/25		
	Actual (1)	Est. (2)	Col.1/Col.2 %	Actual (4)	Est. (5)	Col.4/Col.5 %	Est. (7)	Projected (6)X(7)	Max. Est.
Project:									
Salaries	4000	3900	102.6%	11800	11400	103.5%	54520	56428	68000
Equipment	0	0	-	100	0	*	3100	9300	8000
Materials	0	0	-	0	0	-	1000	1000	2000
Other	0	0	-	100	0	*	0	1000	500
Total Project	4000	3900	102.6%	12000	11400	103.5%	58620	61727	78500
Operations:									
Salaries	30500	31000	98.4%	126500	127000	99.6%	200000	199200	244500
Equipment	589	500	117.8%	2143	2000	107.2%	25500	27336	40000
Materials	611	600	101.8%	2424	2400	101.0%	10100	10201	15000
Other	40	100	40.0%	40	400	10.0%	1600	160	3000
Total Operations	31740	32200	88.6%	131107	131800	99.5%	237200	236897	302500
TOTAL COSTS	35740	36100	99.0%	143107	143200	99.9%	295820	295524	380500
Profits from:									
Increased sales	0	0	0	0	0	0	0	0	0
New Products	0	0	0	0	0	0	0	0	0
Other	0	0	0	0	0	0	0	0	0
Total Profits	0	0	0	0	0	0	0	0	0
GRAND TOTAL	35740	36100	99.0%	143107	143200	99.9%	295820	295524	380500

* Percentage is infinite - the larger of 300% or $1000 will be used for projection.
\- No basis for calculation - 100% will be used for projection.

Figure 8-7. Cost Variance Report

PAYBACK PERIOD

The payback period is the amount of time, after the system has been installed, that will be required before the cumulative savings and/or increased income generated by the system equals the cost of developing and installing the system. Figure 8-8 illustrates a typical three-point (average, minimum, maximum) payback analysis.

Detailed comparison with the cash flow analysis (Figure 8-6) will uncover differences between the present costs (in the payback analysis) and the operations costs (in the cash flow analysis) during the same time period. These differences simulate the utilization of user personnel on the project and the inclusion of their salaries in the project costs until the project is implemented.

The payback analysis should be used by top management while it is considering project authorization (Chapter Three). It provides information about the rate of payback, the payback period, and (if extended through sufficient periods) the rate of payoff after the development costs have been paid back. For large amounts of money yearly (over $100,000 generally) and long (30 or more months) periods of time, some methods of discounting the future value of money (such as discounted cash flow) should be applied. Most books on accounting techniques contain one or more such methods.

PAYBACK ANALYSIS

Period Ending	Pres. Cost	Average Cost			Minimum Cost			Maximum Cost		
		Cost	Diff.	Cum. Diff.	Cost	Diff.	Cum. Diff.	Cost	Diff.	Cum. Diff.
June 14	33200	35300	2100	2100	34700	1500	1500	36200	3000	3000
June 28	33200	35300	2100	4200	35200	2000	3500	36200	3000	6000
July 12	33200	36500	3300	7500	35200	2000	5500	37200	4000	10000
July 26	32200	36100	3900	11400	35200	3000	8500	38200	6000	16000
August 9	31200	37200	6000	17400	36100	4900	13400	38700	7500	23500
August 23	31200	41230	10030	27430	40200	9000	22400	42200	11000	34500
September 4	32200	42280	10680	38110	42200	10000	32400	43200	11000	45500
September 18	33200	47190	7990	46100	42200	9000	41400	48200	15000	60500
October 2	33200	41280	10080	55180	43200	10000	51400	55900	12700	73200
October 16	33200	41040	7840	64020	43200	10000	61400	55200	12000	85200
October 30	34200	11000	(23200)A	40820	9500	(24700)A	36700	37200	3000	88200
November 13	34200	10000	(24200)	15620	9500	(24700)	12000	15000	(19200)A	69000
November 27	34200	10000	(24200)	(7580)B	9500	(24700)	(12700)B	15000	(19200)	49800
December 14	34200	10000	(24200)	(31780)	9500	(24700)	(37400)	15000	(19200)	30600
December 25	33200	10000	(23200)	(54980)	9500	(23700)	(61100)	15000	(18200)	12400
January 8	33200	8900	(24300)	(81280)	8000	(25200)	(86300)	17000	(16200)	(3800) B
January 22	34200	8800	(25400)	(105680)	8000	(27200)	(113500)	17000	(17200)	(21000)

NOTES: ( ) indicates profit.
A indicates the period in which the project is complete and payback begins.
B indicates the period in which all development costs are fully paid back.

For simplicity, this project has abnormally fast payback. The payback period for most projects is one to three years after project completion.

Figure 8-8. Payback Analysis

9

Using Informal and Multi-Project Controls

No project exists in a vacuum. Other projects and activities take place within the EDP area and affect the project personnel and the conduct of the project. These effects are caused by interpersonal relationships and by the general environment in which the project exists.

Thus far, the formal controls for the establishment and conduct of a single project have been discussed in some detail. Of equal importance are the informal methods that should be used to control a project and the techniques for synthesizing the controls of a number of single projects into multi-project controls. Used correctly, informal and multi-project controls provide the means for harnessing interpersonal relationships and the EDP environment for the company's good.

Anyone who has had to answer a charge similar to the one that follows will readily understand the need for informal and multi-project controls.

> Look! I understand that you have problems but you're significantly behind schedule and over budget. I'm really not interested in whether your people aren't performing as you thought they would, or whether your key people quit. Those are your problems. What really disturbs me is your feeling that the project has changed so much since it was initiated that you shouldn't be held to your commitments. That just doesn't make sense. I'm not even sure how or whether we can bail you out of this. Why wasn't I informed earlier?

From this complaint it becomes apparent that the project manager has either encountered the three major causes of project delay or is using them as excuses for poor performance. The three major causes are:

1. poor initial estimates or controls
2. turnover and morale problems
3. changes in project scope.

This chapter recommends specific informal and multiproject controls that will aid the project manager and EDP manager in eliminating or alleviating them.

INFORMAL CONTROLS

Informal controls are the regulatory mechanisms exercised upon a project during the normal course of the project manager's daily activities. The three primary controls are:

1. project initiation
2. personal contacts
3. review meetings

The purpose of these informal controls is to determine whether, and to what degree, the project staff and users have begun to put into use their own controls, and to continually motivate the project staff to exercise a larger degree of individual control. When successful, informal controls produce a somewhat autonomous project staff, because the degree of control that each person is exercising on his own portion of the project requires little control from the project manager.

Project Initiation

Because the project personnel usually will not be available at one time and will join the project staff at various points in time, project initiation is conducted for each person as he joins the project. This initiation can be conducted by a subordinate to the project manager (project leader) if the new person is going to work for that project leader. However, the project initiation is much more effective if conducted by the project manager, assisted by the project leader.

The project initiation begins with a meeting during which the project's purpose, benefits, scope, and conceptual design are explained to the new staff member. When he understands these factors, he is informed of his area of responsibility (and authority), others areas of responsibility, and how these areas interface. Finally, the new staff member is acquainted with the project standards, project control mechanisms, and the project completion date and budget, and is provided with all other available information pertaining to his areas of responsibility.

The new staff member is then requested to consider what he has learned, to deliberate for a period of time proportional to the scope of his responsibilities (two hours to two days), and to return with:

1. A detailed schedule for the completion of these activities.
2. An estimate of the cost involved in completing these activities.
3. An estimate of the computer run time for his responsibility area.
4. Recommendations for changes to projects standards, controls or any other area.

Before preparing this information, the new staff member is informed that his initial responses will indicate his understanding of his responsibility area and that all schedules and budgets, *WHEN AGREED UPON*, will be viewed as his personal commitments. Thereafter, it will be his responsibility to meet these commitments.

While the new staff member is preparing his responses, the project manager (and/or project leader) will thoroughly review the information. The review will provide sufficient data so that the project manager can fully substantiate the schedule and costs for at least two major segments within the new staff member's area of responsibility.

When the new staff member submits his initial responses, there will be a review during which the schedule and costs will be:

1. Significantly less than the original schedule and costs contained in the "Project Justification." In these cases, the project manager must review the schedule and costs and show where elements have been omitted or efforts underestimated. Revision upward is usually relatively easy but, in problem cases, the major segments in which the project manager is confident should be emphasized.
2. Very close to the original schedule and costs. In these cases, no further review is required by the manager other than to ensure that all benchmarks are estimated properly.
3. Significantly larger than the original schedule and costs. In these cases, the project manager should concentrate upon the major segments that he has studied in depth and convince the new staff member that there are areas that are being overestimated. When this agreement has been reached, the new staff member is requested to review and revise his schedules and costs.

During some initiation reviews, the project manager may check schedules and costs with another project manager to obtain confirmation. This is always done in cases of serious disagreements with a new staff member. In some cases, because of the experience of the staff member or because the original estimates were incorrect, the schedule and/or costs will have to be increased to agree with the staff member's estimates.

After all segments of the project have been scheduled by the personnel who will be responsible for the actual work, an initial project schedule and an initial project cash flow are prepared based upon these estimates. If they are significantly different from the project schedule and cash flow analysis in the "Project Justification," these (new) documents are submitted to top management and, from this point on, all controls are based upon the schedules and costs contained in these documents.

During the initiation review, the project manager must also give serious consideration to including or revising any standards, controls, or other facets of the project that have been recommended by the staff. When the review is complete and all agreements have been made, the project manager must make clear that the new staff member fully understands his project responsibilities and that he will be expected to meet all his commitments with regard to schedule, costs, standards, and controls. If there are no questions, the project initiation has been completed.

Follow up. After the conclusion of the project initiation, the project manager, to maintain control of the project, must:

1. Monitor activities to ensure that all commitments will be met.
2. Advise, assist, and support any staff member having trouble meeting his commitments.
3. Maintain records of each person's success in meeting his commitments so that he may be rewarded accordingly.

The methods, forms, and techniques presented in other sections of this book provide more than adequate means for accomplishing these functions.

Personal Contact

Because the project initiation relieves the project manager from any (project-related) responsibilities such as ensuring that his project staff is present, conforming to regular working hours, or working rather than socializing, he can devote his personal contacts with staff members to informal project controls. Therefore, the project manager can spend his personal contact time validating the formal control mechanisms and ensuring that each staff member is fulfilling his commitments to project schedule, quality, and cost.

To be productive in personal contacts you must:

1. Know whom you should contact.
2. Review prior formal controls from these people.
3. Establish the purposes of the contact.
4. Make the contact.
5. Document the results.

If possible, every staff member should be contacted every day. If, however, time and circumstances do not permit this, a simple Contact Log (Figure 9-1) provides the basic information required to determine who should be contacted. This log should be briefly reviewed at the start of each day. The criticality of each person's efforts, the amount of time since the last contact, and any pertinent comments must be considered in the making of a list of people that should be contacted.

If you are thoroughly acquainted with the prior efforts of the people you are about to contact, no additional review of their work is required. However, it is usually necessary to periodically review the work they have already done to determine how well they have met their schedule, quality and cost commitments. This review can be accomplished by checking specific sections of the project schedule, the "System Documentation," and the cost controls. Because the review is intended to convey general rather than detailed knowledge, no review for an individual should require more than five minutes.

Purpose. After the contacts with the staff members have been determined and their prior work has been reviewed, you must establish the purposes for the next contact. There will usually be one primary purpose, but skillful managers will have

(sample) PROJECT

CONTACT LOG

Date of Next Update ____

Name	Working On	Last Benchmark	Date	Next Bench-mark	Last Con-tact	Comments
1.P.Williams	DD-O-SA4	DD-I-SA4	6/25	7/5	6/28	Check standards, conformance
2.B.Brown	DD-I-Vendor-SA1	DD-I-Mainline-SA1	6/28	6/28	6/30	Check schedule
3.J.Jones	DD-MF-SA3	DD-I-SA3	6/27	7/12	6/27	Check standards, documentation
4.W.Walsh	DD-F-Dealer-SA5	DD-O-Control SA5	6/26	7/12	6/26	Check quality
5.D.Dawn	--	--	--	7/15	--	Initiate 7/13
6.L.Lane	--	--	--	7/29	--	Initiate 7/23
7.C.Clark	MS-W-SA3	MS-S-SA4	6/27	7/14	6/27	Check schedule and morale

NOTE: All project personnel would normally appear on this log. Many personnel are not included in this sample because of space requirements.

CODING: Format (1)-(2)-(3)-(4): (1)Function (2)Task (3)Subtask or program (4)Program

Functions	Tasks		Subtasks	Program
CD Conceptual Design	I Input	P Program Test	Clear Language See Estimate of Development	Same Code as in Estimate of Development
DD Detail Design	O Output	L Linkage Test		
P Programming	MF Master File	S System Test		
T Testing	F Flow Chart	PI Pilot Test		
C Conversion	D Documentation	PL Parallel Test		
MS Manual Systems	S Study	W Write Procedures		
	C Code	TR Train		
	T Test	CW Condition		

Figure 9-1. Contact Log

several purposes for contacting any individual. As examples, a person might be contacted because:

1. Prior performance indicates that the person performs better if certain areas are reviewed and emphasized periodically.
2. The time between benchmarks may be sufficient to require interim checking.
3. The person's work habits are not well known and interim contacts provide additional information.
4. The formal reports indicate contradictory or improbable achievements.
5. The person's morale and general attitude can be assessed and perhaps improved.

6. The informal social structures and/or grapevine are to be used to obtain or disseminate information.
7. Public praise is in order for significantly improved or meritorious efforts.

Obviously, there are a vast number of purposes that can exist. Your problem is to determine what you expect to accomplish before the contact is made.

Conduct. Informal contacts occur throughout each day as part of normal activities. They occur in halls, in offices, at the water cooler, on the telephone, and in many other ways. If you leave your office periodically during business hours, informal contacts may occur by chance. If you also develop the habit of "dropping by" each staff member's work area for a minute or two each day, informal contacts are assured.

Regardless of the manner in which these contacts occur, the conduct of the contact must be strictly informal. You will be aware of the purposes of your contact and the results you wish to obtain. You should not, however, simply conduct the contact to achieve your purposes. It should be natural and your purpose should be served by directing the flow of conversation to the project without exerting undue influence. If the conversation begins with (or strays to) other topics, you should listen, contribute, and learn until you can naturally divert the thinking back to the project.

The conduct of any informal contact can take a good deal of time, because the person may be interested in discussing matters other than the project. The perceptive project manager will decide whether he should spend the time or terminate the contact depending upon:

1. The importance of his purpose in contacting this staff member.
2. The worth of the additional information that he is obtaining about other topics.
3. The effect that the termination of the contact will have on the staff member.
4. His skill and success in directing the conversation back to the project matters.

If the purposes are so important that time cannot be taken to divert the conversation, or that the contact cannot be terminated and resumed another time, it should be terminated and a meeting between the participants should be arranged. This is accomplished by simply suggesting that you'd like to discuss some things further but, at the present, you do not have the time; therefore, you would like the other participants to drop by your office at a specified time.

Improvement. Conducting successful informal contacts is a skill. This skill should be measured and can be increased by:

1. continual exercise
2. documentation of the success of each contact
3. analysis of your problem areas
4. attempting to overcome problem areas

Of these activities, the documentation of the success of each contact is the activity that is most usually avoided or overlooked. Whether this is so because it is not considered necessary or because it is humbling to admit a totally unsuccessful contact, the fact remains that no logical and systematic attempt to improve informal contacts can be made without documenting the results of these contacts. In addition, if the results of informal contacts are not documented they tend either to deteriorate into general non-project oriented conversations (bull sessions) or tend to decrease in frequency.

Figure 9-2 illustrates a Contact Results Form that can be used to document the results of informal contacts. By simply keeping these forms on your desk and developing the habit of filling them in when you return to your office, the documentation of each informal contact can be accomplished in about a minute. If significant results are obtained, additional system (or program) documentation may be required. In these cases, the reference number on the Contact Results Form may be used to cross-reference the source of the information.

CONTACT RESULTS

Reference #__________

Person Contacted:______________________ Date:__________ Time:__________

Contact Occurred When:____

____

Project______________ Function______________ Task______________

Purpose: 1.____

2.____

3.____

RESULTS:____

____

____

____

Time Spent________________________________ Initials______________

Figure 9-2. Contact Results Form

Review Meetings

Review meetings are composed of five basic types:

1. Personal
2. Benchmark
3. Functional
4. User
5. Top management

These meetings are conducted to ensure that the project is progressing in a satisfactory fashion. They are important to overall control because they provide the forum necessary for reviewing past performance.

Personal. Personal review is conducted when consideration of a staff member's performance indicates that he will probably be unable to fulfill his project commitments. The purpose of the personal review is to discuss his situation and to motivate and assist him so that his commitments are met. Because each personal review indicates that a staff member has not achieved agreed-upon goals, these meetings should be conducted in private, on a face-to-face basis. The tone or theme that is usually most effective is one of paternalistic support. "What seems to be the problem?" and "What can I do to help?" typify this theme.

Benchmark. A benchmark review is conducted each time that a benchmark is attained and a Benchmark Control Report (Figure 5-6) received. The purposes of the benchmark review are to compliment the staff member for completing the project task, to remark upon the degree to which the staff member has fulfilled his commitments (to schedule, quality and cost), and to motivate him to improve his performance. Benchmark reviews should be conducted privately if there are any negative points to discuss but can be conducted publicly, on an informal basis, if all of the comments are positive. The theme of these meetings should be congratulatory to the highest degree possible, and comments like "I'm really happy that you finished this segment of the project. I can understand some of the difficulties you overcame" should predominate.

Functional. Functional reviews are conducted when all of the tasks within each computer-related function (i.e. detail design, programming, testing and conversion) are completed. The primary purpose of the functional review is to assess the overall quality of the project. To accomplish this objective, the "System Documentation" is duplicated and sent to the operations group and the user group (see Chapter Two).

Within one week, a meeting of the project staff and these groups is held. At this meeting, the documentation is summarized by the project staff and any areas that were unclear or did not conform to standards are discussed. During the meeting, the user group and operations group are expected to comment on any areas that they do not understand. When the meeting concludes, all necessary changes should be documented and the staff members should understand their individual responsibilities for making these changes. These meetings should be conducted in a conference room setting whenever possible. The theme should be one of constructive criticism which also improves the communication among groups.

User. User reviews are conducted when the project is authorized, upon completion of every manual systems-related function (i.e. study, write, train, and condition) and when required at other points within the project. The purpose of user reviews is to begin to inform all the users of the project's progress as it affects or will affect the users, to clear up any misconceptions, and to interest and involve the users in the completion of the project. User reviews should be conducted among (required) staff members and representative user personnel in a conference room setting. The staff members should conduct the meeting so that the user representatives are interested and become involved, and should not simply inform the user personnel of the progress of the project. This requires a good deal of preparation and insight into the psychological needs of the user group. Therefore, manual systems personnel (and user group personnel) can be of great assistance when preparing for a user review. Because involvement is required, the theme of these meetings must be the accomplishments to date and the requirements for the future. The staff members should emphasize that the system belongs to the users by stressing that "*your* system is progressing satisfactorily but we cannot afford to relax. To achieve all the benefits that *your* system can produce we must . . ."

Top management. Top management reviews are conducted periodically (monthly) in many companies. A preferable schedule is to conduct a top management review at the project manager's instigation whenever sufficient progress has been made to warrant such a review, with the stipulation that, in any project, no six-week period can elapse without a top management review. The purpose of these reviews is to inform top management of the progress of the project, of any deviations from commitments, and the prognosis for the future. These meetings also provide the means for communicating any points that cannot be communicated by, or that might not be fully understood from, the formal reports submitted to top management. These meetings should be conducted among the project manager, the development manager, and representatives of top management in a conference room environment. The theme should be informative and questions and recommendations should be solicited.

Conduct. Other meetings will also be held during the project. These meetings will usually involve staff members and/or user personnel and will be conducted to provide specific training or to solve specific problems.

Before conducting any meeting, the following factors should be considered:

1. Each individual and the composite group.
2. The purpose of the meeting and the situation at the time of the meeting.
3. Your personality, skills, and experience.

Based upon these factors, you should:

1. Invite participants to meetings in groupings that will be conducive to your purposes.
2. Select an environment (time, room, etc.) and establish seating so that they serve your purposes.
3. Supply any necessary information (agenda, summaries, etc.) to the participants in a manner that either encourages or discourages their perusal dependent upon which activity best suits your purpose.
4. Thoroughly prepare your (or the staff's) presentation so that the media (slides, charts, lecture, etc.) complement each other, the theme, and the environment.

These considerations and recommended practices must be substantially amplified and expanded to conform to individual company practices and procedures. However, they provide a general basis for conducting efficient and successful meetings.

MULTI-PROJECT CONTROLS

Generally, as soon as a person begins to demonstrate that he can manage a single project, he is made responsible for several projects. Multi-project controls are the reports and procedures required (in addition to normal project controls) to enable one person to maintain control over a number of projects. In addition to being control media for a multi-project manager such as the manager of development, the reports and procedures recommended in this section also provide an understandable method of communicating the progress and requirements of single and multiple projects to top management and/or other (operations) managers.

To control single and multiple projects, the following four basic reports are required:

1. Project progress report (Figure 9-3).
2. Multi-project progress report (Figure 9-4).
3. Manpower schedule (Figure 9-5).
4. New project computer time requirements (Figure 9-6).

While these four reports provide basic control and communication media for multiple projects, their formats can also be readily adapted for other reports required by top management or other managers.

The remainder of this section describes, in some detail, the four basic reports and the procedures required for their preparation and dissemination.

Project Progress Report

The project progress report summarizes the expected and actual progress of the project for each key control element during each base period. It also provides subjective evaluations of the criticality of any problems, and illustrates the effort remaining with regard to costs, cash flow, schedule, and quality. In addition the project progress report provides an understandable vehicle for communicating with top management.

Initiation. As each project is begun, the basic format is established. It includes an abstract of the project and pictorial (graphical) representations of the estimates of the project's:

1. Cash flow
2. Costs
3. Main schedule elements
4. Review points
5. Documentation points

These representations are constructed on a base period basis. As was explained in Chapter Eight, the base period that is selected should be the same as the company's pay period to facilitate cost comparisons.

(sample) PROJECT

SUMMARY OF PROGRESS

Period Ending ________

Signature:____________________Project Manager

Date ____________

ABSTRACT: Project includes Detail Design, Programming, Testing, and Conversion of basic Inventory Functions. After payback, by re-allocating personnel and from increased income, the company will save approximately $____________ per year.

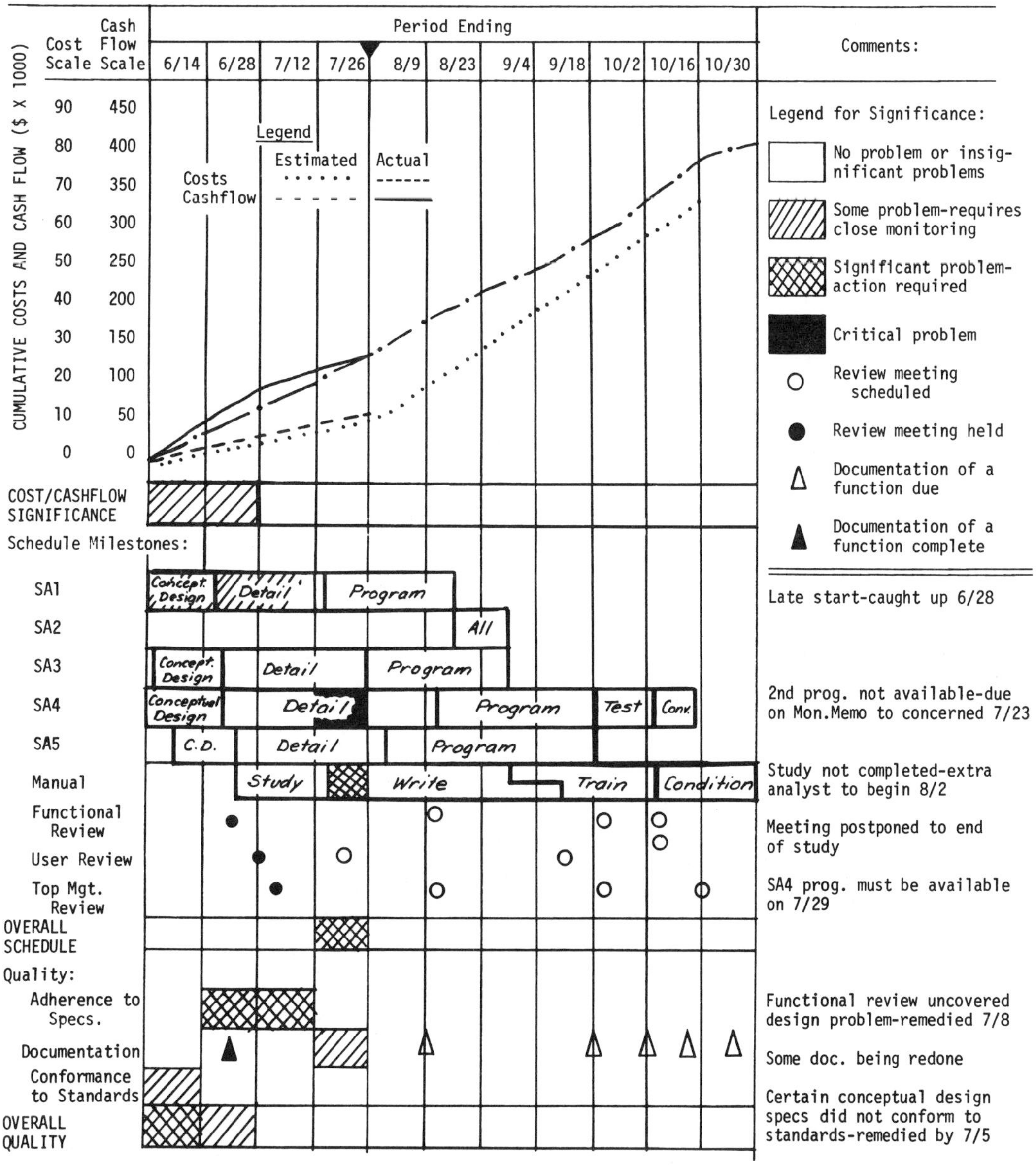

SUMMARY: All quality and cost problems are under control. Lack of a programmer on SA4 is causing delay in a critical path item. This will be helped when the programmer begins on 7/29. Other personnel will assist and attempt to get this area back on schedule.

APPROVED: ____________________ Development Manager ____________________ EDP Manager

Figure 9-3. Project Progress Report

In addition to the pictorial representations, lines in the project progress summary are devoted to subjective judgments of project progress that include:

1. The significance of any deviations from estimated cost and cash flow.
2. The significance of deviations from schedule.
3. The significance of deviations in quality.
4. Elements of quality:
   a. Adherence to specifications.
   b. Documentation.
   c. Conformance to standards.
5. Any other elements that the project manager believes to be significant.

Finally, the project progress summary is concluded by a brief, written summary of the project's progress to date and the steps that are being taken to remedy any problems.

Completion. As the project progresses, at the end of each base period, the project manager completes the project progress summary by:

1. Updating the line graphs of the actual cash flow and cost information.
2. Coding the elements of the schedule and quality to indicate problem occurrences and severity. The coding that is used is:
   a. Blank ▭ if there is no significant problem.
   b. Striped ▨ if there is a problem but it is minor and can be corrected by close monitoring without taking additional action. Commentary is optional.
   c. Crosshatched ▩ if there is a significant problem that requires action. Commentary is required.
   d. Black ■ if the problems solution is critical to the successful completion of the project. Commentary is mandatory and an accompanying or preceding memo is recommended.
3. Writing the required and optional commentary to clarify any problem areas.
4. Summarizing the cost/cash flow, schedule, and quality via similar coding.
5. Writing the brief summary.

Other coding schemes may be utilized. Color coding is much easier to perceive but cannot be easily copied.

Submission. When the project progress summary for a period has been completed, the project manager should have copies prepared for the development manager and the EDP manager. These managers should review the report to assure its understandability and completeness and to confirm the subjective estimates of the project manager.

When the report has been reviewed, the EDP manager should have a brief (ten minute) meeting with the development manager and the project manager. At the meeting, report approvals are given (signed), any additional questions are answered, and the project manager is motivated to improve the progress of the project. Without periodic meetings of this type, project managers may tend to function without being truly managed.

After approval, the report should be distributed to top management.

Multi-Project Progress Report

The multi-project progress report presents a pictorial and statistical summary of the progress of the:

1. cost/cash flow
2. schedule
3. quality
4. top management reviews

for a number of projects. It provides very general information about each project's individual progress and about its progress with respect to other projects. It is used by the multi-project manager to determine whether (and how) to reallocate resources. In addition to allowing top management to also review resource allocation, this report can also be used as one basis for assessing the multi-project manager's efforts.

Initiation. This report is initiated whenever a person becomes responsible for the simultaneous conduct of more than one project. The number of periods that are summarized in this report can vary according to the preference of top management but should be consistent on all such reports; between one and three years is usual.

The format is developed by listing, as illustrated by Figure 9-4:

1. The projects for which you are responsible
2. Their respective costs and completion dates
3. Cost (C), schedule (S), quality (Q) and top management points (R) lines for each project
4. A total segment at the bottom of the page with a line for each problem criticality code. (The same coding should be used as is used in the Project Progress Summary, Figure 9-3.)

The format is completed by heading each column with the correct base period identification. Naturally, since the period just completed is the last period that can be reported upon, the right hand column will be identified as the last completed period and the preferred number of reporting periods appear sequentially to its left.

The efficient multi-project manager will prepare all main heading, basic project information, and legend information on one (masking) sheet from which the columnar space (area for column headings and information) will be cut out. The column headings (base period identifications) will then be prepared on a much wider (progress section) sheet of paper and will be arranged so that the preferred number of periods (columns) fit the total column space on the mask. However, column headings should be prepared for a year or so in the future as well as for the original (preferred) number of periods.

Completion. When a period is completed, the coded summary information from the project progress summary is copied onto the corresponding lines and columns in the progress section of the multi-project progress report. As new project responsibilities

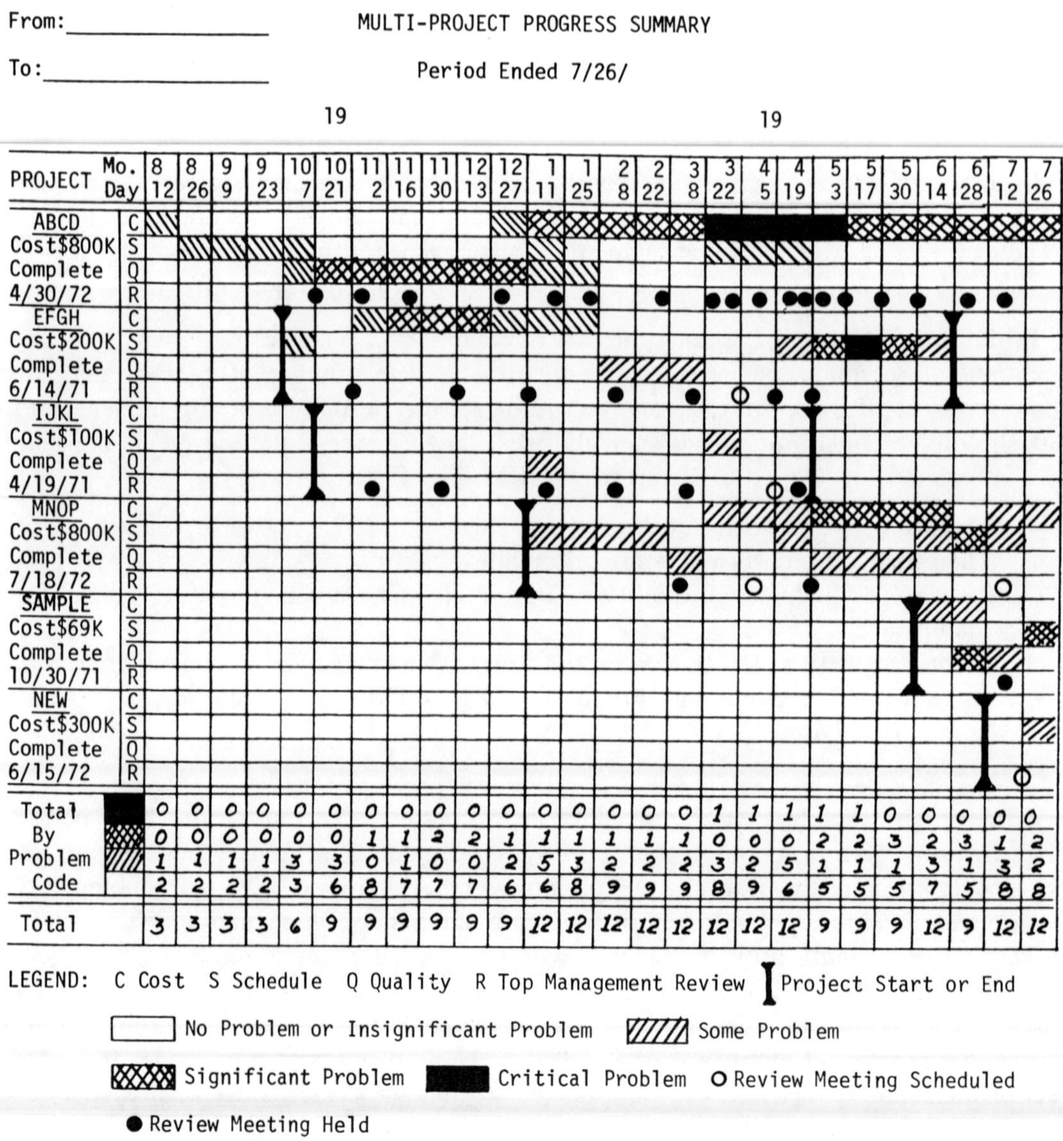

Figure 9-4. Multi-Project Progress Report

are added, new project information lines are added to the masking sheet. Finally, for each period, the number of rows containing each of the criticality codes are totaled, these totals are written in their respective lines and are summed. The sum total must equal three (the number of codes per project) times the number of projects for that period.

The totals by criticality code are statistics which indicate the multi-project manager's overall effectiveness. Each line may also be expressed as a percentage of the sum total and the total figures or percentages can be graphed (line or bar graph) on a period by period basis to illustrate changes in effectiveness. Given the basic figures, other statistical analyses (e.g. percentage of costs that are critical, significant problems, or insignificant) can be developed as required.

Submission. The multi-project progress report is submitted by the multi-project manager to the development manager, the EDP manager, and all the top management personnel identified by the development manager as being interested. This report is a summarization of project progress summaries, and usually does not require managerial approval.

Manpower Schedule and New Project Computer Time Requirements

The manpower schedule (Figure 9-5) and the new project computer time requirement (Figure 9-6) illustrate two methods of summarizing information about the utilization of specific resources among various projects. They are used by the multi-project manager to:

1. determine how resources might be allocated;
2. estimate when new projects might be begun;
3. convince top management of the need to add resources;
4. develop a perspective of the possible utilization of resources for future projects with respect to ongoing projects.

Other formats may be used for summarizing multi-project resource allocation, but the maintenance of updated resource information in some form is a necessity for logical multi-project control. If good resource information does not exist, decisions affecting resource allocation are usually made without it because of the extensive time required to prepare this information initially.

The initiation, completion, and submission of this information are very straightforward. All information can be obtained and summarized from the basic, single project controls described in other chapters. These reports should only be submitted to top management when the multi-project manager wishes to document the reasons behind his requests for additional resources.

MANPOWER SCHEDULE
Project Personnel

Updated on 7/26/71

Personnel	Present	Start-Complete	Second	Start-Complete	Third	Start-Complete	Unsched. Beg.	*
Managers & Leaders								
R. Rough	NEW	7/1/71-6/15/72					6/15/72	3
S. Stuff	MNOP	1/1/71-7/18/72					7/18/72	4
T. Tough	MNOP	1/1/7/-5/20/72					5/20/72	2
P. Williams	sample	6/1/71-10/30/71					10/30/71	1
Analysts-System								
L. Light	StudyQRST	7/20/71-8/7/71	StudyUVWX	8/8/71-8/15/71			8/15/71	1
P. Pure	NEW	7/1/71-9/10/71					8/11/71	2
S. Straight	NEW	7/1/71-11/5/71					11/5/71	3
Analysts-Manual								
C.Clerk	MNOP	2/20/71-8/28/72					8/28/72	4
M.Main	sample	6/21/71-11/15/71	NEW	11/15/71-7/15/72			7/15/72	2
P.Pram	MNOP	2/15/71-8/2/71	sample	8/2/71-11/1/71	MNOP	11/1/71-8/5/72	8/5/72	3
W. Wall	sample	6/28/71-10/16/71	NEW	10/16/71-7/1/72			7/1/72	1
Programmer-Analysts								
B. Brown	sample	6/1/71-10/30/71					10/30/71	1
C. Chart	MNOP	2/25/71-7/18/72					7/18/72	4
J. Jones	sample	6/5/71-2/5/72	NEW	8/30/71-2/5/72			2/5/72	2
S. Smith	MNOP	3/1/71-7/18/72					7/18/72	5
W. Walsh	sample	6/10/71-9/21/71	NEW	9/21/71-5/15/72			5/15/72	3
Programmers								
A. Adams	MNOP	3/1/71-5/15/72					5/15/72	4
D. Dawn	sample	7/15/71-9/11/71	NEW	9/11/71-6/15/72			6/15/72	6
G. Green	MNOP	3/15/71-8/7/71	NEW	8/7/71-4/5/72			4/5/72	3
L. Lane	MNOP	5/16/71-7/21/72	sample	7/29/71-9/9/71	MNOP	9/10/71-4/3/72	4/3/72	2
N. North	MNOP	3/8/71-7/18/72					7/18/72	9
W. Paine	MNOP	4/18/71-11/5/71	NEW	11/5/71-6/1/72			6/1/72	5
B. Prime	NEW	7/15/71-6/15/72					6/15/72	7
W. West	MNOP	4/17/71-12/5/71	NEW	12/5/71-3/1/72			3/1/72	1
(New Recruit)	Training	8/18/71-10/1/71	MNOP	10/1/71-7/1/72			7/1/72	8

NOTE: * = Availability Number indicates the order of availability for work on new projects for the personnel in each category.

Figure 9-5. Manpower Schedule

NEW PROJECT

Hours/ week by Time Period

COMPUTER TIME REQUIREMENTS
360/40 Configuration A

Updated ____________
By ____________

Project	Function	Mo. / Day	1/11	1/25	2/8	2/22	3/8	3/22	4/5	4/19	5/3	5/17	5/31	6/14	6/28	7/12	7/26	8/9	8/22	9/4	9/18	10/2	10/16	10/30	11/13	11/27	12/11	12/25	1/7	1/21	2/4	2/18	3/4
ABCD	Testing		-	-	-	-	-	5	5	10	0	0	0	0	5	5	10	5	0	0	0	5	5	5	5	10	10	25	15	20	20	10	30
	Operation		-	-	-	-	-	-	-	-	-	-	-	-	-	-	-	-	-	-	-	-	-	-	-	-	-	-	-	-	-	-	-
EFGH	Testing		-	-	-	-	3	5	5	8	10	15	18	20	3	3	-	-	-	-	-	-	-	-	-	-	-	-	-	-	-	-	-
	Operation		-	-	-	-	-	-	-	-	-	-	-	-	12	12	12	12	12	12	12	15	12	12	12	12	12	12	15	12	12	12	12
IJKL	Testing		0	3	3	3	5	5	10	10	-	-	-	-	-	-	-	-	-	-	-	-	-	-	-	-	-	-	-	-	-	-	-
	Operation		-	-	-	-	-	-	-	-	3	3	3	3	3	3	3	3	3	3	3	3	3	3	3	3	3	3	4	3	3	3	2
MNOP	Testing		-	-	-	-	-	-	-	-	-	-	-	-	-	-	-	-	-	-	-	-	-	-	5	10	5	0	0	0	5	10	3
	Operation		-	-	-	-	-	-	-	-	-	-	-	-	-	-	-	-	-	-	-	-	-	-	-	-	-	-	-	-	-	-	-
SAMPLE	Testing		-	-	-	-	-	-	-	-	-	-	-	3	5	10	5	5	10	10	10	10	15	20	5	-	-	-	-	-	-	-	-
	Operation		-	-	-	-	-	-	-	-	-	-	-	-	-	-	-	-	-	-	-	-	-	-	10	10	10	10	15	10	10	10	10
NEW	Testing		-	-	-	-	-	-	-	-	-	-	-	-	-	-	-	-	-	-	-	-	-	-	-	-	-	-	-	3	5	5	5
	Operation		-	-	-	-	-	-	-	-	-	-	-	-	-	-	-	-	-	-	-	-	-	-	-	-	-	-	-	-	-	-	-
TOTALS FOR	Testing		0	3	3	3	8	15	20	28	10	15	18	23	13	18	15	10	10	10	10	15	20	25	15	20	15	15	15	23	30	25	35
	Operation		0	0	0	0	0	0	0	0	3	3	3	3	15	15	15	15	15	15	15	18	15	15	25	25	25	25	34	25	25	25	24
PROJECTS	TOTAL		0	3	3	3	8	15	20	28	13	18	21	26	28	33	30	25	25	25	25	33	35	40	40	45	40	40	49	48	55	50	59
Contingency-All Projects			5	2	2	2	2	5	5	2	7	2	4	4	7	2	5	5	5	5	10	7	5	5	10	5	10	10	6	7	0	10	1
TOTAL REQUESTED			5	5	5	5	10	20	25	30	20	20	25	30	35	35	35	30	30	30	35	40	40	45	50	50	50	50	55	55	55	60	60
Total Used			0	0	3	7	12	18	32	31	27	24	25	29	29	40	34																
Unused (Extra Usage)			5	5	2	(2)	(2)	2	(7)	(1)	(7)	(4)	0	1	6	(5)	1																
Cumulative Unused (Extra Usage)			5	10	12	10	8	10	3	2	(5)	(9)	(9)	(8)	(2)	(7)	(6)																

Figure 9-6. Computer Time Requirements

10

Managing Production Areas for Successful Projects

Everyone appreciates how important development personnel are to the ultimate success of a project. Less commonly understood or appreciated is the importance of the personnel in the production (or operations) areas. The production areas are composed of:

1. user operations
2. EDP operations

and the personnel in these areas are equally, if not more, important to the success of a project than are the development personnel.

When production personnel are unable or unwilling to operate the system efficiently, discussions similar to the one that follows occur:

Development Manager: I understand that there have been some complaints about the order entry system we installed a few months ago.

User Manager: That's correct. My people have been killing themselves trying to achieve the benefits that were forecasted for this system but we can't even dent the surface. For every dollar we can save, the computer area charges us two.

EDP Operations Manager: It's true our charges to you are higher than forecast but we've had to make a lot of changes. We've only charged you for making the changes and operating the system.

User Manager: I don't know anything about your changes. All I want to do is to get some of the benefits out of this system and get the treasurer off my back.

Development Manager: Well, let's take a look and see what can be done.

This discussion implies a basic understanding of the various responsibilities and a concern for costs. It also indicates that several basic controls on system operation are not being used and alludes to the fact that changes are the primary cause of problems in operational systems.

This chapter describes:

1. methods and procedures for controlling operational:
    a. costs.
    b. schedules.
    c. quality.
2. techniques for managing systems modifications by:
    a. evaluating their necessity and effect.
    b. controlling their preparation and installation.

The operational controls and systems modifications management techniques are described as they would be applied, during and after system implementation, *to ensure that the benefits expected of a project are obtained.* Most of these controls and techniques can be effectively applied in managing any production area.

OPERATIONAL CONTROLS

Operational controls consist of the methods, reports, and procedures that are used to monitor and determine areas for improvement within the production processes. These controls are of three main types:

1. Cost Controls.
2. Schedule Contols.
3. Quality Controls.

Together they should monitor the significant elements of production within every user and EDP group or area.

To be able to monitor every significant element within every area requires a good knowledge of control techniques and an excellent knowledge of the production areas and processes. The following sections describe a variety of control methods and procedures that can be applied. This knowledge must be combined with knowledge of specific production areas and processes in order to produce viable operational controls.

Cost Controls

Chapter Eight describes a method of utilizing the three-point estimate of cash flow to determine payback. By comparing actual figures with these estimates via a graph of the cumulative cash flows, excellent control media can be established for the project implementation and payback periods.

After payback has been completed, basic operational controls on cumulative cost figures, while possible, are quite tedious. Moreover, because the figures become extremely large, significant variations from expectations are not readily apparent.

Basic period-by-period cost comparisons are also not a reliable basis for controlling operational costs because they tend to obscure changes in trend and are significantly affected by seasonal and volume variations.

This section describes two basis indicators of cost and cost effectiveness that:

1. Provide the ability to rapidly analyze trend.
2. Eliminate seasonal variation.
3. Pinpoint significant variations.
4. Correlate costs and volume.

These two indicators, the cost moving annual total (MAT); and the cost/volume MAT, provide viable bases for comparing (single or) three-point estimates of operational costs with actual operational costs.

In addition to describing the two basic indicators, this section also describes the general procedures for diagnosing the causes of cost variations and the reports or analyses that could be referenced.

Cost moving annual total (MAT). Moving annual totals (MATs) are used to eliminate seasonal variations. The cost MAT for any period is composed of the total costs for all periods in the year that ends with the period under consideration, and can be calculated by simply adding together the costs for all periods during the preceding year. However, once a cost MAT is developed for one period, the cost MAT for the next period can be calculated by adding the MAT that has already been developed to the costs for the next period and subtracting the costs for the oldest period in the preceding year. Figure 10-1 illustrates the basis for calculating cost MATs and provides representative cost MAT figures.

While cost MAT figures are quite informative, their real worth becomes apparent when translated into graphical form. Figure 10-2 is a graph of the representative cost MAT figures in Figure 10-1. As can be seen, the general trend of costs was increasing in year two and is decreasing in year three.

Lacking any specific knowledge to the contrary, the remainder of year three could be estimated by simply continuing the general trend as shown in Figure 10-2. While this method of estimation is not extremely accurate, it is usually sufficient for most purposes.

Obviously, if the cost MAT can be projected, raw costs can be derived from this projection. For example, if the cost MAT for Period 24, Year 3 in Figure 10-1 were to be graphically projected to be 2605, then by calculation:

$$2605 = 2610 + x - 125$$
$$120 = x$$

the cost for Period 24, Year 3, is determined to be 120. The cost for the other missing periods could be similarly calculated.

Worthwhile as the graphical presentation of the cost MAT is for projecting purposes, it is even more beneficial when used as an operational control technique. To use cost MATs as operational controls, for new projects:

1. translate the three-point cash flow estimates into cost MATs;
2. graph these cost MATs as the control MATs (Figure 10-2);
3. develop a MAT of the actual cost and graph it on the control MATs.

REPRESENTATIVE COST MAT

	Year 1		Year 2		Year 3	
Period	Cost	Cumulative	Cost	MAT	Cost	MAT
1	100	100	105	2650	110	2740
2	105	205	110	2655	100	2730
3	110	315	110	2655	105	2725
4	115	430	110	2650	105	2720
5	110	540	115	2655	110	2715
6	105	645	110	2660	105	2710
7	100	745	105	2665	95	2700
8	90	835	100	2675	90	2690
9	70	905	80	2685	80	2690
10	60	965	60	2685	70	2700
11	70	1035	60	2675	60	2700
12	80	1115	85	2680	70	2685
13	90	1205	90	2680	80	2675
14	100	1305	105	2685	95	2665
15	100	1405	100	2685	100	2665
16	100	1505	110	2695	100	2655
17	100	1605	110	2705	95	2640
18	105	1715	100	2700	100	2640
19	110	1825	110	2700	105	2635
20	110	1935	115	2705	110	2630
21	115	2050	120	2710	110	2620
22	115	2165	125	2720	115	2610
23	120	2285	125	2725	--	--
24	120	2405	130	2735	--	--
25	125	2530	130	2740	--	--
26	115	2645(MAT)	120	2735	--	--

Basis: MAT for any period= MAT of previous period + cost this period - cost this period in previous year.

Sample: MAT for period 1, year 2= MAT period 26, year 1 + cost period 1, year 2 - cost period 1, year 1.

2650=2645+105-100

Figure 10-1. Representative Cost MAT

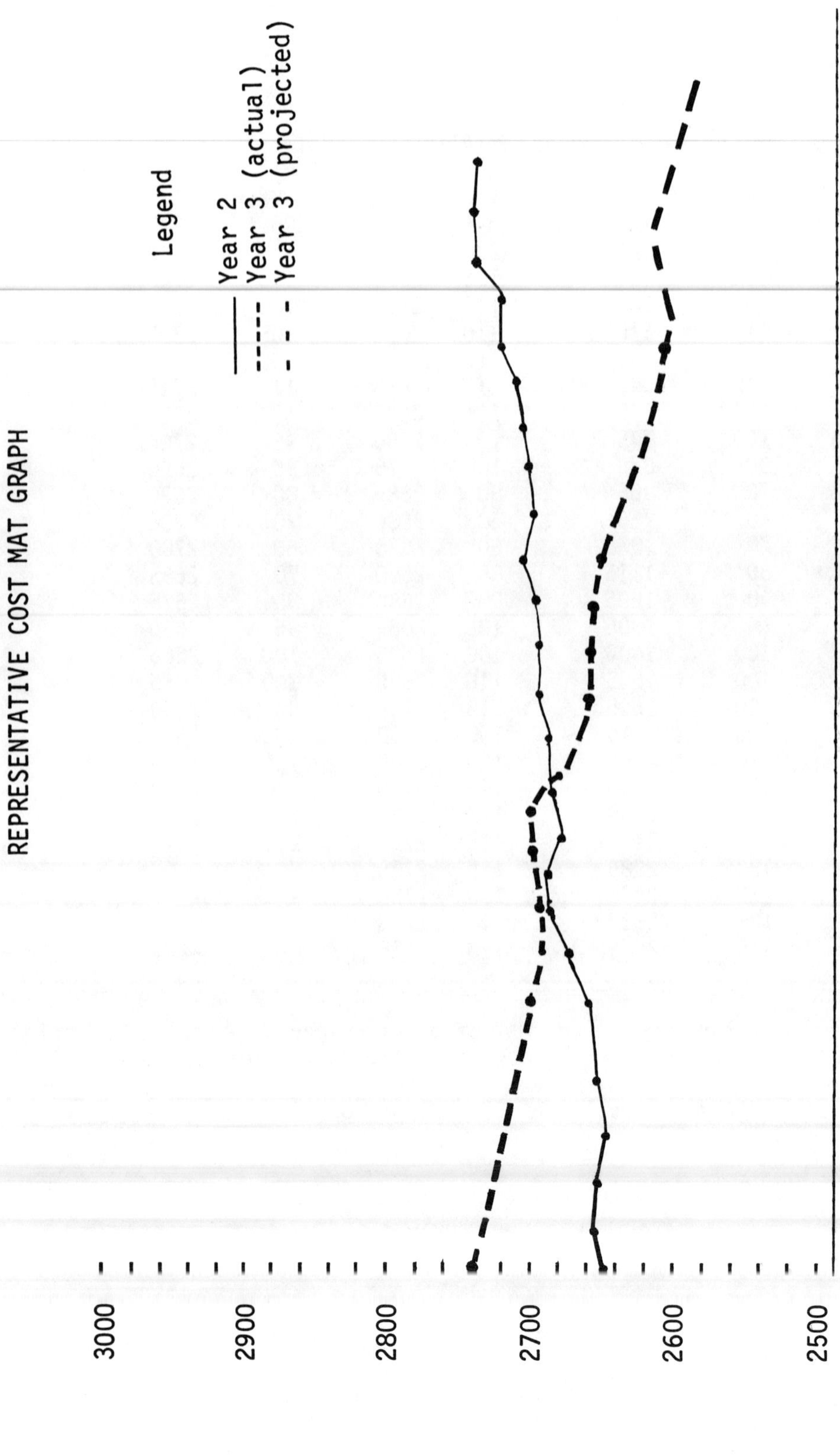

Figure 10-2. Representative Cost MAT Graph

The first year (cumulative portion) of these MATs should be identical to the cumulative cash flow graphs and need not be duplicated. However, after the first year, comparison of the performance of the actual MAT and the control MATs will provide an additional method of controlling costs during any remaining project implementation and a method for determining the trend of actual costs during the periods after implementation. Additionally, the graph of control MATs and actual MATs provides an important operational control by highlighting any significant deviations from cost expectations.

Cost/volume MAT. While the cost MAT indicates the trend of operational costs and emphasizes these deviations from cost expectations, it does not provide information about their causes. One major cause of cost deviation is a fluctuation in the volume of work that is processed. To determine whether such fluctuations are the primary causes of cost variations, a cost/volume MAT should be developed and maintained.

A cost/volume MAT is simply the moving annual total of periodic cost per unit of volume of production. To develop a cost/volume MAT:

1. Determine the primary production unit for the system (stockkeeping units moved, invoices, checks, orders entered, etc.).
2. Keep records on the quantity (volume) of these units that are processed in each period.
3. Divide each period's cash flow by its volume to develop a cost/volume indicator.
4. Develop MATs based on cost/volume indicators.
5. Graph the cost/volume indicator and the cost/volume MAT.

The cost/volume indicator depicts period-by-period changes in the cost of producing a primary unit of work, while the cost/volume MAT presents the trend of the cost.

Diagnosis. After you have determined whether there are any significant variations from cost estimates by reviewing the cost MAT, the cost/volume indicator and cost/volume MAT should be reviewed.

1. If there are significant variations on the cost MAT but none appear on the cost/volume indicator or cost/volume MAT, a substantial deviation from expected volume has occurred. Further diagnosis into the types and causes of volume variance should be conducted to determine whether the apparent trend in volume will continue.
2. If there are no significant variations in the cost MAT but the cost/volume indicator and cost/volume MAT indicate significant variations, the costs are not sensitive to variations in volume. While this may be very good, further checking should be done to ensure that the costs and volumes are accurate and that additional cost elements cannot be eliminated.
3. If the cost MAT and cost/volume MAT both increase or both decrease significantly, the problem is in the cost area. Therefore, each element of cost (salaries, equipment, etc.) must be reviewed to determine which element(s) is causing the cost variations. Then further analysis is necessary to determine why the variation is occurring in that element.

4. If the cost MAT and the cost/volume MAT vary significantly in opposite directions (increase and decrease or decrease and increase) the problem is again volume.
5. If no significant variations are observed, all is as expected. Normal effort should be expended to reduce all costs still further.

Many times, for specific companies and production areas, additional analyses will be maintained. Among the more common analyses (indicators or MATs) are:

1. Cost/Production Person
2. Cost/$ Value of Production
3. Cost/Income $ (Gross and/or Net)
4. Personnel (Salaries and Fringe) Cost/Volume
5. Equipment Cost/Volume
6. Fringe $/Salary $
7. Personnel Cost/Total Cost
8. Equipment Cost/Total Cost

Each person must determine which analyses will be maintained because they provide enough information to pay for their maintenance. Other analyses may be developed as required.

Schedule Controls

The main control over the production schedule should be the EDP scheduling area. As the group who must schedule all input, outputs and computer processing (see Chapter One) the scheduling personnel must be constantly aware of any areas that will not meet their schedules, and must adjust them to accomodate necessary variations. If variations are continuing, the scheduling area should inform the user manager, the computer operations manager, and all others responsible for reviewing and accomplishing the production function (see Chapter Two). The information should be conveyed via a memorandum and should describe the cause for the schedule variation as the effect.

Periodic (daily or weekly) production reports provide the second control on the production schedule. Designed correctly, these reports contain information about the quantities of work received, processed, and backlogged, by the type of work, priority of work, and in total, as well as the dates of the oldest work, and any pertinent remarks or observations. Figure 10-3 illustrates a typical production report.

These two basic controls can be validated and expanded by informal interviews with the managers, supervisors, and production personnel in the areas that prepare, process, and use the system data. Additional, unannounced spot checks and rough inventories of work-on-hand can also be used to ensure that the information on schedules is complete and accurate. Naturally, each interview and/or spot check should be followed with a memo to the area supervisor (or manager) and all other personnel responsible for production and review. This memo should outline the intent, findings, and recommendations and should praise all concerned whenever possible.

To: ____________________

From: __________________

__________ Department

PRODUCTION STATUS

Inventory Work

Date ____________

Type of Work	Received	Processed	Diff.	Previous Balance	New Balance	Date of Oldest Work
Priority Work: Cutoff 10/28						
Receipts	500	900	(400)	400	0	-
Shipments	1000	1800	(800)	810	10	10/26
New Vendors	40	36	4	10	14	10/25A
Changes	150	120	30	20	50	10/27
Error Corrections	100	180	(80)	100	20	10/27
TOTAL	1790	3036	(1246)	1340	94	10/25D
Normal Work:						
Receipts	1000	100	900	1000	1900	10/27
Shipments	700	500	200	1900	2100	10/27
New Vendors	40	0	40	0	40	10/27
Changes	500B	0	500	100	600	10/27
Error Corrections	20	0	20	0	20	10/24C
TOTAL	2260	600	1660	3000	4660	10/24D
Total Work						
Receipts	1500	1000	500	1400	1900	10/27
Shipments	1700	2300	600	2710	3310	10/26
New Vendors	80	36	44	10	54	10/25
Changes	650	120	530	120	650	10/27
Error Corrections	120	180	60	100	40	10/24
TOTAL	4050	3636	414	4340	4754	10/24D

REMARKS:
A. 10/25 New Vendor was received in Keypunch on 10/28
B. Changes abnormally high. Three extra Punchers begin tomorrow.
C. Single error - rejected again 10/26 - off punched. Will enter 10/29.
D. Oldest work in area.

Figure 10-3. Production Status Report

Quality Controls

The overall quality of a system is composed of its functional quality and technical quality. The functional quality of a system is monitored by determining the quantity, source, type, and severity of the errors that are produced in relation to the work that is processed correctly. The technical quality of a system is monitored by determining the ease of operation of the system, the efficient utilization of the computer, and the amount of program modification required. Each element of the system's functional and technical quality must be continually monitored so that problems in the system are identified and their causes pinpointed to the correct manual or computer portion of the system.

Functional quality. Functional quality information is usually obtained by means of error analyses or reports. A comprehensive Complaint, Error, and Reject Report is illustrated by Figure 10-4. This report provides information about the quantities, sources, types and general severity of each day's errors and also about the source, quantity, and complainants for the month's complaints. Obviously, to be effective, error analyses must be tailored for each specific system and procedures must be established for obtaining this information. The basic sources for obtaining the raw information are the control totals produced by each computer program (see Chapter Six). Secondary sources are the processing logs of the groups handling the physical inputs, outputs, errors and rejects. Primary and secondary information should be assembled and the totals balanced to ensure complete processing of all data and thorough distribution of all outputs. Specifics as to who performs these functions and how they are performed must be determined by the individual company for each specific system.

When the raw error, reject, and complaint information has been collected and the (periodic) daily analysis has been prepared, the daily totals of the most significant elements should be compared to the same totals from the analyses of preceding days. This can be done by developing moving weekly (monthly, quarterly, or yearly) totals, by graphing the daily or the developed figures, by visually comparing several reports, or by any other means that will highlight significant variations. If the method used also summarizes the information and is readily understandable, it should be used as a method of communicating the trend of the system's functional quality to higher management.

Technical quality. Other than the subjective opinions of the computer operators, the raw information pertaining to a system's technical quality is contained in the Computer Operations Log. A Computer Operations Log is usually a book wherein the computer operator indicates the

1. system identification (and any associated charge numbers)
2. program identification
3. priority
4. time the program entered into the processing queue
5. time the program began operation

To: ______________________

From: ____________________ Quality Control Supervisor Date _________

COMPLAINT, ERROR, AND REJECT REPORT

(sample) System

ERRORS AND REJECTS	Receipts	Shipments	New Vendor	Changes	Error Correct	Total
Input Total 10/28/70	900	1800	36	120	180	3036
Input Error:						
Editing	5	45 A	3	0	0	53
Coding	5	10	0	0	0	15
Keypunching	20 B	5	3	5	1	34
Miscellaneous	0	0	0	1	0	1
TOTAL INPUT ERRORS	30	60	6	6	1	103
Computer Rejects:						
C/T	20	0	0	1	0	21
Edit	0	10	6	5	0	21
Update - Input	10	50	0	0	1	61
TOTAL INPUT REJECTS	30	60	6	6	1	103
Update File	5 C	25 D	0	0	0	30
TOTAL COMPUTER REJECTS	35	85	6	6	1	133
Computer Accepts	865	1715	30	114	179	2903

OUTPUT COMPLAINTS on:	Invoices (number)	Status Report (items)	Vendor Activity (lines)	Rec.&Sched. Discreps. (lines)	Backorder Report (lines)	Stat. Control (lines)
Total Produced this mo.	56,217	42,176	10,789	8,100	1,209	1,917
Complaints By:						
Quality Control	0	0	0	0	0	0
Inventory Control	-	1,076 E	-	-	-	0
Purchasing	-	-	1	3	-	-
Sales - System Problem	16 F	0	-	-	3	-
Accounting	1	-	0	-	-	-
Receiving and Shipping	-	-	0	0	-	-
Customers - System Problem	230 F	-	-	-	-	-
TOTAL COMPLAINTS	247	1,076	1	3	3	0
Last Complaint Received	10/15	10/28	10/28	10/6	10/19	7/3

REMARKS: A-Shipping notified B-One new keypuncher caused receipt C-Item not on file D-Balance too low to ship E-Improper inventory levels-physical inventory figures used to change F-Print program error-duplicates sent 10/15-total sent 493

Figure 10-4. Complaint, Error, and Reject Report

6. time the program completed operation
7. causes and duration of any delays during processing
8. causes for any termination before completion
9. his initials (or employee number)
10. any significant remarks, production volumes, or statistics

for each program that he runs on the computer. All unused time (downtime) between programs should also be logged and coded (as to cause) in this book.

Periodically (weekly, bi-weekly, monthly, etc.) information in the Computer Operations Log is summarized and analyzed. While this can be done manually, many companies have developed their own (or have purchased) programs to produce these analyses which include Machine Utilization and Efficiency, Operator Efficiency, and Delay and Rerun reports.

The Machine Utilization and Efficiency Report lists and totals, for every system and program run during the period, the total amount of computer time spent by each computer configuration:

1. In total
2. Productively
3. Unproductive, because of:
   a. Delays caused by:
      1) Machine malfunction
      2) Operator error or absence
      3) Tape or disk error
      4) Input problems
      5) Program malfunction
      6) Other causes
   b. Reruns (by the same causes)
   c. Unknown causes.

The report also lists for each system and program:

1. Maintenance time—scheduled and unscheduled.
2. Machine efficiency, which equals the total computer time minus the maintenance time and minus the delay and rerun times caused by machine malfunctions; divided by the total (computer) time.
3. Productive efficiency which equals the productive time divided by the total time.
4. Total utilization percentage which equals each system's (and program's) total time divided by the grand total time.
5. Productive utilization percentage which equals each system's productive time divided by the total productive time.
6. Significant production (volume per productive hour) statistics.

The Operator Efficiency Report lists and totals the same types of information categorized by the operator rather than the computer configuration. The Delay and Rerun Report includes similar information about the programs involved in delays and reruns, grouped by the cause and also by the frequency of occurrence.

The information provided by the Machine Utilization and Efficiency Reports must be reviewed. Summary totals within the information should be graphed, and significant variations noted. Then the Operator Efficiency Reports should be checked to ensure that the cause of the variations is not operator-induced. Finally, the Delay and Rerun Report should be checked to determine the frequency of problems.

Based on the information provided by the review of these reports, suspect problem areas should be defined including the programs and/or system, the effect of the problem, and the probable cause (operation, inefficient utilization, or excessive modification) of the program's problems. With this knowledge, detailed investigation of the operation, procedures, computer efficiency and program modifications can be accomplished by either EDP personnel or available (manufacturer's, proprietary, or the company's) diagnostic software.

Summary

No single chapter can begin to cover all of the methods, media and procedures required to control user and EDP operations for all systems in all companies. However, those presented in this chapter illustrate what can be done to diagnose the causes of cost, schedule, and quality problems. You must determine when, where, how, by whom and to what extent these operational controls can be profitably used both during and after implementation.

MANAGING SYSTEMS MODIFICATIONS

Systems modifications are the changes made to programs and/or procedures in order to correct or improve the functioning of the system after it is in operation. These changes are necessitated by:

1. Uncorrected errors in the system itself.
2. Changes in the computer equipment or supporting software.
3. Changes in system requirements.

Because the frequency and scope of systems modifications for a particular system (usually) require a great deal less effort than did its development, fewer (and usually different) personnel are required to modify the system than were required to develop it. These personnel are organized in two operational groups:

1. The manufacturer's systems modification (MSM) group.
2. The applications systems modification (ASM) group.

The functions of these two groups are described in Chapter One but, generally, they are responsible for ensuring that the programs in all computer systems operate and function correctly and efficiently.

To fulfill this responsibility, many personnel in these groups begin by monitoring and/or reviewing the previously described controls. Based on their determination of problems within the system, the personnel in the MSM group and ASM group decide whether, how, when, and to what extent the programs will be changed and then perform the changes.

Properly managed, the MSM and ASM groups provide additional controls for the operation and are significant factors in achieving additional operational improvements and benefits. Improperly managed, these groups can negate operational controls, breed confusion, and eliminate any benefits from operational systems. The remainder of this chapter describes basic planning and control techniques for managing systems modifications.

Planning

Systems modifications are very similar to the EDP projects that we have previously discussed, but they usually require significantly less effort to achieve successful completion. Therefore, many of the controls previously discussed can be adapted to control systems modifications.

As with regular EDP projects, control of systems modifications must begin with control of the request process. To achieve this control, all requests must be channeled through a single individual (the supervisor-systems modifications) or a designated subordinate. Because problems requiring system modification are very likely to be discovered and require immediate attention during evening and nighttime computer operations, the channeling procedure can be very inconvenient for the responsible individual. However, if systems modification personnel are permitted to be contacted directly, control of request approval, personnel assignments, schedule, and costs becomes a virtual impossibility.

Requests for systems modifications caused by changes in equipment, software and system requirements are seldom difficult to channel. These requests propose systems modifications that will improve the functioning of the system and, although sometimes mandatory, rarely require immediate attention. Therefore, all of these requests can be made on Request for Modification Forms (Figure 10-5) and processed in a normal manner (see Chapter Three).

Corrections of previously undetected system errors require immediate attention when they cause the system to halt or operate incorrectly. In these instances, the requests for systems modifications are almost always initiated by computer operations. These requests should be telephoned directly to the supervisor-systems modifications and should indicate:

1. The program and system where the problem occurred.
2. The effect of the problem and, if known, the cause of the problem.
3. The results of attempts that have been made to correct the error.
4. The diagnostic information that is available.

Based on the request information, the supervisor-systems modifications can:

1. Evaluate the benefits.
2. Approximate the scope of the problem and the time required for modifying the program.

3. Assess the availability of trained personnel.
4. Determine when the system modification should be made.
5. Assign personnel to accomplish the modification and notify them of their assignment.
6. Complete the request for modification form.

If the supervisor-system modification requires assistance when evaluating benefits or approximating the scope of the problem, he will have sufficient information to know whom to contact for assistance. To logically assess the availability of personnel and assign their work, the supervisor must have an updated manpower schedule (see Chapter Nine) available at all times. If telephone numbers are included on the manpower schedule, the supervisor can contact his people at home whenever necessary.

To: Supervisor - Systems Modifications

REQUEST FOR MODIFICATION

______________ SYSTEM

Date: ______________ Time: ______________

Program(s)____

should be modified because ______________________________

____

____

____

Modification is: Mandatory Very Beneficial Beneficial

Modification Required: Immediately As Soon As Possible When Convenient

Comments:____

____

Requester Name ________________ Position ______________ Dept.________

____

Approval Date ________________ Time ____________ Initials ____________

Assignment of ________________ To Begin ______ Expected Completion ______

Figure 10-5. Request for Modification

By taking the basic steps required for project approval, the supervisor-systems modifications maintains control over the work being done, personnel assignments, and personnel availability. Naturally, because of the reduced scope of most system modification projects, formal feasibility study is rarely required prior to approval. With all approval responsibility centered on the supervisor himself, no formal project justification or request for project authorization is required. However, the logging and controls for requests described in Chapter Three can be very beneficial.

Controls

Upon being assigned a systems modification task, system modification personnel (termed R&D or maintenance programmers in many companies) must begin by estimating project scope, schedule, costs, and potential problem areas. These estimates should be conveyed to the supervisor-systems modification at the earliest opportunity. After these estimates have been agreed to by the supervisor and the staff member (see Chapter Nine—Project Initiation) the estimates are used to revise and/or update all multiproject controls.

The main difference between controlling development systems projects and controlling systems modification projects is that, in systems modifications, one person usually completes the entire project from study through conversion and installation in a one or two week period. This necessitates estimating the schedule in hours rather than days and also centralizes much more responsibility in each staff member. Because the responsibilities are centralized and because errors during systems modification can cripple and/or halt operations, the quality controls that are employed must be equivalent to or better than those employed during conversion.

The remainder of this section presents recommendations for controlling the schedule, quality, and costs of systems modification projects. For particular projects, many techniques recommended in other chapters of this book can also be successfully employed.

Schedule. The duration of system modification projects varies from less than an hour to many man weeks. The average project requires about ten man days of effort and is completed in about three weeks of elapsed time. The unexplained five man days (three weeks minus ten days effort) is devoted to making other systems modifications that have higher priority, need immediate attention, and require the staff member's special experience.

To schedule effectively, the number and duration of unanticipated systems modifications requiring immediate attention must be estimated. The soundest bases for this estimation are the machine utilization and efficiency reports and the delay and rerun analyses described in an earlier section of this chapter. They provide the raw data about reruns and delays which required system modification. By combining this information with the time and cost distribution analyses for ASM and MSM personnel provided by accounting, relatively comprehensive statistics can be obtained about the probability of occurrence and duration of unanticipated problems. These statistics, while far from perfect, provide the best possible projections or forecasts of anticipated problems.

Therefore, if it is determined that a particular system has required eight hours of attention, on the average of once a week, during the last month, it is wise to schedule the first working day of each week for modifying (for unknown causes) that system. In this manner, all other scheduled modification efforts will be ahead of schedule until the unanticipated problem occurs.

Given the statistics on unanticipated problems, scheduling of systems modifications efforts consists of the preparation and updating of manpower schedules (see Chapter Nine) for a specific period in the future. Thirteen weeks (one quarter) is usually used because it is short enough to be reasonable and long enough to be worthwhile.

Scheduling is begun by translating the manpower schedule into an overall multiproject schedule (Chapter Nine). Every requested project, and the efforts required because of unanticipated problems, will be indicated if they require more than one man hour per week (overtime is a personal responsibility and is not scheduled); and all efforts requiring more than twenty-four man hours should be segmented to provide benchmarks. The estimates for each project agreed upon by the supervisor and consultant should be used as the basis for the multiproject schedule.

After the overall multiproject schedule is completed, it is updated with information from weekly periodic reports, benchmark reports, exception reports and new (unanticipated) project information. Except for the new (unanticipated) problem information the procedures are the same as for development projects (see Chapter Five).

Because of the changeability of these schedules, their preparation and display may be simplified by using some of the available tools for short-interval scheduling and production scheduling. These tools include magnetic boards, peg boards, segmented acetate roller mechanisms and a variety of other media. These tools are commercially available and are heavily advertised in production, manufacturing, inventory, purchasing, and some management journals.

Quality. To the greatest degree possible, the production of all test data and checking of all test results should be performed by a user group (see Chapters Two and Six). In addition, each systems modification project should incorporate as many of the other quality controls (described in Chapters Two, Six and Seven) as time permits.

Every systems modification must be subjected to certain (minimum) quality controls, so that disastrous errors are averted. The following controls are recommended for all projects:

1. No project can be accepted or begun without approval of the supervisor-systems modifications.
2. No operational program deck is to be modified. A copy of the deck is to be obtained and the copy is to be modified and used for all testing.
3. No modified program disk (tape or card deck) is to be placed in operation without permission of the supervisor-systems modifications. This permission will not be given until at least one person, other than the staff member making the modification, has reviewed the modification and all test results and has informed the supervisor of his findings. Usually, this review will be conducted by another systems modification staff member but, in emergencies, a shift chief from computer operations, a quality control person, or a supervisor from the user area can conduct it.

4. When accepting a new (modified) program deck, the old deck is to be banded, identified, and sent to the supervisor-systems modifications.
5. The staff member, after modifying the program, will not begin any other project until the documentation of the modification has been completed and submitted to his immediate superior.
6. All modification documentation is to be reviewed for completeness, correctness, adherence to standards and understandability by the supervisor-systems modifications (or his delegate) within three days of completion.

Enforcement of these basic controls in all situations will greatly reduce the inadvertent errors made under stress, will ensure the quality of the continuing documentation, and will tend to impress all concerned with the grave responsibilities borne by each systems modification staff member.

Costs

Generally, like any other production area, the overall budget of the systems modification area is considered the area's primary cost control. However, if:

1. the costs for all modifications performed on request of outside areas are isolated and charged to the requesting areas,
2. the costs for all modifications required by changes to equipment and/or software are isolated and charged to computer operations,
3. the costs for all errors, undetected systems problems and overhead (training, sickness, etc.) time remain in the systems modifications areas budget;

then the systems modification budget becomes much more representative. To substantiate the reasonability of the charges to other areas, analyses similar to

1. cost/system modification project,
2. cost/man-hour (or equipment-hour),
3. $ benefit/$ cost (or payback)

may be required. As with development projects, most of the information for these analyses should be available from the company's cost distribution system.

11

Illustrating the Master Control Plan

Many people confuse control and planning; two separate, equally important, management functions. Control provides an assessment of the situation (of the project) with respect to its environment. A control plan, therefore, is an organized set of activities whereby the situation (of the project) can be assessed. Planning is the formulation of an organized set of activities whereby the assessed situation can be transformed into achievement.

A comprehensive control plan for EDP projects is an organized set of activities providing a complete assessment of the situation of the project. To be effective and efficient, each element or activity in the control plan must thoroughly assess one aspect of the situation of the project and all elements or activities must be integrated so that every aspect of the situation is assessed with a minimum of effort.

If a comprehensive control plan is not developed for each and every EDP project, discussions similar to the one that follows will occur quite frequently.

Executive VP: What's happening in EDP? A number of the managers have complained about the way the projects you're doing for them are being handled. What are the problems?

EDP Manager: I don't know who's complained or what they're complaining about. We're having some problems with certain projects but nothing out of the ordinary.

Executive VP: From what I hear, your projects are late, over cost, overstaffed, and don't provide the benefits that are needed. If that's ordinary . . .

There are four basic causes for discussions of this nature:

1. A master control plan has not been developed.
2. The master control plan is not being used.

3. The assessment of the situation (control information) is not being submitted to top management.
4. Top management does not understand the information that it receives.

This chapter illustrates the master control plan for EDP projects that has been developed segment-by-segment in the preceding chapters. It also explains how and when control information is submitted to top management, and illustrates why the information should be understood by top management.

The illustration describes how the control plan would be employed during an actual project. The project whose control is described is the sample project. The description of the control plan begins with the request for a new project and proceeds step-by-step through the operation of the system. To assist in this description, throughout this book, the most important figures have been prepared so that their contents illustrate exactly how the forms and schedules would have been completed for the sample project.

PROJECT ORIGINATION AND STUDY

Toward the end of June 19 , J. Jefferies, a warehouse supervisor for the *EZT* Time Company, became irritated by the amount of overtime work required during the semi-annual physical inventory. Most of the overtime was spent re-checking the inventories of items whose physical counts disagreed significantly from the records that were being kept on cards.

Request

Noticing the set of project request forms attached to the warehouse bulletin board, Mr. Jefferies decided that he might vent his anger by completing and submitting one of the forms. After looking at the form, he felt that he could easily complete it correctly. He, therefore, removed one of the forms and took it back to his desk, completed the information and sent it to the EDP manager. Feeling much better, Mr. Jefferies returned to work and promptly forgot the form entirely.

Preliminary Review

The next day, the form was given to the EDP manager's secretary with the other (daily) mail. The secretary then logged the request, noted the receipt date on the form, and placed the form in the EDP manager's incoming mail.

The EDP manager, upon reading his mail that afternoon, found and preliminarily reviewed the request. Deciding that sufficient information was present to warrant further study, the EDP manager returned the form to his secretary and told her to issue a preliminary review memorandum and named the project "sample inventory project" or "sample" for short.

The next morning, after finding the form in her typing, the secretary typed the preliminary review memorandum, logged the date of submission, noted the manager's calendar for a 7/10/ follow-up, had the manager sign the preliminary review, and put it in the mail. One carbon copy of the preliminary review was then sent to the development manager and the other copy was placed in the EDP manager's incoming mail.

Initial Survey

Reminded by their copies of the preliminary review form, the EDP manager and development manager discussed the initial study at the end of an afternoon meeting on an ongoing project. P. Williams, an analyst and project leader, was immediately available and was selected to conduct the initial study. The EDP manager and development manager also set 10:30 the next morning for a meeting between the EDP manager and the analyst.

The next day, prior to the morning's meeting, the development manager advised the analyst of his assignment, the general concept of the study, and the time and place of his appointment. Meanwhile, the EDP manager had the preliminary review form copied and sent to the analyst, planned the survey, and estimated the completion date.

At the 10:30 meeting, the EDP manager outlined his concepts of the initial study, assessed the analyst's abilities, discussed the study, and obtained agreement on the completion date. P. Williams, elated by the opportunity to work directly for the EDP manager again, and not fully aware of the problems he would encounter, readily agreed to a completion date of 7/7/ and departed to begin the study.

During this same morning, J. Jefferies, while reading the mail that had come in the previous afternoon, found and read the preliminary review memorandum. Astounded at receiving an answer from anyone, and especially the EDP manager, Mr. Jefferies decided to let the phone call wait for a day or so until he could gather his wits. Not five minutes later, he received a call from the EDP manager and learned of the EDP manager's appreciation for the request. Able to add little to the request information, Mr. Jefferies learned that he would soon be contacted by Mr. Williams for the purposes of the initial study. Mr. Jefferies then suggested that his superior, Mr. Fowler, also be contacted. As this was already planned, the EDP manager, relieved of the problem of convincing Mr. Jefferies of the soundness of this idea, thanked him profusely and politely ended the conversation.

Shortly after this conversation, Mr. Jefferies was contacted by Mr. Williams, a meeting was arranged, and the initial survey was begun. During the initial survey, Mr. Williams interviewed personnel from Purchasing and Sales in addition to Mr. Jefferies and Mr. Fowler. Mr. Williams also spent three days studying the present inventory files and procedures. Based on the information gathered, Mr. Williams determined whether and how the proposed system might be implemented, what the benefits and costs might be, and completed the initial survey report. The report was typed on 7/9/ , copied and distributed to Mr. Williams, Mr. Jefferies, the EDP manager, and the development manager.

The EDP manager's secretary received the EDP manager's copy of the initial survey report in the regular 7/10/ mail, noted completion of the survey in the log, and placed the initial survey report in the EDP manager's incoming mail.

Upon reading the report, the EDP manager determined that, at worst, the project would save $50,000 per year, would cost $115,000 and would pay back its cost in about three years. Then, after checking the projects pending notebook and the manpower schedule, the EDP manager determined that the project was worthy of further study because, if the estimates in the initial study proved correct, the sample project would probably rank high enough to be implemented during the next year. The EDP manager then telephoned the development manager, the analyst and Mr. Jefferies and arranged a meeting for 2:00 on 7/12/ . During the telephone conversation, the EDP manager indicated that the topic of the meeting would be the initial study report and implied that the results looked very interesting. However, only the development manager was informed of his tentative decision to continue with a feasibility study.

Prior to the meeting, the EDP manager and development manager decided who would conduct the feasibility study and when it would start. Because P. Williams would be able to begin the study within a month, he was named study manager and the study was scheduled to begin on 8/15/ . The EDP manager and development manager also discussed the scope of the project and agreed that it should be completed by Mr. Williams, with the help of Mrs. L. Light, another analyst, by 9/15/ .

During the meeting on 7/12/ , Mr. Jefferies was thanked for submitting his idea and congratulated on its merit. A discussion of the initial study report did not add any new information. The analyst, Mr. Williams, was then congratulated on his thoroughness and informed that he had been selected to begin the feasibility study. The starting date, scope, conduct, and Mrs. Light's assistance were then discussed. Mr. Williams was asked to estimate the completion date of the feasibility study by the next morning.

The next morning, Mr. Williams presented detailed schedule for the feasibility study to the development manager. The completion date for the study was 10/7/ . After thorough review, a number of activities that had been included in the development of the conceptual design were determined to be unnecessary for project justification and were eliminated (to be done during the detail design function of the actual project). Elimination of these times and re-scheduling established the new completion date as 9/19/ . This date was then agreed to during a telephone conversation between the development manager and the EDP manager. Mr. Williams was instructed to report any problems that might delay the start of the study, and the initial study was concluded.

Feasibility Study

Between the end of the initial study on 7/13/ and the beginning of the feasibility study on 8/15/ , the EDP manager and the development manager, during the normal course of business, informally contacted as many top management personnel and managers of user areas as possible. Before, during or after normal discussions of other matters, the concept of the new project was introduced, attitudes toward the project were determined, negative attitudes were changed or lessened, and all were informed that a feasibility study would start in the near future. Usually, because they had specific knowledge of the proposed benefits, source of request, and costs, the EDP manager and development manager encountered little trouble in creating interest in the project. Whenever possible, by using tact and diplomacy, they also created an impression that the idea for further study came from the person(s) to whom they were speaking. By the time the study began, almost all important managers would have enthusiastically supported the study, if asked.

On 8/8/ the development manager met P. Williams in the hall and determined that Mr. Williams would complete the project he was working on by 8/14/ . Upon receiving this assurance, the development manager requested that Mr. Williams begin the feasibility study by meeting with the EDP manager and him at 9:00 on 8/15/ . He also indicated that, during this meeting, Mr. Williams would be asked to detail his interviewing schedule and data collection activities. Mr. Williams agreed to have this information ready.

Conceptual design. On 8/15/ , the feasibility study began. Mr. Williams met with the EDP manager and the development manager and described his immediate schedule in detail and overall schedule in general. The EDP manager and development manager agreed with Mr. Williams' planning and provided Mr. Williams with a synopsis of their knowledge about each proposed interviewee. This knowledge was gleaned from their memories and from various contact results forms that they had completed on these people from past contacts. Thus, forewarned to some degree, Mr. Williams began the feasibility study. Because of Mr. Williams' extensive experience in conducting feasibility studies for the EDP manager and development manager, the usual explanation of project responsibilities, reporting, and the need for tact and diplomacy was reduced to reminders of Mr. Williams' specific problems in these areas.

Two days later, on Friday 8/17/ , Mr. Williams submitted the first periodic report on the conduct of the feasibility study and, as a courtesy, included copies of the interviewee reports for the five people whom he had interviewed. The project was on schedule and no significant problems had been encountered. The interviewee reports provided little new information but were included in the development manager's contact file.

During the following week, the development manager informally contacted Mr. Williams four times, received the first benchmark report (8/22/) and the next (8/24/) periodic report. No problems were reported, but Mr. Williams had not been able to arrange an interview with the purchasing manager as he had expected. In fact, it appeared that the purchasing manager might be avoiding Mr. Williams as he had not answered any of the eight messages left for him.

On Tuesday (8/28/), the development manager, via an informal meeting, determined that the project was still going well but that the purchasing manager was still unavailable. The development manager, who was not acquainted with the purchasing manager, said nothing to Mr. Williams but called and informed the EDP manager of the situation. The EDP manager, who knew the purchasing manager from several previous meetings, happened to drop in and say hello to the purchasing manager that afternoon. During their discussion, the importance of the project, its intent and the potential benefits to Purchasing were mentioned. Mr. Williams was also mentioned by name but his inability to arrange a meeting was not mentioned. Later that day

Mr. Williams called the development manager to report that a meeting had been arranged with the purchasing manager. This was noted by the development manager and the information was passed along to the EDP manager. This situation illustrates an excellent use of the informal interview for conveying political information that should not be included in the project file.

As the study progressed, other benchmarks were achieved on or ahead of schedule:

8/30/	Initial interviews complete
9/4/	Inputs defined
9/7/	Outputs defined
9/10/	Master file defined
9/11/	Functional and technical flow charts complete (Figures 3-4, 3-5)
9/14/	Follow-up interviews complete
9/14/	Conceptual design complete

However, because Mrs. Light was not available until 9/17 (although promised for 9/12/ , the analysis portion of the study was not begun on time.

Analysis. On 9/12/ , when he was informed of Mrs. Light's inability to join the project until 9/17/ , Mr. Williams determined that no other person could be made available and replanned the remainder of the project. By working evenings and during the weekend (9/15 and 9/16), Mr. Williams planned to complete the study on schedule.

Mr. Williams submitted an exception report on 9/13/ and held discussions with the EDP manager and the development manager wherein he described the problem and his solution. From 9/12/ on, the original schedule was missed but the 9/13/ schedule was met with no significant delays. However, the completion of the project justification (report) in draft form took three days rather than one day. It, therefore, was not ready until 9/21/ . Writing, editing, and typing were the main problems.

During the period 9/13 to 9/19, all analyses were complete as follows:

9/14	Estimate of computer operations
9/15	Project standards - general
9/15	Input/output matrix
9/15	Estimate of development
9/16	Project schedule and modified CPM
9/16	Production schedule
9/17	Development cost estimate and detailed development cost estimate
9/17	Personnel requirements listing - development, and personnel requirements listing - operations
9/18	Cash flow analysis and payback analysis

As each analysis was completed, it was copied and sent to the development manager and the EDP manager. They, in turn, initiated the formation of the user group and the technical review team (Chapter Nine) and copied and submitted all analyses and the conceptual design to these groups.

Project justification. From 9/15 through 9/20, the study manager, Mr. Williams, answered all major questions from the user group and the technical review team. On 9/21 Mr. Williams held meetings with the user group, the technical review team, the EDP manager, and the development manager. At these meetings, the (draft) project justification was reviewed and minor discrepancies were changed. During these meetings, Mr. Williams publicly thanked each and every participant for the work he had done and the promptness with which they all had completed their work. As no problems existed at the end of these meetings, the corrected draft of the project justification was given to the EDP manager. He, upon returning to the office, obtained the latest EDP Projects - Point Assignment Table and, based upon the analyses in the project justification, completed the Weighted Point Evaluation, rewrote the "Section I - Summary" and "Section II - Recommendations," reviewed the remainder of the project justification, and had it sent out for typing and copying.

On 9/27 the copies were received by the EDP manager's secretary. She immediately distributed them to the development manager, the user group, the technical review team, the study manager (Mr. Williams), and the user manager (Mr. Fowler). She also informed those concerned that the user review meeting would be held on 10/5 at 9:00 and the technical review meeting would be held on 10/5 at 1:30.

On 10/3, Mr. Sams, the representative from Purchasing, called the study manager and requested the inclusion of additional data in the vendor file and two additional vendor analysis reports. Mr. Williams reviewed the changes necessary, called on other user group and technical review team personnel and asked their opinion about the impact of the change. By noon on 10/4, it was determined that the changes requested by Mr. Sams would be minimal and could be included without further study. Again, Mr. Williams contacted all reviewers and asked them to make the necessary corrections (which he spelled out in detail).

On 10/5, the review meetings were held. Apart from typographical and editorial changes, the project justification was agreed upon by all reviewers. At these meetings, when agreement was reached, the directors of the user group (development manager and user manager) and of the technical review team (development manager and operations manager) submitted their written approvals of the conceptual design and project justification. The EDP manager and the directors all conveyed to the members of the groups their appreciation for the work done and the speed of accomplishment. Outstanding performers were praised and the benefits of the project were emphasized.

On 10/8, while passing by Mr. Williams' office area, the EDP manager and development manager stopped and publicly complimented Mr. Williams and Mrs. Light for the accomplishment of the study. Mr. Williams was especially praised for his efforts which brought the project back on schedule and was asked to thoroughly review the study.

Request for Project Authorization

The EDP manager reviewed a draft of the Request for Project Authorization and asked Mr. Williams if he would like the responsibility for implementing the project and achieving the indicated goals if the project were to be approved. When Mr. Williams answered affirmatively, he was reminded that errors in estimates of the same magnitude as the error in estimating the time to prepare the draft of the project justification would cause serious schedule and cost problems in the implementation, and was asked again if he would still like the responsibility. Mr. Williams indicated that he had learned from the estimation error and that if the projected personnel had been available when expected, he might well have had the additional time required to meet the schedule, even with the error in the estimate. Mr. Williams again expressed confidence in all estimates and a willingness to assume project management responsibilities. The EDP manager and development manager said that, if at all possible, they would try to ensure that Mr. Williams would be assigned as project manager because of the exemplary manner in which he had conducted the feasibility study. They also told Mr. Williams that he would be informed of top management's decision as soon as it was made, and then ended the meeting.

The EDP manager and the development manager then discussed the "Project Justification" and the meetings with the review groups and Mr. Williams. Based on its information and the confidence of Mr. Williams and the review groups in that information, the EDP manager and development manager agreed to submit the Request for Project Authorization without any further checking or review. The "Project Justification," with corrections from the review meetings, and the Request for Project Authorization were given to the EDP manager's secretary for correction, copying, proofreading, and distribution.

On 10/12, the Request for Project Authorization and Project Justification were distributed to top management, the user group, the technical review team, the user manager, the EDP manager, the development manager, the requester (Mr. Jefferies), and the study manager (Mr. Williams).

Authorization

During October 19 , the EDP manager answered a variety of questions from top management personnel. He also presented the request to the Planning Committee on 10/22. On 11/8, approval for the sample project was verbally given by the financial vice president (Mr. J. J. Jones) and the copy of the Request for Authorization with his concurrence was received on 11/9/ .

PROJECT IMPLEMENTATION

The period from 11/9/ , when the sample project was authorized, until 6/1/ when project implementation began was not wasted. During this period the EDP manager, the development manager and the project manager (Mr. Williams) spent their spare time in the user areas. The EDP manager and the development manager discussed the project with managerial and supervisory personnel, building the user's interest and involvement in the project. Mr. Williams also participated in these activities but his main efforts were directed toward collecting more data from the user department personnel and toward developing more detailed plans.

The conceptual design and analyses in the project justification provided a good basis for planning controls. Starting with the detailed development cost estimate, Mr. Williams developed the total development cost summary and cumulative graph. From the cash flow analysis, he developed a cost variance report for each period (minus the actuals) and the project progress report. From the project schedule and the conceptual design, Mr. Williams developed detailed computer time requirements. However, the greatest portion of Mr. Williams' spare time was spent determining, defining, and describing each staff member's specific responsibilities and the detailed standards for the project.

On 10/12/ , Project ABCD was being implemented, implementation of Project EFGH had just begun and Project IJKL was proposed as the next project (see the multi-project progress report). At that time, it was expected that the sample project would begin when analysts were free from EFGH and IJKL (about January 15, 19). However, the MNOP project was requested in October and, because it would produce a great deal ($100,000 per month gross, $70,000 per month net) of revenue by performing a function that could not be performed manually, it was requested and authorized to be implemented first. This delayed the start of the sample project until 6/1/ .

On 5/10/ , Mr. Williams was notified by the development manager that the required systems personnel would become available beginning with B. Brown on 6/1/ . Mr. Brown was to be followed by J. Jones on 6/3, W. Walsh on 6/10, D. Dawn on 7/15, and L. Lane on 7/29. Manual systems analysts were to be available as follows: C. Clark 6/21 and W. Wall 6/28.

Initiation

On 5/24/ , Mr. Williams contacted Mr. B. Brown to arrange a meeting, prior to 6/1/ , for his initiation to the project. At that time, Mr. Brown informed Mr. Williams that he would not be available until 6/10 because of a problem in finishing his current assignment. Mr. Williams thanked him for the information and contacted J. Jones and W. Walsh. Mr. Jones would be ready on 6/3/ and Miss Walsh would be available on 6/10. Mr. Williams then set appointments for 5/30 and 6/7.

Mr. Williams then assigned SA 4 to himself, SA 3 to Mr. Jones, SA 5 to Miss Walsh and SA 1 (the least critical) to Mr. Brown whose availability was still in doubt. Based on these assignments, Mr. Williams prepared for the project initiation meetings (Chapter Nine). The meeting with Mr. Jones was conducted on 5/30 and went very well. On 6/3, Mr. Jones submitted his schedule and costs to Mr. Williams. Except for minor discrepancies Mr. Jones' schedule was almost exactly the same as Mr. Williams. The discrepancies were discussed and a final schedule was agreed upon.

Miss Walsh's project initiation was conducted on 6/7 but proved to be somewhat more difficult. Because the total responsibilities were not made clear, Miss Walsh's first schedule and costs were 30 per cent too low when she submitted them on 6/10. During the meeting on 6/10, Miss Walsh and Mr. Williams found that Miss Walsh had not fully understood that the conceptual design of the print program (SA 5) was not complete. This misunderstanding and a very low estimation of the programming effort had caused the 30 per cent understatement. By 6/11, Miss Walsh had produced a schedule and costs that were agreeable to Mr. Williams.

Mr. Brown became available on 6/12. His project initiation, conducted on 6/11, was the most difficult. Mr. Williams asked Mr. Brown to prepare a schedule that would, if possible, complete programs SA 1 and SA 2 by 8/30. Mr. Brown contended that this couldn't be done and that he was being asked to make up the delay caused by his unavailability. This was true. Mr. Williams then requested Mr. Brown to schedule and cost the effort without regard for the end date. On 6/12, Mr. Brown's schedule indicated completion on 10/2. Review of this schedule indicated proportional overestimation of every category. Mr. Williams then concentrated on the review of the two factors he knew best. Long discussion centering on these points finally resulted in Mr. Brown's declaration, "O.K. There is about 30 per cent fudge in my schedule. I just got chewed out for missing a completion date on my last project. I'm not going to do it again." Mr. Williams then indicated that, if the fudge were removed, an 8/30 completion date might be possible and that this would remove Mr. Brown's work from the critical path, therefore reducing the pressure on him. On 6/13 Mr. Brown and Mr. Williams agreed to a new schedule with a completion date of 8/30/ .

Implementation Through 7/26/

On 6/7, the first periodic reports were submitted by Mr. Williams and Mr. Jones. Mr. Williams, because of his work prior to 6/1, was well ahead of schedule and had completed three benchmarks: 5/28 CD of Input, 5/30 CD of Output, and 6/6 CD of Master File. Mr. Jones, because of an early start, was also ahead of schedule and had completed one benchmark: DC input. No cost information was available and the quality of the conceptual design still looked fine.

On 6/12, Miss Walsh submitted an exception report indicating that the conceptual design specifications did not meet standards but that she would correct the situation during detailed design.

On 6/14, the periodic, benchmark, and exception reports indicated: SA 3 and SA 4 ahead of schedule, SA 5 on schedule but with slight quality problems, SA 1 behind schedule but would catch up, SA 2 not scheduled to start.

On 6/17, the cost analyses from Accounting indicated an overrun of $400 or about 25%. This was attributed to charges for the early work done by Mr. Williams and Mr. Jones, but required watching. On 6/18 Mr. Williams submitted his first project progress summary.

By 6/21, periodic and benchmark reports indicated that SA 3 and SA 4 were ahead of schedule, SA 5 was on schedule but that quality problems still existed, and SA 1 was almost back on schedule. However, as all conceptual design was completed, a functional review was held on 6/21. This review uncovered a serious design discrepancy between SA 4 and SA 5. A general solution was proposed that would only affect Mr. Williams' tasks. Mr. Williams decided to implement this solution and expected to remedy the problem by 7/15.

The project initiation for Mr. Clark (manual systems analyst) was begun on 6/20. However, due to the functional review on 6/21, Mr. Clark's schedule and costs were not reviewed until 6/24. Mr. Clark's schedule and costs for manual analysis generally conformed with Mr. Williams' and were agreed upon.

Between 6/21 and 6/28, Mr. Brown caught up with schedule on SA 1, Mr. Williams and Mr. Jones stayed ahead of schedule on SA 4 and SA 3 and Miss Walsh maintained schedule on SA 5 while bringing the conceptual design specifications up to standard. Therefore, except for the serious design problem being worked on by Mr. Williams, as of 6/28, all areas were on (or ahead of) schedule with good quality.

On 7/2 the cost analyses (through 6/28) from Accounting indicated an additional \$400 cost overrun. This 25% variation could not be simply explained. Mr. Williams contacted Accounting and beginning with the cost variance report and with Accounting's aid reviewed the cost allocations. This review uncovered the fact that overtime costs were being charged to the project even when the people accumulating the overtime were salaried. This error in the program was corrected and a \$300 manual adjustment was entered for the next cost distribution. Additional costs were found to be caused by higher salaries than anticipated and a 2% higher fringe factor. The fringe had been caused by the initiation of a new (and 5% higher) hospitalization package on 4/1. Having discerned that the costs could only be eliminated by increasing production, Mr. Williams began to devote himself to that end.

Mrs. W. Wall was not available to begin until 7/1. Her project initiation was conducted by Mr. Clark with Mr. Williams in attendance. Mrs. Wall had never estimated a task. Therefore, Mr. Clark worked with her until, on 7/4, agreeable schedules and costs were obtained.

By 7/12, all programs were on or ahead of schedule and (by 7/7) Mr. Williams had cleared up the design problem. The user review and top management review of the conceptual design were held on 7/3 and 7/9 respectively. No additional discrepancies were found during these reviews. On 7/15 the cost analyses reflected the \$300 correction and the project appeared to be in excellent shape. However, the addition of Miss Dawn on 7/15 was delayed because Miss Dawn was ill, and informal contacts by Mr. Williams (with Mr. Clark) indicated that the study portion of the manual analysis was going slower than expected because of vacations in the user area.

On 7/16, Miss Dawn was confined to the hospital with pneumonia. No other programmer would be available until Mr. Lane finished his project (7/29). SA 4 began to fall seriously behind schedule. In addition, when reviewing the SA 1 documentation, Mr. Williams determined that Mr. Brown would have to redo most of the detail design documentation because it was so cryptic that it could not be easily understood. Mr. Brown agreed to improve the documentation without affecting his schedule.

On 7/18, a functional review of the study (manual systems) was delayed because the study was not complete. Vacations in the user area continued to be the problem. As all critical vacations would be finished by 8/2, an additional manual systems analyst (P. Pram) was requisitioned and obtained to begin on that date. This, it was felt, would bring manual systems back on schedule. All possible writing was begun while waiting for the completion of study.

As of 7/26, (see Figure 8-3), the outstanding problems were: the lack of a programmer on SA 4, the delay in completing the study caused by vacations, and the improper documentation of SA 1. Miss Dawn was scheduled (per her doctor and herself) to return on 7/29. She would be assigned SA 2. Mr. Lane, who had completed his project initiation with Mr. Williams, would undertake to bring SA 4 back on schedule. The addition of a manual systems analyst on 8/2 and Mr. Brown's efforts in redoing SA 1 documentation were expected to bring the project back to schedule with no problems by 8/16.

Implementation 7/26/71–10/2/71

After 7/26, Mr. Williams, the project manager, continued to control the project by reviewing periodic reports, benchmark reports, exception reports, project documentation and cost analyses. These reviews were supported by his informal contacts and meetings and his reports to top management continued.

The project manager's controls detected a variety of potential problems early enough to eliminate the source of the problem as they had prior to 7/26.

About 7/26, Mr. Williams began to receive support from the operations group and the user group (see Chapter Nine). These groups were formed and began to thoroughly review each segment of the detail design as it was completed. The formation and initiation of these groups were conducted by the development manager and the EDP manager working in close cooperation with the operations manager and the user manager. While the operations group was only concerned with reviewing the detail design, the user group also worked with Mr. Williams to develop a plan and schedule for developing the test data required to thoroughly test the system and with Mr. Clark to study new procedures.

By 8/2 all detail design had been completed and the programming of SA 1, SA 3 and SA 5 was on or ahead of schedule. Costs had been no problem and were within \$500 of estimate (1% of cost 0.4% of cash flow). All design problems were solved and the manual systems study was completed 8/9.

The functional reviews, user reviews and top management review of the detail design took place on 8/15 (ahead of schedule) and no serious errors were detected. The user review of the study results (manual systems) took place on 8/18 and was also without problems. On 8/9, only the manual systems portion of the project was behind schedule and, because of the additional analyst, would be on schedule by 8/23.

By 8/23, everything was on schedule, on cost and of excellent quality, except for the documentation of SA 1 which Mr. Brown would have to redo for clarity. Mr. Brown agreed to redo the documentation when he finished SA 2.

By 9/4, everything was on schedule: Programs SA 1, SA 2, and SA 3 were completed and programmer and linkage tested; SA 5 was being desk checked; the coding of SA 4 was within three days of completion; and all manual procedures were written and being tested. All documentation was up to date and indicated adherence to specifications and conformance to standards. Mr. Brown and Mr. Jones had completed their responsibilities and were working on other projects. Mr. Williams had completed an appraisal of activity (performance reviews) for each of them and had scheduled meetings (on 9/11) with them to review his appraisals on 9/11. Mr. Brown and Miss

Lane were completing the coding of SA 4 and Mr. Williams was checking their work. Miss Walsh was desk checking SA 5 and Mr. Clark, Mrs. Wall and Mrs. Pram were training user personnel. The user group had completed all test data and had reviewed and approved the results of the linkage test of SA 1, SA 2, and SA 3. Costs were well within control. Everything looked excellent.

On 9/8, Mr. Sams, the representative from Purchasing to the user group, requested that four new reports be produced from the system. Unfortunately, Mr. Sams made the request of Miss Walsh directly. As she was already testing her program, Miss Walsh, somewhat tactlessly, asked Mr. Sams if he had lost *all* his marbles and would only laugh at further questions from Mr. Sams. Within a half hour, Mr. Sams' request was being discussed by him, the purchasing manager, the EDP manager, and the project manager.

After apologizing to Mr. Sams for Miss Walsh's lack of tact and explaining the pressures under which she was working, the EDP manager requested that Mr. Sams again explain his requests. Mr. Sams, somewhat mollified, repeated his request. The purchasing manager described the benefits these reports would provide. Mr. Williams, who had been forewarned and had reviewed the general requests, indicated that he could understand the benefits but, if the request were implemented immediately, the project would be delayed at least four weeks. Mr. Williams also pointed out that, at a later date, the request could be complied with without using much more effort because the files contained the correct information. The EDP manager then asked the purchasing manager if he thought that the immediate implementation of the reports was worth delaying a project that would save $270,000 per year. The purchasing manager admitted that he couldn't justify the delay but wanted to know when he would get the reports. The EDP manager indicated that, at that time, he did not know the exact date but it would be after November 16 and probably before May 1, 1972. The EDP manager also agreed to try to determine the date more exactly by checking the application system modification (ASM) staffing and plans. This meeting is a classic example of the use of cost and schedule controls to eliminate (or delay) changes in the scope of a project during implementation.

On 9/15, testing of SA 4 indicated that new vendor records were not being correctly produced. The error was traced to coding on 9/17 but, as of 9/18, the coding error had not been found. Mr. Williams, Miss Dawn and Mr. Lane worked during the weekend (9/19/20) and found the coding error in Mr. Lane's vendor routines. Mr. Lane corrected his coding and, by 9/21, the problem was eliminated.

All other problems were minor, and by 10/2 all program and linkage testing was satisfactorily completed and systems testing had been begun. Costs were $2,000 over estimate because of extra test time usage by Miss Walsh and the SA 4 group. Quality was very fine. The user group was checking final linkage test results and preparing to check system test results. The operations group had checked all operations times and documentation and was prepared to use the systems test as a dress rehearsal of actual operations. Training of user personnel was complete, the user manager had assumed responsibility, and conditioning was being accomplished during system test and conversion. Everything looked very good.

Implementation 10/2/ —10/30/

On Sunday 10/4/ , during the second complete pass of the system, the system stopped operation. Error messages indicated interface problems between the manufacturer's software and the systems software. As these errors had not occurred previously, all programmers who had made changes were called to check whether their changes should have caused the errors. Thorough review by the programmers who could be contacted that Sunday afternoon indicated no changes that would cause the error. Miss Dawn and Mr. Brown could not be contacted.

Mr. Williams contacted the development manager and requested permission to check with the supervisor of the manufacturer's system modifications. Permission was granted and the contact was made at 6:00 P.M. on 10/4. No manufacturer system modifications were to have been made during the weekend. The system programs were again reviewed.

At 8:00 P.M., Mr. Williams contacted the computer operations shift chief to try and get computer time for another test. The shift chief indicated that time was not available because a number of jobs were being re-run. Mr. Williams again contacted the development manager and requested that he contact the shift chief to increase the priority of the sample project testing and obtain computer time that evening.

While talking to the shift chief, the development manager learned that nothing had been processed correctly since the end of the night shift on Saturday (8:00 Sunday). Then, by checking the operations log, the shift chief learned that an MSM test was the last successful run and that it had completed at 8:07 Sunday morning. Subsequent checking with the programmer of the MSM run indicated that special instructions existed for run completion. If the procedures were not followed, the equipment would operate under control of the MSM programs being tested and not the normal MSM system. The procedures had not been followed because of the change in shifts.

The procedures were then followed at 8:45 P.M. on Sunday. As a favor for finding the problem, the sample project testing was used to check the system. Everything performed well.

By 10/15, all testing was complete. Conversion of the files took place on the evening of 10/31 to obtain a month-end cutover. Conversions went perfectly as had been predicted by the results of a 100% pilot run on 10/24. On 11/1, the sample system began operation.

Final assessment of implementation: quality excellent, schedule met, costs overrun by $1500 or 2.2%. Very fine performance overall.

OPERATION

During the first two weeks of November, Mr. Williams remained on the sample project. During this time he evaluated and completed an appraisal of activity for each staff member, discussed these appraisals with the staff members, checked the user and operations areas for problems and to determine the efficiency of the system, checked on the reduction of personnel necessary to achieve the benefits and completed turnover of all system documentation to the supervisor of the application systems modification area.

Since only minor problems had occurred which had been handled by user and operations personnel, Mr. Williams made sure that he would get copies of the various operations controls (cost, schedule and quality—see Chapter Ten) that he, the user manager, and the operations manager considered to be necessary to control the project. Receiving this assurance; Mr. Williams spent an additional day visiting and publicly congratulating and thanking every person who had worked on the project staff, user group, operations group, technical review team or in any other capacity. On 11/18/ , Mr. Williams began another study.

During the weeks that followed, the development manager, the user manager, and the EDP manager informally contacted, thanked and congratulated all personnel who had worked on the project. As time passed, they also told all concerned how benefits were actually being achieved.

On December 6, 19 , all participants in the project and wives, husbands, or dates were invited to a party celebrating the project's success on 12/13/ . Mr. J. Jones, financial vice president, issued the invitations. At the party he indicated that this was a token of appreciation for the effort expended and congratulated all concerned, especially the requester, user manager, EDP manager, development manager, and project manager. Mr. Jones also indicated that, based on one month's operation, the system would provide all expected benefits. However, he noted, the same diligent effort would be needed during operation as was given during implementation. (While a party may not be necessary, a similar meeting charted by top management provides incentive for the future.)

Until February 19 , the EDP manager, development manager, and project manager received copies of operational control reports. By February, it was apparent that the project had reduced costs sufficiently and was meeting all schedule and quality commitments. Therefore, by agreement, the copies for these managers were discontinued and the user manager assumed full responsibility for future operations.

SUMMARY

This edited version of the chronological utilization of project controls describes the control of the hypothetical sample project from origination through operation. Of necessity many of the minor problems have been eliminated. However, this description should be sufficient to illustrate and amplify the manner in which the individual controls, described in previous chapters, are developed and used to provide a master control plan.

12

Implementing the Master Control Plan

Before all the benefits that can be derived from the utilization of the master control plan can be achieved, the entire control plan must be implemented. Until this is done, uncontrolled elements in the project can cause significant, irreversible problems for all concerned before they are detected. If not controlled from the outset, time cannot be regained, money cannot be spent elsewhere, and poor quality can negate the benefits expected from the project.

If the control plan is implemented incorrectly, control of a project will be very much like trying to flatten a water-filled balloon with your hands. As you press it down and bring it into control in one area, it bulges out of control in another. The following discussion could well have been caused by an improperly implemented control plan.

Executive VP: Well, now that the order entry debacle has been concluded, how do you expect to eliminate similar tragedies in the future?

EDP manager: I'm glad you asked that question. During the order entry project, we found that, quite often, a few necessary project controls were not effective or missing entirely. Order entry showed us our weaknesses. Now we'll be able to control our projects in a better fashion.

Executive VP: I certainly hope so.

EDP manager: I'm sure of it. Now we can simply use all the order entry controls on our other projects.

If you have attempted to use one project's controls on another project, you will realize the futility of the EDP manager's suggestion. Unfortunately, this EDP manager does not understand the exact composition of an overall control plan, how to implement a new control plan or the difficulty (and time required) to implement a control plan.

To assist in the implementation of the master control plan, this chapter describes the structure of the control plan and a method of modular implementation for the plan.

The structure of the control plan includes:

1. The two main partitions of the structure.
2. The elements that comprise each partition.
3. The levels within each partition.
4. The relationships among the elements and levels.

The method of modular implementation describes:

1. The implementation of the critical elements in the control plan structure.
2. How to maintain control when only the critical elements have been implemented.
3. The most efficient sequence for implementing the remaining elements.

These descriptions provide a logical basis for successful implementation of the master control plan in any company. Naturally, this information must be amplified by a knowledge of the company and its specific requirements before final implementation plans are developed.

CONTROL PLAN STRUCTURE

An understanding of the structure or underlying logic of the control plan is required before the method for implementing the plan can be described. Until the structure of the control plan is understood, it would seem that any method of implementing the control plan would be as efficient as any other method. However, because of relationships among the elements of the control plan one method of implementing the control plan is more efficient and beneficial than are others.

The control plan can be thought of as being composed of two main partitions: control yardsticks and control data. Control yardsticks consist of all of the goals, schedules, project standards, cost estimations, and resource material requirements that are developed during the planning or study phase of the project. Control data consists of the information about the actual progress, costs, and quality produced during the course of the project. Project control is maintained by comparing the control data with the control yardsticks to ensure that, whenever expectations are not being met, significant discrepancies will be noticed and the causes of these discrepancies determined.

The control yardsticks and control data partitions each consist of several levels or layers and each level consists of a number of (control) elements. Each level in a partition is based on the level below, and every element is also related in some way to the other elements in its levels. The following description of the structure of the control plan, defines the levels, elements, and relationships within the partitions and also defines the media recommended for comparisons between partitions.

Control Yardstick

The control yardstick partition is composed of seven levels. (See Figure 12-1.) From the based upward these levels can be generally described as:

1. Base
2. Expectations
3. Estimations
4. Resources
5. Costs
6. Benefits
7. Acceptance

Included in these levels are all of the control elements that are developed during the study portion of the project. Individually, each of these elements simulates, describes, illustrates, or portrays the manner in which a segment of the project's resources will be used. Together, the control yardstick elements provide a simulation or model of the proposed project.

In the pictorial representation of the control yardstick partition, the relationships among the control elements are indicated by each control element's size, position in the partition, and the manner in which it appears to abut its neighboring cost elements; for example:

1. Control of requests provides the entire base of the partition because, if requests are not controlled in some manner, any development staff member can begin a project, thereby rendering all other controls useless.
2. In the costs level, conceptual design and project standards for a project are based, in part, on the expected results and the expected results are based, in part, on the conceptual design and project standards.
3. In the estimations level, the project schedule is the basis for developing the modified CPM and is validated by the modified CPM. The project schedule is also based upon the estimate of development and, in turn, causes changes in the estimate of development.

The remaining relationships are indicated by Figure 12-1. Because these relationships have been discussed (or implied) in previous chapters when the individual control elements were described, they are not discussed again in this section.

Control Data

The control data partition is composed of seven levels. (See Figure 12-2.) From the base upward, these levels can generally be described as:

1. Base Records
2. Analysis
3. Results
4. Time
5. Costs

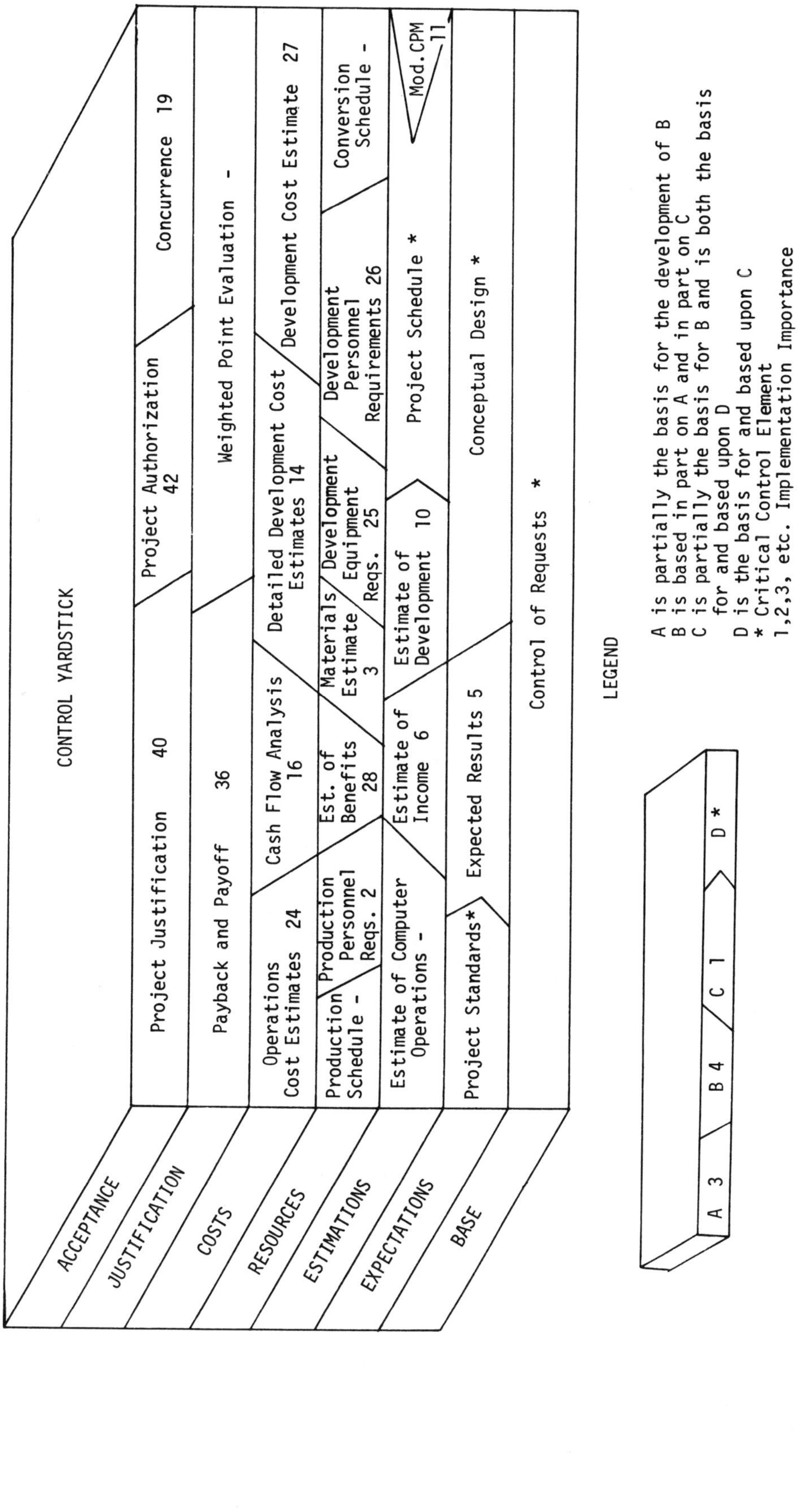

Figure 12-1. Control Yardstick Partition

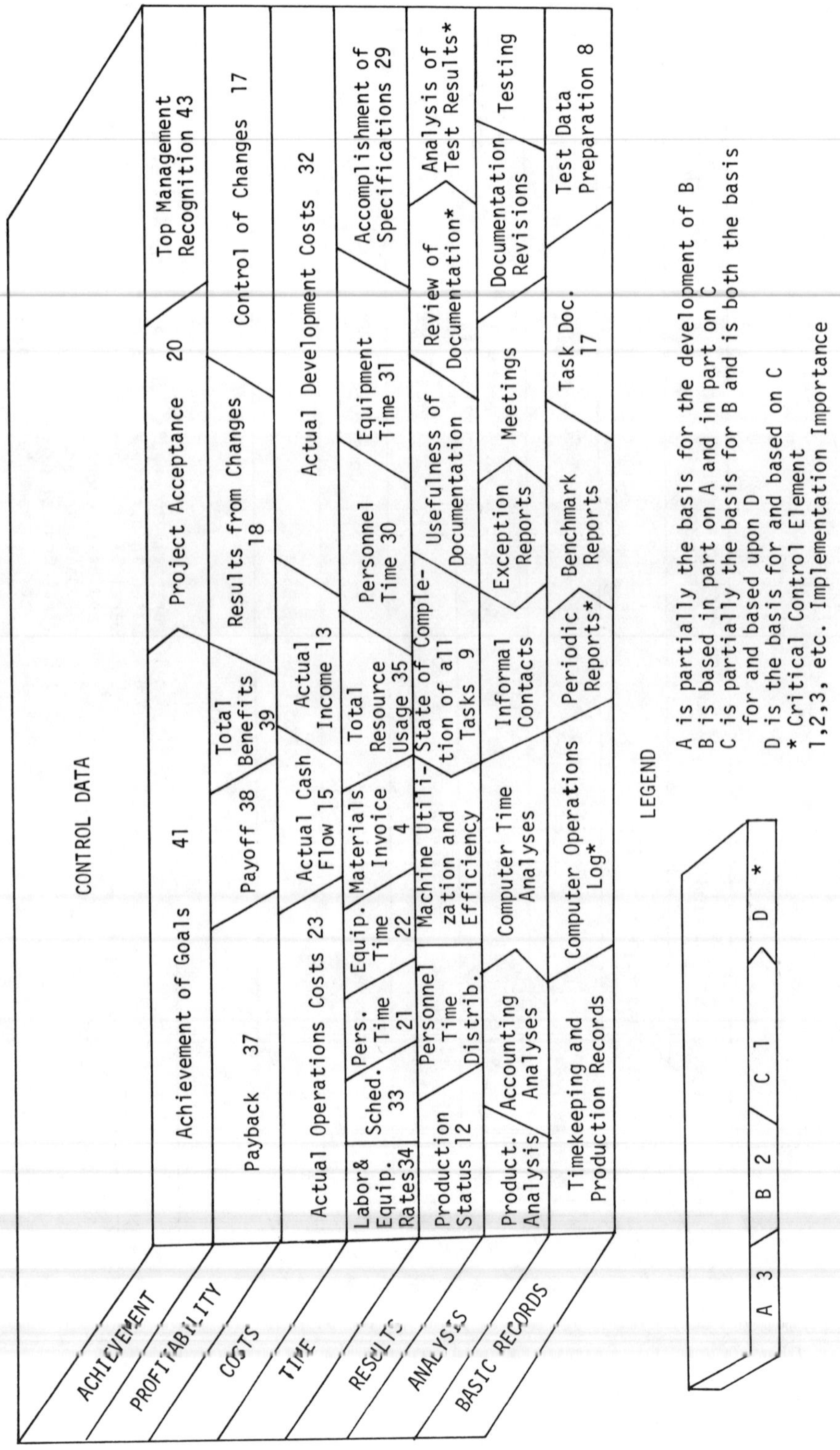

Figure 12-2. Control Data Partition

6. Profitability
7. Achievement

All of the control elements produced during the implementation and operation portions of the project are included in these levels. Individually, each of these elements provides actual data about the manner in which a particular portion of the project has been accomplished. Together, the control data elements portray or illustrate the success with which the overall system has been accomplished.

The pictorial representation of the control data partition (Figure 12-2) has been developed in the same manner as was the representation of the control yardstick partition (Figure 12-1). Therefore, relationships among the elements are indicated by the size and position of each element and its method of abutment with its neighbor. For example:

1. The basic records level contains control elements which make up the record-keeping activities that provide the data upon which all other control data elements are based.
2. Within the basic records level:
    a. test data preparation and benchmark report are, in part, based upon the completion of task documentation.
    b. periodic reports and benchmark reports provide mutual validation.
    c. the computer operations log provides run times for the operations section of the periodic reports and its production is validated by the timekeeping and production records.

Because the other relationships indicated in Figure 12-2 have been included in discussions of the individual control elements in previous chapters, they are not discussed again in this section.

Primary Control Comparisons

Controls are feedback mechanisms that inform management of the occurrence of significant variations from expectations. Therefore, project control is the comparison of elements in the control data partition with comparable elements in the control yardstick partition.

While comparisons could be made of every element in the control data partition that has a comparable element in the control yardstick partition, certain comparisons highlight significant variations in the most important elements of scheduling, costs, and quality. The primary control comparisons, the media used to present them, and the sources of the information contained therein are illustrated in Figure 12-3.

If significant variations are indicated by a primary control comparison, the causes of these variations are deduced by:

1. Reviewing the other primary control comparisons to determine whether the variation is restricted to one area. For example: a variation in a period's cash flow would cause the period's development costs, operations costs and income comparisons to be reviewed.

PRIMARY CONTROL COMPARISONS

CONTROL COMPARISONS		SOURCE OF INFORMATION	
Information Compared	Media	Control Data	Control Yardstick
A. Schedule			
1. Overall Progress vs. Sched.	Summary of Progress (8-3)	State of Completion of Tasks	Project Schedule
2. Act. Task Comple. vs. Schedule	Project Schedule (4-2)	Benchmark Reports	Project Schedule
3. State of Tasks vs. Schedule	Project Schedule (4-2)	Periodic Reports	Project Schedule
4. Delay Information Schedule	Project Schedule (4-2)	Exception Reports	Project Schedule
B. Cost			
1. Cashflow-Actual vs. Estimate	Summary of Progress (8-3)	Actual Cashflow	Cashflow Analysis
2. Payback/Payoff-Act. vs. Est.	Graph-Cum. Pres. Cost vs. Act. Cum. Cashflow	Cumulative Cashflow	Cumulative Present Cost
3. Projection-Cashflow Varia.	Cost Variance Report (7-6)	Actual Cashflow	Cashflow Analysis
4. Dev. Costs-Actual vs. Est.	Total Development Cost Summary (7-4)	Development Costs	Dev. Cost Estimates
5. Op. Costs-Actual vs. Est.	Cashflow Analysis (7-5)	Operations Cost	Operations Cost Est.
6. Income-Actual vs. Estimate	Cashflow Analysis (7-5)	Income	Estimated Income
7. Signif. Changes in Cost	Cashflow Analysis (7-5)	Exception Report	Cashflow Analysis
C. Quality			
1. Operation vs. Expectation	Actual System Operation	Production Schedule&Results	Prod. Sched. &Concep. Des.
2. Test Results vs. Expect.	Review of Test Results	Test Results	Conceptual Design
3. Doc. vs. Expectations	Review of Documentation	Task Documentation	Concept. Design&Standards
4. Changes vs. Cause for Change	Analysis of Causes for Change	Control of Changes	System Documentation
5. Overall Quality vs. Expect.	Summary of Progress (8-3)	All Quality Control Data	Design, Doc. & Standards
D. Overall			
1. Data vs. Intuition	Informal Controls & Meetings	Informal Controls & Meetings	All Control Yardsticks
2. Project vs. Project Summary	Multi-project Progress Report (8-4)	Summary of Progress (8-3)	--
3. Manpower used vs. Expect.	Manpower Schedule (8-5)	Personnel Assignments	Personnel Requirements
4. Computer Util. vs. Expect.	New Project Computer Time Reqs. (8-6)	Comp. Util. &Efficiency Report	Computer Time Estimations

Figure 12-3. Primary Control Comparisons

2. Producing comparisons of the more detailed control elements which make up the primary control. For example, development: salaries, fringe, equipment, and materials costs would be compared if the variation was detected in development costs.
3. Producing comparisons of smaller (more detailed) control elements and/or special analyses to further isolate the cause. For example: salaries variations might be isolated to a department and a cost/unit volume analysis of that department might indicate that either salary increases or production rate decreases were the cause.

Methodical, step-by-step deduction is not always necessary. Often the cause of variations is immediately suspected and final comparisons and/or analyses are performed to confirm the suspicion.

MODULAR IMPLEMENTATION

All EDP areas control their projects in one way or another. The speed with which present methods of control are transformed into the master control plan is dependent upon:

1. The success of the present methods.
2. The number of control elements that are missing and the resources that are required for their implementation.
3. The resources that can be applied to the implementation of new control elements.

Because these factors vary widely from company to company, an optimum implementation plan cannot be described. However, because certain control elements are more critical than others, the method of modular implementation that is outlined in this section provides effective overall control during the implementation period.

The method defines the critical control elements and describes their implementation, recommends methods for approximating non-critical control elements, and suggests for them a sequence of implementation.

Critical Control Elements

A critical control element is defined as any element used for primary control comparison when significant variations cannot be detected by other control elements. Based on this definition, there are four critical control elements in the control yardstick partition:

1. Control of requests
2. Conceptual design
3. Project standards
4. Project schedule

and four critical control elements in the control data partition:

1. Periodic reports
2. Computer operations logs
3. Review of documentation
4. Analysis of test results

The information provided by these eight control elements is necessary for adequate project control. When it is available, the information contained in all other control elements is very beneficial. However, it can be roughly estimated from that provided by the critical control elements until all are implemented.

Implementation of Critical Control Elements

If they are not already implemented in some form, the implementation of seven of the eight critical control elements can almost always be accomplished by any project manager who desires it. Control of requests, although not usually the direct responsibility of a project manager, will cause many problems for him, and can be (narrowly) considered to be under the control of the project manager. If this interpretation is accepted, all eight critical control elements can be implemented by the project manager and, therefore, by any person superior to him. The methods that he might use to implement the eight critical control elements are described in the remainder of this section.

Control of requests. For a project manager, control of requests consists of ensuring that no person working on his project(s) begins working on any task, project or change without the project manager's approval. This rule and the necessity for this rule can be explained during the project initiation of each staff member. If any staff member must work on two projects simultaneously and be shared with another project manager (a practice that should be strongly discouraged), the two project managers should agree upon and jointly inform the staff member of this rule and the specific timetable for his work on each project.

The managers and each member of the review groups should be informed that their function is advisory in nature and that it ends with the suggestion of changes and does not include any actual implementation activity.

The tone of these discussions with staff members, other project managers, and review personnel should be conducive to understanding and should result in agreement and acceptance. However, any violations of this rule discovered during the course of the project should be dealt with immediately (in private) and severely enough to eliminate further violations.

Conceptual design, project standards, project schedule and periodic reports. The project manager can implement the conceptual design, project standards, project schedule and periodic requests control elements at will. Each of these elements can be developed by the project manager whenever he wishes to expend the effort necessary for their development. If the required efforts are expended prior to project development, these elements can be introduced to each staff member as requirements during project initiation.

The only factors that can influence the implementation of these four critical control elements are the amount of effort necessary for their development and the time available. As the project manager controls the level of detail in each of these elements, acceptable controls can usually be developed. Obviously, if the level of detail in these elements approximates the level suggested in this book, the control elements will be most efficient.

Review of documentation and analysis of test results. For most efficient control, the review of documentation and analysis of test results should be performed by the operations group, the user group, and the development manager in addition to the project manager. However, if he lacks the position or persuasiveness required to convince the people that can organize these reviews, the project manager can depend solely upon the reviews and analyses made by himself and his staff.

The project manager should devote a great deal of effort toward the organization of these groups. His efforts will transfer work from his project staff and will produce many tangential benefits such as:

1. Involvement of the review groups.
2. Training for the review groups.
3. Automatic approval from the review groups.

These benefits are lost if these groups are not formed and do not participate in the reviews analyses.

Computer operations log. The implementation of a computer operations log poses the greatest difficulty for the project manager. If he cannot convince the supervisor of computer operations that the implementation of such a log would be beneficial, the project manager must implement procedures whereby the staff members record some of the basic data that is usually found in the computer operations log. Minimally, this data must include the purpose, system, programs, programmer, equipment configuration, duration of run, reason and duration of delays; cause of termination or rerun, and volume of data processed for each utilization of the computer. These data, when recorded, can be collected and summarized by administrative personnel or by the project manager himself. The summary should sequence the data by configuration, system, program, and programmer and should include totals at each of these levels.

Maintaining Control During Implementation

By intelligently manipulating the information provided by the eight critical control elements, the project manager can maintain primitive, yet comprehensive, control of the project until the other control elements can be implemented. This section describes how the eight critical control elements can be used to maintain control over the project schedule, quality, and costs. Naturally, the project manager should fully utilize as many other control elements as are available.

Schedule. Significant variations in schedule can be determined by comparing the expected progress of the project, as pictured by the project schedule, with the information about the actual status of the tasks as described by the periodic reports. If he listens carefully, additional information for validating the periodic reports data will be gleaned from informal contacts and meetings without any preplanning on the part of the project manager. By graphing the progress information from the periodic reports and other sources on the project schedule, significant variations from schedule are easily detected.

Quality. The quality of a project might best be described as the degree to which the end product (system) meets or exceeds the specifications for that product. The project specifications are summarized by the conceptual design and the project standards. The primary determination of how well these specifications have been met occurs during the review of the documentation and analysis of test results when the task documentation and test results are compared with the project specifications.

A secondary determination of project quality is derived from the control of requests. By noting the frequency, sources, and cause of requests for change during and after project implementation, a different basis is provided for evaluating the quality of the project and system.

Together, these methods of determining project quality make up most of the primary control comparisons for quality. When information on system operation (derived from informal contacts and meetings) is added, all primary control comparisons for quality have been implemented.

To accomplish the implementation of all primary control comparisons, five of the eight critical control elements are required. This stress of the criticality of the quality control elements is essential because all other control elements depend upon the control of the quality of the project. It is meaningless to determine that the project is on schedule or within budget, unless one is assured that the efforts that have been expended have produced the products that were specified.

Development costs. The control of development costs is extremely important. To top management, it is probably the most important project control. However, implementation of methods, procedures, and systems for calculating costs is time consuming, costly, and often requires a high degree of tact and diplomacy.

Until the efforts that are required to implement all necessary cost control elements can be expended and coordinated, significant variations in development costs can almost always be detected by analyzing the information provided by the eight critical control elements.

Significant variations in project development costs can be detected by observing significant variations in the following:

1. The number of people working on the project (salaried employees).
2. The number of hours worked by these people (hourly employees).
3. The computer hours used (by equipment configuration).
4. The materials used.
5. Fringe as a percentage of salaries.

Without basic timekeeping records, the number of actual people and hours can be determined if a "Number of hours worked on project ______" line is added to the periodic report and if periodic reports are obtained from review personnel as well as all staff members. These figures can then be compared with the number of (staff and review) people and hours that were estimated on the project schedule. All variations in people or hours can be easily translated into salaries (and fringe) to determine their significance.

The computer operations log provides the information about the number of computer hours used for a project. The estimate of computer hours is contained in the testing schedule and requirements. Therefore, by obtaining and reviewing the actual computer hours, the project manager can detect utilization that varies significantly. By applying the standard cost rates for the equipment, variations in computer utilization can be projected into approximate development cost variations.

Materials and fringe percentage are not controlled directly because they rarely have an appreciable effect on the overall cost. However, by occasionally asking the project staff and review groups about materials usage and by checking with Accounting (or Personnel), the project manager can usually detect significant unexpected costs variations in these areas.

Operations costs. Operations costs, like development costs, are based on people hours, and (to a smaller extent) materials and fringe percentage. However, unless basic timekeeping procedures are implemented, the control over operations costs is quite weak. But, because the control of operations costs is not a primary responsibility of the project manager, this weak control can be acceptable to the project manager. If the user manager wishes stronger control, he only needs to implement additional, more stringent timekeeping procedures.

Without primitive timekeeping or estimation procedures, the project manager can monitor personnel by making periodic head counts in the operations areas. These observations can be supported during discussions (with user personnel) about the general operation of the system after it has been installed. The actual figures on personnel that are developed can then be compared to the number of personnel that the project manager estimated from reviewing the conceptual design and determining which manual functions were being replaced by the system. In this way, a crude estimate of variations from expected operations personnel levels can be obtained.

Computer costs can be estimated much more directly. Actual computer times can be obtained from the computer operations log during the testing function. Program times that appear to vary significantly from general expectations should be reviewed and corrected during the test effort.

Materials and fringe percentage are monitored in the same informal manner as during development.

Although these controls are quite weak, most companies require timekeeping and budgeting activities in all production areas. If these activities exist, the area's budget vs. actual reports will reflect the cost impact of the system after implementation. The timekeeping activities, as previously noted, provide a basis for projecting the actual costs for comparison. In any company that lacks these basic activities, even the weak control of operational costs that is provided will be an improvement over present procedures.

Summary

The preceding portions of this section describe how a project can be primitively controlled if only the eight critical control elements are implemented. While only rough approximations of estimated and actual cash flow, payback, and payoff can be obtained (by combining development and operations costs), these approximations would be a giant step forward for a company that lacks all non-critical control elements. As was mentioned in the beginning of this section, any additional control elements that are already implemented should be used to their fullest extent by the project manager.

Non-Critical Control Elements

When the critical control elements have been implemented, the project manager should begin to implement the non-critical control elements. While the specific implementations, methods, procedures, and sequences are determined to a large extent by each company's individual requirements, this section recommends a method of implementing the non-critical control elements. This method consists of descriptions of the general procedures involved in the implementation and the most efficient priority for implementation. These descriptions should simplify the planning that is required for any company to transform a primitive control plan into an efficient master control plan.

Procedures. These procedures for implementing non-critical control elements are, of necessity, general in nature. It is impossible to describe specific implementation procedures or the handling of interdepartmental contacts without knowing the individual company, environment, and personnel. However, the general procedures that are described should provide a basis for detailed implementation planning.

The procedures for implementing non-critical control elements consist of:

1. Selection of a pilot area, function, or project.
2. Implementation of the control elements in (or for) the pilot.
3. Checking, verifying, refining, and ensuring that the benefits provided by the pilot are satisfactory.
4. Implementation of the control elements in other areas.

These procedures are recommended because they provide a simple platform for exhibiting and proving the usefulness of new techniques. This exhibition is necessary because new techniques must be proven to be useful for each individual company because of peoples' natural resistance to change, and because there are a variety of factors within a specific company that could easily negate any benefits that could be provided by the new technique (see Chapter Thirteen). After they are proven useful in one (pilot) area of a specific company, the implementation of a new control element in other areas is accomplished more efficiently and with much less resistance.

Priority. While final priority for implementing control elements is primarily dependent upon specific project and company requirements, the non-critical control element priority analysis (Figure 12-4):

1. Divides the control elements into those which increase control information and those which simplify the efforts necessary to effect control comparisons.
2. Indicates the implementation priority of each control element within its division. This priority is based upon the importance of the element in the master control plan, its individual difficulty of implementation, and the other elements that must be implemented before this element.
3. Generally describes the difficulty that will be encountered in implementing each control element *if all control elements are implemented in priority order.*
4. Rates the importance of each control element in the overall control plan. These importance ratings are also indicated in Figures 12-1 and 12-2. A dash (–) indicates that the control element provides a base (must be implemented before) for a more important item but that the specific control element's individual importance does not justify its priority.

A logical and efficient implementation schedule can be developed for a specific company by considering: project requirements, company requirements, the importance of the control element to the master control plan, and the priority of each control element.

IMPLEMENTATION PRIORITY ANALYSIS

Non-Critical Control Elements

Increase Control				Simplify Control			
P*	Control Element	Implementation*	I*	P*	Control Element	Implementation*	I*
1	Timekeeping	Easy or In	1	1	Accounting Analyses	Medium	-
2	Estimate of Computer Operations	Easy	-	2	Personnel Time Distribution	Difficult	-
3	Production Schedule	Easy	-	3	Personnel Time	Easy	21
4	Production Personnel Requirements	Easy	2	4	Equipment Time	Easy	22
5	Materials Estimate	Medium	3	5	Actual Operating Costs	Medium	23
6	Materials Invoices	Medium	4	6	Operations Cost Estimate	Easy	24
7	Expected Results	Easy	5	7	Development Personnel Requirements	Easy	25
8	Estimate of Income	Hard	6	8	Development Equipment Requirements	Easy	26
9	Task Documentation	Medium	7	9	Development Cost Estimate	Easy	27
10	Testing	In or Easy	-	10	Estimate of Benefits	Medium	28
11	Documentation Revision	In or Easy	-	11	Usefulness of Documentation	Medium	-
12	Test Data Preparation	Difficult	8	12	Accomplishment of Specifications	Easy	29
13	Exception Reports	Very Easy	-	13	Personnel Time - Development	Easy	30
14	Benchmark Reports	Very Easy	-	14	Computer Time Analysis	Medium	-
15	Informal Contacts	Very Easy	-	15	Machine Utilization & Efficiency	Medium	-
16	Meetings	Very Easy	-	16	Equipment Time - Development	Easy	31
17	State of Completion - Analysis	Very Easy	9	17	Actual Development Costs	Easy	32
18	Estimate of Development	Easy	10	18	Conversion Schedule	Medium	-
19	Modified CPM	Medium	11	19	Schedule (Actual Production)	Medium	33
20	Production Analysis	Medium	-	20	Labor and Equipment Rates	Medium	34
21	Production Status	Easy	12	21	Total Resource Usage	Easy	35
22	Actual Income	Medium	13	22	Payback and Payoff - Estimate	Easy	36
23	Detailed Development Cost Estimate	Easy	14	23	Payback - Actual	Easy	37
24	Actual Cash Flow	Easy	15	24	Payoff - Actual	Easy	38
25	Cash Flow Analysis	Easy	16	25	Total Benefits	Easy	39
26	Control of Changes	Medium	17	26	Project Justification	Medium	40
27	Results from Changes	Easy	18	27	Achievement of Goals	Medium	41
28	Concurrence	Medium	19	28	Project Authorization	Easy	42
29	Project Acceptance	Medium	20	29	Top Management Recognition	Medium	43
30	Weighted Point Evaluation	Difficult	-				

* P - Priority   I - Importance   Implementation - Ease of implementation descriptions assume that all higher priority controls have been implemented.

Figure 12-4. Non-Critical Control Element Priority Analysis

13

Avoiding Problems During Implementation

The problems encountered in implementing a comprehensive control plan are not solved by the development of an implementation plan. Equally as many, and probably more serious, problems are encountered while organizing, directing and controlling the implementation effort.

Many of the problems that are encountered will be inherent to the specific industry, company, or EDP area. However, there are some that are likely to occur wherever the implementation of a master control plan is attempted. Acknowledgment of the likelihood of these problems and an understanding of their causes provide forewarning. The consideration and selection of techniques for eliminating these potential problems constitute forearming.

Unless he is forewarned and forearmed, the implementor will probably engage in a discussion similar to the one that follows.

President: I understand that you are trying to get us to use some sophisticated new method for judging what projects we want to put in.

Implementor: Yes, I really believe that by using the weighted point evaluation technique we will be able to judge the priority that should be given to proposed projects.

President: What do you think is the matter with the way we've always judged projects? We've done all right so far, haven't we?

Although the implementor may be able to extricate himself from this situation, it would be to his advantage if he had avoided the situation entirely.

This chapter describes four general sources of problems that should be expected when implementing the master control plan. These are:

1. People's natural resistance to change.
2. The increased coordination that is required.

3. The potential basis for responsibility accounting.
4. The lack of measurable benefits.

The description of each problem source includes:

1. A brief summation of the (major) possible causes.
2. Generally effective methods of eliminating the causes of problems.
3. An example indicating how the method might be used.

From these descriptions, the implementor should gain an understanding of the underlying causes of many implementation problems and of general methods for negating or eliminating these causes. When added to the implementor's knowledge, experience, and abilities in planning, directing, motivating, and controlling EDP projects, this knowledge should provide the basis for successful and efficient implementation of the master control plan.

RESISTANCE TO CHANGE

Resistance to change is a normal, common, and serious source of many of the problems encountered whenever any new technique, project or plan is implemented in any business. Because it is based primarily upon a person's fear of the unknown and relative comfort with known situations, resistance to change is probably present, to some degree, in everyone. Each person's satisfaction with (or acceptance of) his present environment determines the strength of his resistance to change, with the strongest reaction coming from those who are dissatisfied with their environment.

The basis for people's fears of the unknown are very real. Until a person can begin to understand the elements of the change—how the new procedures will be performed, where he will be required to assist, how his responsibilities will be affected, what the benefits (to him) will be, and whether he can cope with the change and will be able to perform creditably—his lack of knowledge in these areas will pose a continuing threat and he will resist the change.

Method of Elimination

The pilot implementation (see Chapter Twelve) for each control element can produce many of the factors that are most effective in eliminating people's resistance to change. By carefully selecting the area in which it will be conducted, the pilot implementation can be used to demonstrate:

1. Operation of the new procedures.
2. Various responsibilities and responsibility relationships.
3. Specific benefits.
4. All skills required.
5. Ease of implementation.

Demonstration of these factors in an actual operating area that is known to be typical or, preferably, slightly below average in the quality of its personnel is usually very effective in eliminating many of the fears upon which resistance to change is based.

Selection of the area in which the pilot implementation of a control element will be conducted should be based upon two factors: the composite reputation of the area's personnel and the degree of interest that the area's management shows towards the control element. If not known, these factors can be determined by informal contacts with managers outside and inside potential pilot implementation departments.

It should be noted that modular implementation of the control elements also decreases resistance to change. By segmenting the entire control plan into a number of control modules, each of which contains one to four control elements, the total implementation is effected much more gradually. A series of small changes, effected over a period of time, is not as threatening as a single, major change. When change is effected in small doses it can be absorbed and understood more easily and in a cumulative fashion rather than in one mind-boggling lump. Modular implementation also permits distribution of pilot implementations to a number of areas so that modules can be worked on simultaneously by the groups whose resistance to the required changes is minimal.

Illustration – Weighted Point Evaluation Technique

As explained in detail in Chapter Four, the weighted point evaluation technique translates the basic project information that is assembled during the feasibility study into a quantitative description of the project's worth. To implement the weighted point evaluation technique, the EDP manager must interest and involve top management because he requires its concurrence and approval on:

1. The definition of the factors that contribute to the worth of a project.
2. The relative importance (weight) of each factor with respect to the other factors.
3. The method of assigning points (point assignment table).

Resistance to change on the part of most top management personnel would be expected to be very strong because this control element would appear to be:

1. Very complex and difficult to understand or use.
2. An automation and diminution of top management's decision-making responsibility.
3. A way of learning how top management makes decisions.
4. Worthless and error prone.

To eliminate these feelings and implement the weighted point evaluation technique, the EDP manager should:

1. Define all factors, weights and points to the best of his own ability.
2. Develop ratings for a number of projects whose results have been estimated or are known.
3. Revise weighting and ratings necessary to correlate ratings with (intuitive) worth.

4. Integrate comments about his efforts into discussions with top management personnel when this can be done naturally.
5. Select a pilot manager who is influential and interested, but not known for his ability with figures.
6. Show and discuss the results of his previous ratings with the pilot manager.
7. Assist the pilot manager in rating several more projects.
8. Refine all factors with the pilot manager and demonstrate that the technique assists rather than supersedes decision-making.
9. Let the pilot manager rate a project.
10. Show how the technique could be applied to rate non-EDP projects (e.g. capital budgeting).
11. Indicate the benefits to be gained if all (representative) top management could assist in refining the factors and reviewing the results.

This procedure may have to be repeated before enough interest is generated to support full implementation. However, if the EDP manager is a skillful motivator and has selected the right pilot manager, implementation can be demanded by top management in less than a month.

INCREASED COORDINATION

Implementation of the control elements requires increased coordination and cooperation among a variety of diverse areas. This coordination and cooperation can, in itself, be a source of problems because it usually increases the work of the areas' managers, or supersedes (and/or contravenes) organizational, social, and political groupings or structures. Because people's status, recognition, friendship, esteem, and sense of achievement are primarily dependent upon themselves and their organizational, social and political environments, the implementation of control elements that require increased cooperation necessitates the use of methods beyond those required for eliminating resistance to change.

Methods of Elimination

The modular pilot implementation technique is also useful in eliminating the problems caused by the need for increased cooperation, because it eliminates resistance to change and reduces the extent of the cooperation required among areas and isolates the increase to a few control elements at a time. However, the following modification should be made to the methods previously described:

1. Selection of a pilot area should be based upon the area manager's dissatisfaction with his present environment, in addition to the factors previously described.
2. Benefits to the individual include the inherent added esteem, new friendships, increased recognition, and self-achievement. These benefits must be continually emphasized to the individual.

Selection of a dissatisfied pilot manager will facilitate his involvement and the benefits will appear proportionally greater. His enthusiasm will help during full implementation because others will perceive the benefits that he obtained. The additional emphasis of benefits in terms of psychological need fulfillment allows participants to directly compare their gains (from cooperation and coordination) with potential losses from superseding structural boundaries. As long as the potential benefits seem to be sufficient to warrant the risk of loss through cooperation, each participant will be encouraged to cooperate fully.

Illustration — Accounting Analysis

The accounting analysis control element translates the timekeeping reports (or logs) into the personnel times and production statistics upon which operations costs are based. To implement these analyses, the cooperation among user areas, the project manager, the project staff, the EDP manager, the development manager, the operations manager, and the operations staff is mandatory. These people must all understand the correct usage of cost distribution codes, know the codes to use and use them correctly. Additionally, media, procedures and responsibilities must be established for recording, collecting, analyzing, and reporting cost distribution data.

Implementation would begin with the selection of a pilot implementation area. Because Accounting could cause (and enforce) implementation, the manager of an Accounting area that performed work for a number of areas, was constantly under pressure, and that continually received requests for additional analyses (e.g. payroll) would be (informally) contacted and his dissatisfaction would be noted. Control of requests by back-charging would be suggested and, if an interest developed, the benefits of an accounting analysis system would be described. Then, "just to see what the figures would look like," a crude analysis system would be developed and implemented for the area.

If the results warranted, accounting management could be informed of the costs of requests by source, and informed of the need either for additional staff or decreased requests based on the analyses. Any further action by accounting management would be a direct benefit upon which expanded implementation could be based.

If the results did not warrant informing accounting management or if accounting management would not take action, the pilot implementation would be attempted area-by-area until total implementation was achieved. During the interim, inter-area coordination would be achieved because each group's costs would be established on the same basis, and because each group would have the pilot implementation experience in common with the other groups. From this, by emphasizing benefits, a common bond could be formed from which further implementation could be generated.

RESPONSIBILITY ACCOUNTING

The more perceptive managers may discover that the master control plan contains a number of control elements that can be adapted to almost any area to provide a basis for responsibility accounting. This, in itself, may be the source of problems because many of today's managers fear responsibility accounting. They feel that, in addition to being new and a change, it will expose their weaknesses and may not be fair to them. Because of their feelings, these managers tend to resist any hint of or form of responsibility accounting much more strenuously than most other changes.

Method of Elimination

Because it illustrates the ability with which each manager has fulfilled each of his various responsibilities, thorough responsibility accounting does expose weaknesses. However, it also highlights, strengthens and, in total, strikes a balance between strengths and weaknesses. After this has been demonstrated (by the pilot implementation) and is understood, much of the opposition disappears.

Responsibility accounting techniques can also be unfair in what they present or in the methods of presentation. Emphasis of this fact and use of it as an argument for involvement during implementation assures the involvement of managers who distrust the technique.

Therefore, in addition to previously presented methods and procedures, when implementing any control element that might be used for responsibility accounting:

1. The manner in which this element highlights strengths must be demonstrated;
2. Each manager must be very interested and involved in the implementation of the technique to ensure that the results fairly depict the facts in his individual case.

As can be seen in the following illustration, these methods, when applied with tact and diplomacy, can help to eliminate the fear of responsibility accounting and obtain extra assistance during implementation.

Illustration—Three-Point Estimate of Income

To obtain a three-point (minimum, average, and maximum) estimate of income (see Chapter Eight) from the vice president of Sales is difficult. To obtain a three-point estimation from the VP of Sales of the change in income that would result from the implementation of a computer system is considered, by many, impossible. It is not impossible and often is so easy that it should be considered for a pilot implementation.

The vice president of Sales and his staff are continually being asked for their estimations of sales income under diverse and unique circumstances. In most companies one of their prime responsibilities is to forecast sales volume and income. These forecasts must be redone for every significant change in the environment, industry, and company. In comparison with many of these forecasts, changes caused by systems implementations can be estimated with a fair degree of accuracy.

Therefore, to implement a three-point estimate:

1. They should have been used effectively to control a project's development costs or some other factor.
2. Their use should be discussed with the VP of Sales.
3. Benefits to Sales should be emphasized. These include:
   a. The fact that three-point estimates directly indicate the degree of uncertainty.
   b. The fact that Sales would be evaluated by their proximity to average but that they would only be seriously wrong if the actual turned out to be beyond the maximum or minimum.
   c. The elimination of arbitrary fudge factors from estimates would be possible.
4. If the VP of Sales is not yet interested in implementing three-point estimates, the potential for bias if these estimates are implemented without the involvement of the VP should be described.
5. The ease of implementation should be described.

These arguments, properly presented, almost always obtain interest and involvement in the implementation of three-point estimates. They should never fail in obtaining a trial estimate because:

6. It can be presented: "As a demonstration, to see if three-point estimations can be useful to Sales."

In this case the implementor will probably have to do the work while Sales personnel observe and review. If a demonstration is made, the results can usually be used to persuade Sales to try one of their own.

The demonstration consists of:

1. Presenting all pertinent facts to five "estimators" from Sales.
2. Obtaining secret, anonymous estimates of the minimum, average, and maximum change in income from each estimator.
3. Discussing any wide variances in estimates of minimum, average or maximum changes with the estimators.
4. After any changes have been made, the average of the five minimums becomes the Minimum, the average of the five averages becomes the Average and the average of the five maximums becomes the Maximum.

The procedure can include three-point estimates in as many time periods as is necessary. After the demonstration project, the benefits and ease of implementation will have been demonstrated. Further implementation can usually be based upon these results.

LACK OF MEASURABLE BENEFITS

Because the benefits from the implementation of a control element will usually not result in a direct reduction of people or computer time, savings in materials, or increase in gross income, the benefits from its implementation are difficult to estimate and/or measure. This lack of measurable benefits is a source of problems because if people do not perceive measurable benefits resulting from the implementation, they tend to:

1. Believe that the implementation is being done for the good of the EDP area rather than the good of the company. This generates jealousy and/or anger.
2. Raise the question of whether the control might not be effected in some other, more profitable, manner.
3. Disregard the overall importance of the control element and delay implementation.
4. Confuse control with management and demand results as soon as the causes of problems are defined.

These feelings and actions can cause a variety of implementation problems.

Method of Elimination

The lack of measurable benefits is most effectively eliminated as a source of implementation problems by:

1. Emphasizing that each control element is implemented as a part of a master control plan. The benefits of the control plan which are easier to perceive, are then stressed; thereby:
   a. Indicating the benefits to all areas.
   b. Demonstrating the logical approach to implementation.
   c. Emphasizing the importance of the control in relation to the plan.
   d. Defining control and its place in management.
2. Using pilot implementation to prove that benefits can be achieved. The additional methods that were previously described can also aid in eliminating the lack of measurable benefits, but the two methods outlined above are usually most effective.

Illustration—Using Outside Resources

The decision to use outside (EDP) resources, rather than waiting for resources to become available internally, is difficult when made subjectively. Although there is no single control element whose implementation could significantly reduce the difficulty of this decision, the implementation of the master control plan can reduce this decision to a simple review.

By demanding that the source of the outside resources supply the control yardstick elements pertaining to Quality, Schedule, and Development Costs as a part of its proposal and by developing the operations cost estimates, income estimates, detailed cash flow, payoff/payback estimates, and weighted point evaluation, the EDP manager can determine the priority rating that should be given to the project, if it were to be done with outside resources. This can be compared with the priority rating of the project if it were to be done internally, and with the priority rating of other potential projects. Based on these comparisons, the decision of whether to proceed is reduced to a simple review. This provides a logical basis for ensuring that outside resources are not purchased needlessly.

Because everyone can usually understand the benefit of the control plan when illustrated by examples like "using outside resources," a number of actual and dramatic illustrations should be developed for use in combating and eliminating the lack of measurable benefits of a single control element.

SUMMARY

Many of the problems in implementing the comprehensive control plan can be avoided by:

1. Implementing modules of (one to four) control elements over an extended period of time.
2. Using carefully selected pilot implementations.
3. Describing and emphasizing the benefits to each individual.
4. Relating the problems that may occur if implementation is not supported.
5. Explaining that each module provides the basis for the overall plan and illustrating the benefits of the master plan.

These are very general. To be successful, they must be supported, modified, and added to by the efforts, experience, knowledge, tact, diplomacy, charisma, and influence of every person within the company who supports the implementation of the master control plan.

Index

F

G

I

M

N

O

P

Q

R

S